Dispatches from the Revolution

Dispatches from the Revolution

Russia 1916–18

Morgan Philips Price

Edited by Tania Rose

Pluto Press

LONDON · CHICAGO, ILLINOIS

First published 1997 by Pluto Press
345 Archway Road, London N6 5AA

Copyright © Tania Rose on behalf of the
Morgan Philips Price estate 1997
Foreword © 1997 Eric Hobsbawm

British Library Cataloguing-in-Publication Data
A catalogue record for this book is available from the British Library

ISBN 0 7453 1210 1 hbk

Designed and produced for Pluto Press by
Chase Production Services, Chadlington, OX7 3LN
Typeset from disk by Stanford DTP Services, Northampton
Printed in the EC by WSOY

Contents

Acknowledgements

The editor and publishers are grateful to the *Guardian* for permission to reprint some of Morgan Philips Price's dispatches to the *Manchester Guardian* in 1917 and 1918; to HarperCollins for permission to quote passages from his book *My Reminiscences of the Russian Revolution* (Allen and Unwin, 1921) and from some of Price's articles quoted by Roger Pethybridge in his *Witnesses to the Russian Revolution* (Allen and Unwin, 1964); to John Murray for permission to requote from Harvey Pitcher's *Witnesses to the Russian Revolution* (1994); and to Frank Cass for permission to quote some of the censored cables published in 'What the Papers Didn't Say' by Jonathan Smele in *Revolutionary Russia* (1996).

Foreword

Eric Hobsbawm

Of all the foreign eyewitnesses to the Russian Revolution of 1917, Morgan Philips Price was almost certainly the best qualified. He knew Russia well, spoke the language fluently, and had travelled widely in the country since 1910, particularly in its Asian regions. He had come to Russia through his family's business interests in the timber trade, as well as his own passion for adventure, country pursuits, scientific exploration and forests – one of the rare official positions he was ever to hold in the British establishment was as an enthusiastic Forestry Commissioner – but also as a young man from a wealthy and well-connected political family, whose members had sat in Parliament in the Liberal interest since Manchester first got the vote after the Great Reform Bill of 1832. Price's father had sat for Tewkesbury, his grandfather for Gloucester, and he himself, adopted Liberal candidate for Gloucester in 1912 at the age of 27, was confidently preparing himself for a parliamentary career, which would certainly be advanced by a young politician's expert knowledge of an important part of the world. In fact Price, who opposed the 1914 war, resigned his Liberal candidature in 1915 and, when he returned to politics, joined the Labour Party which remained his home except for a brief spell in the Communist Party between 1922 and 1924. He failed to win Gloucester, but in the end he returned to his family's political territory as a popular and much-respected Labour member for the Forest of Dean/Gloucestershire West from 1935 to 1959.

Meanwhile he had returned to Russia in 1914 as special correspondent for the *Manchester Guardian* and, unofficially, for the anti-war *Union of Democratic Control* of his cousin Charles Trevelyan. He remained in Russia until the end of 1918, after which he became the correspondent of George Lansbury's *Daily Herald* – a far cry from its remote descendant, today's *Sun* – in Berlin, and did not return to Britain until 1923. As his obituary in the *Manchester Guardian* observed, 'He was immensely moved by his experiences and became a passionate advocate of the Revolution against the Allied interventionists', but later 'his deep knowledge and feeling for Russia made him understanding of but unsympathetic to

Communist imperialism'. However it is only fair to recall the less political aspects of this 'singularly attractive personality', but one 'who did not fit well into the present-day Labour Party'. On being congratulated on his eightieth birthday, he wrote: 'I had a splendid day. Hounds met at my house. We hunted all day in the woods I have looked after for 60 years, and in the evening we had a splendid party.' It seems a good way to conclude a good life.

Price's books and pamphlets on the Russian Revolution have been largely forgotten, although his *My Reminiscences of the Russian Revolution*, published in 1921, has long been recognised as the best of the contemporary British eyewitness accounts. The present volume, prepared by Philips Price's daughter, is an extraordinarily valuable compilation of Price's published and unpublished writings about the Russian Revolution, many of them hitherto virtually or entirely inaccessible. They are particularly, one might say uniquely, valuable because Price was one of the few witnesses whose perspective on the Revolution was not metropolitan. He had reported the war largely from the Russian provinces and the Caucasus. He experienced the February Revolution in Georgia, travelled via Moscow to Petrograd (reporting on Finland and Kronstadt), and in the last months before the October Revolution undertook a tremendous seven weeks' tour of the provinces for the *Manchester Guardian*, filing from Samara, Orenburg, Nijni Novgorod and Yaroslav, before returning to Petrograd in time for the Bolshevik Revolution. Talking to peasants, merchants, soldiers, overhearing conversations on Volga boats, Price recorded what he correctly described as 'the only true voice of Russia'. And he got it right. Nothing shows the dramatic pro-Bolshevik radicalisation of the masses in the autumn of 1917 more vividly than the reports, filed from Yaroslav on 25 October – i.e. before the October Revolution – and printed under the heading 'How the Maximalists (i.e. Bolsheviks) have come to gain control'. These reports were still written with a distinct lack of sympathy for the 'Maximalist fanatics' and for Lenin ('a short man with a round head, small pig-like eyes and close-cropped hair'), which Price later revised.

The value of Price's writings lies not so much in the good journalist's nose for the headline event as in the background of intelligent knowledge about the Russian Empire he brought to his reporting. Price not only kept his eyes open, but knew how to recognise the significance of what he saw. That is what gives his writings their interest for historical readers. How many reporters on a quick flip into central Asia would have observed that 'the Revolution has had the effect of developing among the more intelligent Moslem natives a distinctly national feeling' but no pan-Islamism, or that 'needless to say [the peasants] in Turkestan are quite unaffected by the programme of the Russian Socialist

Revolutionary Party' because 'Land and Liberty' had no significance for them? In a desert country, not land but water was the problem and this depended not on the political situation in Petrograd but on the snowfall in the Pamir plateau. How many reporters were sufficiently interested in feminism to observe that the women's movement among the Tartars, though advancing dramatically since the February Revolution, had begun with the 1905 Revolution, when the women threw off the veil? 'By 1910 a veiled Moslem woman was unknown in Kazan.' In short, the readers of the *Manchester Guardian* in 1917–18 had as good a guide to what was happening in Russia as anyone – insofar as his reports were not mauled or suppressed by the wartime censorship.

Thanks to Tania's Rose's excellent editing, we can now read him afresh and recognise in his writings an important supplement to the history of the Russian Revolution and a useful corrective to the post-Soviet reaction against it. In his pages we can recover something of the excitement and the harshness and hunger of the times, of the Russian people's sense of liberation and hope, and something of what made a British country gentleman of progressive, but far from Bolshevik, views commit himself to the October Revolution.

Eric Hobsbawm

European Russia c. 1917

Introduction

Morgan Philips Price was Special Correspondent in Russia for the *Manchester Guardian* when the two Russian Revolutions of 1917 – in March and in November – took place. Price was one of the relatively few observers from Western Europe at that time who spoke fluent Russian. He was already an experienced writer, both as journalist and author. He had travelled extensively in the Russian Empire before the war, and in 1915 and 1916 he had travelled even further as a War Correspondent with the Russian armies in Poland and the Caucasus. During those years he sent 141 dispatches to the *Manchester Guardian* about the progress of the war and the political situation; he also wrote a number of long memoranda which were not intended for publication but for the private information of a small group of his political friends in Britain. He himself was a radical Liberal, a Parliamentary candidate indeed, and he had opposed Britain's entry into the First World War on political, not conscientious grounds. What he wrote from Russia was inevitably coloured by his own political creed. He had seen for himself the condition of the Russian peasants, workers and soldiers under Tsarism; he believed that change would have to come, that it was in the making and that it must be welcomed. The opening words of his fullest account of the Russian Revolution are:

> The Russian Revolution came like a thief in the night. How often had its possibility been discussed in Russia during the two-a-half-years that followed the outbreak of the Great War![1]

What follows is an edited selection of Price's unpublished memoranda, letters to his family[2] and some of his published articles with a bearing on the Revolutions which reflect not only the events as they unfolded but also his own reactions to them. Price was, unlike most of the other correspondents in Russia at that time, a sympathetic observer, and one who identified with the aspirations and experiences of the people he was observing, whether they were the leaders or the led. The material has been edited only in the sense that it has been abridged in the interest of producing a collection of manageable length. What has been omitted is either repetitive or a digression from the main theme of the article in question, and of less interest or importance than that theme. Linking passages have been written

1

to provide an indication of the historical background against which the events or developments described took place. Biographical notes on all the major public figures mentioned in the text will be found at the end of it. The primary intention has been to let Price speak for himself.

Price was just 32 at the time of the March Revolution. His parents, William Edwin Price and Margaret Philips, both came from wealthy families each with a strong Unitarian and Liberal tradition. Indeed their marriage epitomised a classical link between these factors which appears throughout the history of radical politics in Britain. His father's family fortunes were based on timber and his mother's on cotton. In the course of the previous half century, beginning in 1832, five members of the two families had sat as Liberal MPs in the House of Commons: his father, both his grandfathers, a great-uncle and an uncle by marriage, Sir George Otto Trevelyan, who was married to his mother's sister. Trevelyan's son Charles then followed his father into politics. As Price once said: 'I think it may safely be said that I was predisposed to a political life.' Politics was then still seen more as a form of public service than as a career. Price came from a section of society which inculcated a strong, almost religious, sense of duty to improve the lot of the less fortunate and which had the means to try to do so without the inconvenience of having to think of earning a living.

Price received a typically upper-middle-class education at public school (Harrow) and university (Trinity College, Cambridge). At Harrow he wrote a book on the flora and fauna of what was then the surrounding countryside. At Cambridge he took a Third in science, which disappointed him, but one of his subjects was geology, which became a lifelong interest. He stayed on to do the then new Diploma in Agriculture. His father had died when he was only one year old and he had inherited a large estate in Gloucestershire. He was genuinely interested in both farming and forestry, had taken part in politics in the Union Debating Society at Cambridge and there was an obvious opening for him in the family timber business. For some time after he left Cambridge he did not – and did not need to – make up his mind what he wanted to do. He and his brother, only a year younger, were both good looking and eligible bachelors. They hunted, fished, shot and danced. Moreover he could afford to indulge a taste for travel which he had perhaps inherited from his parents who had begun their married life adventurously by honeymooning in New Mexico in 1878, and had carried on travelling far from the conventional Victorian tracks until his father became too ill to do so.

The MP for the constituency in which he lived with his mother and brother (the Forest of Dean) was Sir Charles Dilke, the radical republican. Although popular with the Forest miners, Dilke was still being shunned socially by many of the county Liberal grandees because of his involvement in a notorious divorce case.[3] Price's mother was more broad-minded and invited him to her house and Dilke befriended her sons. He soon got Price involved in local Liberal politics by appointing him sub-agent for one of the rural areas of the constituency. They corresponded on topical issues like the reform of the House of Lords. Dilke often invited Price to stay with him when he visited the Forest so that they could discuss things together. By the time Price was 25, Dilke had made it clear that he wanted to help him embark on a political career, but Price still had not made up his mind about this. By 1910 Price had already seen more of the world than most young men his age. In 1908 he had gone to Russia, partly to look at the Russian side of the family timber business, partly to look at primeval forests in Finland, then still part of the Russian Empire. In 1910, when invited to come on an expedition organised by Douglas Carruthers to explore the headwaters of the Yenesai River, Price had useful knowledge to contribute, both of geology and of the Russian language which he had begun to learn in 1908. The party travelled via the trans-Siberian railway, and Price was then put in charge of buying Siberian ponies for the expedition – an experience for which the hunting fields of Gloucestershire had not prepared him. The expedition moved on to Outer Mongolia and began to map the Altai Mountains, where Price left it to return to European Russia via Chinese Turkestan and the Caucasus. He was away for over a year.

He returned to find his mother dying – she died a week after his return – and to learn that Dilke had died a month earlier. In this double bereavement he was rescued from a deep depression by Francis Hirst, the editor of *The Economist*, whom he had known slightly for several years and who now began to take Dilke's place as mentor. He too had tried to tempt Price into standing for Parliament before he went away, but seeing that Price was not yet ready to be tempted he asked him instead to write some reports, which later appeared as articles in *The Economist*, about conditions in Russia and prospects for economic development in Siberia. Price then wrote a whole book about Siberia.[4] By the end of 1911 he had recovered his spirits sufficiently to accept the offer of the Liberal candidature for Gloucester.

For the the next two-and-a-half years Price continued almost obsessively to travel in the Balkans, Turkey, Armenia, Persia, Syria and Palestine. He began to contribute occasional articles to the *Manchester Guardian* and was designated 'Special Correspondent' for the first time. However his travels only occupied a fifth of his time; the rest was devoted to his constituency. He did a great deal of home visiting – 3,000 visits in one year – and he spoke at meetings all over the county as well as in the city. His speeches dealt mainly with land reform and land tax, trade union law, Home Rule and foreign policy. He deplored the burden of armaments which prevented money from being applied to measures of social reform which were urgently needed at home. He saw nothing wrong with Germany's economic aspirations, but he was concerned by the system of alliances which were drawing Britain into what he called 'the vortex of Continental diplomacy'. He described himself later as more or less a socialist in home affairs but a Whig where foreign policy was concerned. Yet most of his constituents and friends, and even some of his family were not only shocked but somewhat surprised by the force of his opposition to Britain's involvement in the First World War. He suddenly found himself one of a very small group who opposed the war not on conscientious but on political grounds. As he saw it, there was absolutely no need for Britain to have become involved in a general war. Russia had been the first to mobilise in support of Serbia but Austria had been the first actually to open fire – against the Serb capital – in retaliation for the murder of the Habsburg heir. Russian mobilisation made German mobilisation inevitable. France was drawn in by her treaty with Russia and Britain by hitherto secret commitments to France. Price was not the only one who thought these were not good enough reasons.

The person who probably more than anyone else had influenced Price to take a stand against the war was his cousin Charles Trevelyan. He was 15 years older than Price and was already a Member of Parliament when Price was still at school. In August 1914 he was a junior member of the government as Parliamentary Secretary to the Board of Education. When it became clear that there would be a war he resigned his post; so did four members of the Cabinet. Two of them withdrew their resignations in response to the Prime Minister's entreaties, but the other two – John Morley and John Burns – did not. Trevelyan immediately became one of the most prominent and pro-active men in the formation of a pressure group – the Union of Democratic Control (UDC) – which argued that foreign policy had hitherto been formulated too secretively and should be made accountable to democratic control.[5] Price was at the dinner at which the first manifesto of the Union was hammered out, and so was Hirst. As editor of a national journal Hirst felt he could not actually join the UDC but he supported it in every way, short of membership. The UDC became one of the most influential focal points of the opposition to the war. By the end of 1917 it had a membership of 10,000 and had become an object of great suspicion to police and military intelligence. It had a monthly journal, *UDC*. All the memoranda which Price later addressed to Hirst and Trevelyan from Russia – many of which appear in the following pages – were intended for use either by *The Economist*, or the journal which Hirst founded in 1916, *Common*

Sense, or by *UDC*. It was through their shared opposition to the war and their support for the Union of Democratic Control that there came into being what was in effect a unique private news service from Russia for Hirst and Trevelyan. But first, Hirst suggested, a campaign to secure fundamental change in the control of foreign policy needed evidence and he proposed that a book should be compiled consisting of all the official documents of all the belligerents leading up to the war. Price undertook to do it and, working day and night in a London hotel, by November he had completed the *Diplomatic History of the War*.[6] He also made his position clear to the Gloucester Liberal Party. Since the country *was* at war he would support the Government in bringing it to a successful conclusion, but his support would not be unconditional and he reserved the right to be critical. Eventually he resigned the candidature, but not until the spring of 1915.

His brother shared his views on the war but nonetheless enlisted. Price felt there was other work that he could more usefully do and that entailed interpreting what was going on in Russia to the West. The British press appeared to believe that Russia was going to become more democratic simply because it was fighting on the same side as Britain and France. Price went to see the editor of the *Manchester Guardian*, C. P. Scott, whom he already knew slightly, and with him 'arranged something that was to become one of the turning points of my life'. It was agreed that he would go to Russia for the winter, longer if it seemed desirable, and send Scott reports, not necessarily for publication, about what was going on there, politically and militarily. But nothing he had ever said or written before gave any hint of the radicalisation that had taken place in him, as indicated by his last letter to his brother:

> I must get in touch with the Social Democrats and other brothers of the faith and see what hope there is. I see there is fighting in the Caucasus. I shall go there as soon as possible, not half ... Wait till the dawn of international socialism. Adieu, my dear Bob.

Price left England expecting to be away for about four months. He did not return for eight years, four of which were spent in Russia.

Perhaps more than any other Western journalist in the war years, Price became the target of official censorship. The Tsarist Russian censors prevented him from reporting as fully as he could have done both the political and the military situations in Russia. Later the British censor effectively closed him down as a source of news on post-Revolutionary Russia. Early in August 1914 an official Press Bureau was set up in London through which all incoming and outgoing news had to pass for the rest of the war. By a system of

Instructions to Censors, 'D' notices and letters to editors, the Bureau ensured that such news as was available should as far as possible not question government policy. The Bureau itself got instructions via the so-called 'Great Departments': the War Office, the Home Office and the Foreign Office. 'D' notices told editors that certain subjects, even if news on them had filtered through, were to be avoided. The Bureau had no sanctions and did not need any: it had the Defence of the Realm Act behind it.[7] Offenders against the Act could be prosecuted in Courts of Summary Jurisdiction.

During the whole of the war, 747 'D' notices were issued, which were overwhelmingly concerned with perfectly legitimate security matters like troop and ship movements. But there were two subjects not directly linked to security on which there was a small but significant concentration: strikes and – from the very start of the war – Russia. As early as October 1914, D 34 expressed the concern of the Foreign Office that Russia's military exertions were not being adequately recognised by the British press. In July 1915, D 253, sent at the request of the Russian Ambassador in London, asked the press not to mention the Russian army's lack of arms and ammunition. In February 1916 the censors were told to refer to the Directors for instruction on 'any reports of Russian atrocities on Jews', some of which Price himself had witnessed but had not been allowed to report by the Russian censors. And so it went on. The exertions of the Official Press Bureau after the Bolshevik Revolution, above all from the spring of 1918, ensured that the worst and most hostile construction would be put by the reading public on events in Russia. Where Price was concerned, this meant that nothing he wrote for the *Manchester Guardian* after June 1918 was ever printed, and there is abundant evidence that, in the three months preceding that date, his dispatches had been carefully doctored before they were released to the editor. The only concession made by the Bureau was to allow the *Manchester Guardian*'s Lobby Correspondent in London, at that time Harold Dore, to come and read them but not make notes. Luckily Dore had an excellent memory and was able to convey the main points of Price's articles to Scott, whose editorials were sometimes clearly influenced by them.

At the end of his first six months in Russia, in June 1915, Price decided that there was no point in staying on in northern Russia. He made a unilateral decision to go to the Caucasus, where the Turks had just occupied the Urumiah plateau, and in this theatre it was clear that a war of movement was about to begin. Price never appeared to receive any instructions from Scott, nor does he appear to have told Scott what he was doing or where he was proposing to go on more than one occasion. From his last letter to his brother, it would seem that Price had always intended to go to the Caucasus front as soon as he decently could. He had ridden most of the way from the Chinese frontier to the Caspian in 1910, and all over Armenia and northern Persia in 1912. It was, as he put it, 'very much my country'. He followed the Russian Army about and perhaps because they were doing well on that front it does not seem that either the Russian or the British censors took offence at what he was writing about that theatre. Officially acting as a Red Cross worker, he went into action with the Armenian Volunteers. In February 1916 he was the first Western journalist to arrive in Erzerum after its capture from the Turks. In all this travelling about the area south and east of the Black Sea he was appalled by the plight of the hundreds of thousands of refugees, both Moslem and Christian, who had been displaced by the fighting. He became involved with the Lord Mayor's Fund in London and acted as one of its agents, personally buying and distributing relief supplies, particularly in the remotest villages in Lazistan.

When he first went to the Caucasus, Price had not decided when, or indeed if, he would return to England. He was still determined not to fight in this war, and when conscription was introduced in 1916 he knew he would be 'just the man they will go for'. Riding about, often alone, in the spectacular landscape of the Caucasus, he became both more radical in his political views and also more fatalistic. In a letter to his brother he said that he had abandoned all thought of a political career and now 'sought salvation within myself in Asia'. His letters to Trevelyan began to contain revolutionary, almost apocalyptic phrases. Whenever he returned to Tiflis – his base during this period – to read, write, pick up his mail, replenish his stores, he made friends among the Social Democrats and intellectuals there. During this period, in addition to his articles for the *Manchester Guardian*, 24 pieces appeared in *The Economist* which can reasonably be attributed to him; some indeed took the form of signed letters to the editor. When the Tsar abdicated in March 1917, Price happened to be in Tiflis. By far the greater part of the pages which follow are devoted to what he wrote about Russia after that date.

As will appear, Price was overjoyed by the March Revolution. Despite the fact that he soon realised that the Provisional Government was not living up to the hopes which had been invested in it, he felt that a great and irreversible change had taken place. For the next eight months he used the umbrella phrase 'the revolutionary democracy' more or less indiscriminately, as applied to any and every instrument of government at any level. It is impossible to tell, sometimes, to which or what body he was referring. It does not seem to matter very much in this account of what he was seeing and hearing in the period between the first and second Revolutions. His choice of words to describe parties and organisations is also often confusing. Indeed he continued for some time, even after November 1917, to use the words Maximalist (meaning Bolshevik) and Minimalist (meaning Menshevik) to describe the Left and Moderate wings of the Social Democratic Party – words which in themselves only meant majority and minority in respect of a vote on party policy taken in 1903. He also continued to use the word 'council' – the literal translation of the word 'soviet' – even after the Russian word had become commonplace. And it is often necessary to retranslate his version of the proper names of government departments and new non-governmental organisations created by the Soviet government.

In the autumn of 1917 Price spent six weeks travelling in the Volga region, as a result of which he clearly saw that some form of second Revolution was now inevitable. The Provisional Government had failed to bring about the land reform which had been so eagerly awaited. Such order as now existed in the countryside emanated almost entirely from the 'councils' which had sprung up in every district through which he had travelled (by train, boat and on horseback). The Bolshevik Revolution took place only days after his return to Petrograd; Price was at first (as will be seen) in two minds about it. Revolution, yes, he appeared to be thinking; but Bolshevik Revolution? By the end of January 1918, however, he had come to the conclusion that the Bolsheviks were the only people capable of holding the country together and ending the war, which – it was now clear – was the essential precondition if any serious measure of reform was to be undertaken.

In the early months of 1918 Russia was still in touch with the rest of the world. There was still a postal service of sorts and the cables continued to work until the early summer, after which wireless became the only form of communication available. Price was able to look at English-language newspapers in the reading room of the British Embassy. He could see the hysterical fear of the Bolshevik government which was being whipped up by the press, and the promotion of the idea that the Allies would have to intervene in Russia 'for her own good'. He now had personal contacts with several prominent Bolsheviks and through them was kept informed of much that was going on outside the capital, indeed outside the country, and which did not appear in any newspaper.

The most important of these contacts was Tchicherin, a career diplomat in Tsarist days and a former Menshevik who happened to be in London when the war began. He was active in support of Russian socialist groups in London, opposed the war, was arrested in August 1917 and put in Brixton jail. When Trotsky became Foreign Minister he was able, in January 1918, to secure Tchicherin's release, and when he became Minister for War Tchicherin succeeded him at the Foreign Office. In London Tchicherin had read some of Price's articles in the *Manchester Guardian* and knew him to be a sympathetic observer. On his return he let his colleagues know that Price deserved their confidence. Indeed he personally saw to it that Price was enabled to draw out some money during the anti-government bank strikes which were going on in January 1918 and which had reduced Price to penury and near starvation. From then onwards, Price appears to have been able to secure an interview with Tchicherin whenever he needed an official statement. Tchicherin also put him in touch with Karl Radek, a Polish Jewish Bolshevik journalist, possibly one of the best informed and verbally gifted of them all, who was at that time in charge of foreign propaganda.

There were some exceptions to the generally hostile mood and attitude to Russia of the British press. The *Manchester Guardian* was obviously one of them. Scott interpreted the information he was getting from Price and backed it up with supportive, open-minded and common-sense leading articles. No less exceptional was the Liberal *Daily News* whose correspondent in Russia was the writer Arthur Ransome. Ransome had been mainly based in Russia for some years before the war and also spoke fluent Russian. Throughout his life – and evidence of this will be seen – Price, when speaking or writing about Russia in 1918, habitually began his sentences with 'Ransome and I ...' The two men were indeed at one in their opposition to the prospect of Allied armed intervention in Russia, which now seemed increasingly likely. Ransome had excellent contacts and appears to have used them with great skill and sophistication. He was later known to boast that he had played chess with Lenin. He had not – like Price – spent half the war years away from the capital and he had not let his political orientation show, as Price had done. To the end of his life he protested that he was a completely apolitical writer. But he believed that the British press was being grossly unfair to the Russian government and he did everything in his power to set the record straight. He too was severely censored in London. But the two men had little in common beyond their desire to see the Bolsheviks given a chance. Ransome left Russia in July 1918 and spent the rest of the war in Stockholm or back in London. He remained in touch with leading Bolsheviks however, notably with Radek, and his information even from outside Russia continued to be well founded. Price and Ransome were sometimes bracketed together as more or less subversive characters in the internal memoranda circulating in the Foreign Office, but the Foreign Office also sometimes used Ransome for their own purposes. He visited London several times in the course of the war and was actually in London at the time of the Bolshevik Revolution. Where Ransome only wanted – his words – to see fair play, Price decided – his words – to sink or swim with the Soviets. Ransome returned to Russia for the *Manchester Guardian* in 1919 and wrote a series of sympathetic and penetrating articles; later still he returned as its resident correspondent. It is ironical however that it is he – not Price – who is now thought of as the sole voice of the *Manchester Guardian* on the Russian Revolution.

The American press correspondents were on the whole more sympathetic to the Revolution than the British ones, and foremost among these was John Reed, author of the classic *Ten Days that Shook the World*. Price met Reed at the Smolny on the night of 7 November 1917; indeed they both reported some of the same speeches. In fact Reed had only a sketchy knowledge of Russian but he never lacked willing translators. His account of the days that followed is both more literary and more immediate than the one that Price recounted in his *Reminiscences* two years later. Both men had all their papers and records confiscated after leaving Russia: Reed on returning to America, Price on crossing into Germany in December 1918. But Reed's papers were returned to him; Price's were not. Nonetheless their books do not contradict but rather complement each other. Reed did not stay long after the Bolshevik Revolution, although he – like Ransome – returned to Russia and indeed died in Russia in 1920. But Price never had the chance to get to know him well.

Nothing that Price wrote after 25 June 1918 was ever actually seen in print. A few of his dispatches, sent by wireless in Morse code were picked up and translated in Royal Navy ships and sent on to the Foreign Office, in whose archives they are still to be found. He kept copies of nearly everything he sent after February 1918, when he began to suspect that he was attracting too much attention in the Official Press Bureau, and some of these are included in what follows. By July, Price had given up hope that Britain would not attack northern Russia. Nothing he wrote was being printed and in any case the British government refused to let either his salary or any of his own money leave the country. He had nothing with which to buy food for the second time that year. The first German journalist to arrive in Russia after the Treaty of Brest-Litovsk – the writer Alfons Paquet – described him that summer as 'emaciated'. When Tchicherin offered Price a job as a translator in the Foreign Office he accepted it. The day after he began work there the Allies landed troops at Murmansk and Archangel. The first work that Price did, therefore, was to translate into English the leaflet appeals of Lenin and Tchicherin to the Allied forces to lay down their arms and return home. These were to be scattered from aeroplanes, smuggled across the lines and pinned to trees, and they were indeed picked up by the soldiers, although immediately confiscated if seen. However copies of them have turned up in libraries all over the world, deposited by soldiers who managed to conceal them from their officers. The most famous – or infamous – of those, which

Price wrote himself, was also the first: 'The Truth about the Allied Intervention in Russia', which appears on pp. 141–9 below.

In a letter to Ransome, who by then was in Stockholm, Radek announced in the summer of 1918 that Price had 'joined the Party'. It is impossible to know what that meant literally. There was at that time no other Communist Party that Price could have joined, and a number of French and other West European sympathisers in Moscow in September 1918 were apparently given some form of membership status. Price had identified himself with the party and the fate of the Government and he considered himself a Marxist. (In later life he said that the only thing he regretted about this experience was the effect it had on his prose style.)

After the end of the war, in November 1918, having discussed with Tchicherin and Radek what he might now most usefully do, Price applied to the Foreign Minister of the first German republican government for permission to visit Berlin and report on developments in Germany for the *Manchester Guardian*. He was not aware that Scott had come under pressure to disown him after his pamphlet had been circulated in Whitehall and had actually written to him terminating the relationship. Price never got the letter, never even saw a copy until shortly before he died. It would have made no difference. He now had only two objectives: to see whether the world revolution had really begun in Germany (as the more hopeful Bolsheviks believed but he personally doubted); and to try to get more accurate information about what was really going on in Russia across to the British press. He appears to have thought he would somehow be able to avoid British censorship if his copy was datelined 'Berlin'.

Price left Russia almost exactly four years after he had first arrived in the role of Special Correspondent for the *Manchester Guardian*. From being an affectionate but still more or less detached observer of 'dear old Russia, where everything is forbidden and everything is possible' (as he put it in a letter to his brother early in 1915), he had become a partisan and a propagandist for the new Russia. Why and how this change came about will become apparent in his account of the events to which he was a witness.

Notes on Russian Political Parties, 1880–1918

The Cadet party, a coalition of Liberal *intelligentsia*, was formed in August 1905 with a programme which included universal suffrage for a national legislative assembly, land redistribution and an eight-hour day. They rejected as inadequate the Tsar's October manifesto promising limited constitutional reform but did not – like the parties of the Left – boycott the elections and in the first Duma emerged as the largest single party. Their conflicts with the executive soon proved irreconcilable and, following the dissolution of the Duma, 120 of them (out of a total of 169) signed the Vyborg Manifesto calling on the whole population to adopt a policy of passive resistance to the Government. For this they were penalised by the loss of their political rights, and the Cadets entered the second Duma with their numbers reduced from 184 deputies to 99. They then adopted a more non-confrontational policy, but this did not save them from virtual annihilation in the election of 1907 under a new, more restrictive, electoral law. However an alliance of Cadets with the Octobrists and Trudoviks in the third and fourth Dumas succeeded in securing a number of modest reforms concerning education and local government. In 1915 they joined the Progressive Bloc. After the March Revolution the Cadets played a leading part in the Provisional Government, but after the November Revolution they no longer played a role in Russian politics and many of them emigrated.

NARODNIKS

The Narodniks, or 'People's Cause' party, was created in 1893 by the union of a number of populist groups active in three centres: Saratov, Orel and Moscow. Through their underground press they issued policy statements calling for freedom of assembly, press and religion and for the right of minorities to self-determination. They were put down by the authorities a year later, but some of them went on to join the Socialist Revolutionaries.

OCTOBRISTS

The party emerged as a group under the main leadership of Alexander Guchkov in November 1905 in response, like the Cadets, to the Tsar's October manifesto. Unlike the Cadets however, they believed the manifesto represented an opportunity to be taken, not rejected. By February 1906, 70 local branches had been established, consisting largely of landowners, businessmen, industrialists and the more conservative professionals. Their liberalism was modest and their representation in the second Duma small. But under the post-1907 electoral system, they became the largest single faction in the third Duma and were thrust into the centre of politics. In 1915 they joined the Progressive Bloc but internal disagreements and lack of discipline undermined their effectiveness. Although individual members like Guchkov and Rodzianko (later Chairman of the Duma) continued to be important, the party gradually faded out.

PROGRESSISTS

The Progressists, also known as the Progressives, began to occupy the ground between the Octobrists and the Cadets in 1907, and represented, primarily, the industrial and commercial community, especially in Moscow. They believed in the supremacy of the state, but a supremacy moderated by respect for the rights of people. They formed a distinct party in 1909 but had no base outside the Duma. Because they called for a constitutional monarchy with accountable ministers they were refused recognition as a legal party, but nonetheless played an important role in the formation of the Progressive Bloc and briefly led the opposition to the Government in 1916. The party ceased to exist as a coherent force shortly before the March Revolution.

SOCIAL DEMOCRATIC PARTY

The party developed out of the first Russian Marxist organisation, the Group for the Emancipation of Labour, which was formed in Zurich in 1883. A formal party organisation was created in 1898 but almost from the start was bedevilled by disputes over ideology. At the Second Party Congress, held in Brussels in 1903, it split over the issue of party organisation. The majority (Bolsheviks) voted with Lenin, the minority (Mensheviks) with Martov. At this time Lenin took the view that conditions in Russia were so repressive that only a disciplined elite, prepared to work underground, could effectively lead the Russian workers. This view coloured his attitude to organisational as well as ideological matters. Between 1903 and 1917 a series of party conferences, held in various European capitals, showed the differences between the two wings becoming ever more clearly defined. The mere fact that they were largely operating in exile tended to exacerbate factionalism.

In 1905 the Social Democrats boycotted the elections to the first Duma, but the Mensheviks changed their minds at the last moment and managed to return five deputies from the Caucasus. The second Duma contained 36 Mensheviks, 18 Bolsheviks and 11 unaffiliated Social Democrats. As deputies they began to use their parliamentary immunity to do legal party work outside the Duma. In December 1907 the Government dissolved the Duma in order to arrest the Social Democrats on the pretext that they were fomenting unrest; 16 of them were sentenced to terms of hard labour, the rest were exiled. Both wings of the party continued to be represented in the third and fourth Dumas, but never numbered more than 5 per cent of the deputies. In 1913 the Bolsheviks formed their own Duma faction. The two wings of the party were broadly united in opposition to the war although some Mensheviks ('defensists') were prepared to co-operate with non-governmental organisations like the War Industries Committees; some ('internationalists') played an important part in the European socialist peace movement, exemplified in the conferences at Zimmerwald and Kienthal; and some ('defeatists'), Lenin among them, thought defeat in an Imperialist war not too a high a price to pay if followed by civil war and the overthrow of the Government. In November 1914 all the Bolshevik deputies were arrested and sent to Siberia. The Mensheviks continued to function in the Duma and after the March Revolution played an important part in the Petrograd Soviet and later in the first Coalition of the Provisional Government. In the Pre-Parliament (October 1917) they argued for a socialist coalition at the forthcoming second Congress of Workers' and Soldiers' Deputies but opposed the seizure of power by the Bolsheviks, after which they were increasingly marginalised, although at first tolerated. At the seventh Party Congress (March 1918) the Bolsheviks renamed the party 'Communist'.

SOCIALIST REVOLUTIONARIES

Formed as a union of various populist groups in 1901, the Socialist Revolutionaries (SRs) began early on to concentrate on peasants' issues but had no official programme until 1905. From the start they were ready to use terrorism as an instrument of policy. As their membership expanded and their organisation improved they began to split into Right and (numerically larger) Left wings. They were, among other things, divided along these lines over the war of 1914. They boycotted the elections to all except the second Duma, when they gained 34 seats. After the March Revolution they played a dominant role in the Petrograd Soviet, at which time Kerensky, formerly a Trudovik, joined the party. They joined the Mensheviks and Cadets in the first and second Coalitions of the Provisional Government, but the two wings drew increasingly apart over the issues of war and peace. At the first All-Russia Congress of Workers and Soldiers Deputies the SRs had been the largest single party but at the second the Bolsheviks were dominant. The SRs walked out of the Congress in protest against the Bolshevik seizure of power but the Left SRs then formed a separate party and joined the Bolsheviks in a coalition. The Treaty of Brest-Litovsk again widened the gap and at the fifth All Russia Congress in July 1918 the Left SRs were ready to take up arms against the Germans in the Ukraine once more. They accused the Bolsheviks of having betrayed the Revolution. Two Left SRs, reverting to their early policy of terrorism, murdered the German Ambassador. An attempted Left SR *coup* was soon liquidated. After a brief appearance in uneasy alliance with the counter-revolutionary Directorate at Ufa, the party disintegrated.

TRUDOVIKS

Never an organised party, the Trudoviks were a loose coalition of Left-ish parties in the first and second Dumas, numerous enough to affect the outcome of important votes. Their primary concern was with the agrarian problem. The changes in electoral law undermined much of their support in the second Duma in 1907 but at the same time the increased representation of Social Democrats and Socialist Revolutionaries gave them allies in their demands for the abolition of private landed property and equal rights to the land for those who worked it. In the fourth Duma there were only ten Trudoviks, one of them being Kerensky. They refused to vote for war credits and lobbied for the 'discontinuance' of the war.

CHAPTER 1

Russia in 1915–16

When Price left England in December 1914 a press campaign led by The Times *was being worked up to convince public opinion that Russia – widely perceived to be a repressive autocracy – was going to become a democracy under the influence of France and Britain and would save Western Europe by 'steamrollering' into Germany. Vast numbers of men were indeed deployed against the Austrian Empire in Galicia and against Germany via Poland, and for a few weeks in the autumn of 1914 the Russian armies had seemed invincible. But by the time Price arrived in Russia they had begun to fall back. There had been an almost incredible lack of preparation for the supply of munitions or even such basic necessities of war as boots. In the first ten months of the war Russian casualties amounted to nearly four million men. By the spring of 1915 the armies were everywhere in retreat. Price made several visits to the fronts, was himself caught in the retreat from Lemburg, and watched the burning of the Galician oil fields by the Austrians. Military control over the civil authorities in the rear of the armies was both extensive and ruthless. He saw whole areas being cleared of their civilian populations and Jews being led away in chains. He had been given introductions to a number of key political figures in the capital, including the Foreign Minister, Sazonov, and the head of the Russian Red Cross, Guchkov. He secured interviews with them but then found that the censors would not pass what he had written about them. 'Rather than bury my conscience in Europe I decided to betake myself to Asia,' he wrote,[8] although in all honesty he was not sorry to go. He set out for Tiflis early in June 1915.*

Anything he wrote about Russian politics and economics between June 1915 and April 1917 was heavily dependent on what he could find in the Russian press, although he talked to soldiers and civilians wherever he went and his articles are full of reported conversations. The first of the letters published in this collection of his writings is an attempt to summarise the events of the ten preceding months for the benefit of his English correspondents, primarily Hirst and Trevelyan. The letter contains some statements that cannot be corroborated in detail, but the general picture he describes is borne out in any history of the period. Thus among the subjects mentioned in this letter, Price had seen for himself the oppression of the Jews in Poland, but had probably only read about the attempts which had been made to impose Russian Orthodoxy upon

*the Roman Catholic populations in territory taken from the Austrians.
Similarly he had seen for himself the shortage of munitions at the front
but could only have read about the dismissal of the War Minister,
Sukhomlinov, when the scandal of his mismanagement finally became
uncontainable.*

*In August 1915 the Duma [Russian Parliament] began to demand
more formal measures for the co-ordination of the war effort, such as the
creation of a Defence Council representing the government departments,
trades, industries and voluntary organisations most concerned, as well
as the Duma itself. Resolutions in favour of political reform began to be
passed. In response to public opinion a number of the most reactionary
ministers were dismissed. On 7 September a Progressive Bloc was formed
consisting of the deputies of virtually all the parties except those on the
extreme Right and the Social Democrats. It began to look as if something
like a constitutional monarchy might be in the process of evolution.*

*Inevitably there was a reaction. The 'plot' to which Price refers was
probably a mixture of fact and rumour, but it was true enough that the
Tsarina, whose theory of autocracy was even more extreme than that of
her husband, began to meddle in government affairs. Five days after the
formation of the Progressive Bloc the Duma was prorogued. All the factories
in Petrograd went on strike as if to confirm the need to reinstate a more
repressive regime. Under the influence of the Tsarina the Tsar took over
as Commander-in-Chief from his uncle, the able and liberal-minded Grand
Duke Nicholas. From now on he was more often away at the Army
Headquarters than in Petrograd, leaving the Tsarina a free hand to pursue
her intrigues. She was able to secure, in her turn, the dismissal of
ministers of whom she, or the Court favourite, Rasputin, disapproved.
It was not true that she was pro-German, but rumours of peace feelers
were already circulating in all the belligerent countries in 1915, and Price's
generalisations about the pro-German-ness of the Court were probably
taken from the Liberal and anti-German press, who were only too willing
to believe in the Tsarina's complicity.*

*The emotional reception of the Tsar at the opening of the following
session of the Duma in February 1916 was possibly due to wishful
thinking about the prospects of internal reform among members of the
Progressive Bloc. But the replacement, on the eve of the opening of the
session, of a merely incompetent Prime Minister, Goremykin, by an out-
and-out reactionary, Sturmer, demonstrated what was really being
proposed. While Price was perhaps a little hazy as to the exact sequence
of events in the summer and autumn of 1915, there is no question but
that he was conveying an accurate impression of the state of the country.
'It is' wrote Sir Bernard Pares in his* Fall of the Russian Monarchy
*'from the autumn of 1915 that we must date the serious growth of
national discontent.'[9]*

Memorandum to C. P. Trevelyan
Tiflis, 30 March 1916

All last year the reaction was very strong. The religious persecution in Galicia, the cruel oppression of the Jews, the failure to carry out any reforms long promised in Poland, was finally crowned by the great scandals of last summer when wholesale bribery and corruption was discovered at the War Office. Popular discontent rose like a whirlwind and the War Minister resigned. Then followed a period of quiescence till the autumn ... In September last a reactionary plot was hatched and the Duma was summarily dismissed without any notice as to when it would be summoned again ... Strikes then broke out in Moscow and at the meeting of the United Provincial Councils of Empire[10] which met at Moscow to discuss methods of organising war supplies in the provinces, some extraordinarily plain speaking took place which got into the press.

Then during November came another crisis. Germany proposed to Russia a separate peace on apparently pretty lenient terms. The Court Party round the Emperor, many of whom are Germans, coupled with some of the higher grades of the Bureaucracy, fearing that the rising popular discontent as a result of the mismanagement of the war would force them to give concessions to the people, favoured a peace with Germany in order to strangle this movement. The influence of Germany, they felt, was not so dangerous to Russian autocracy as that of France and England. The intellectuals, lower grade officials, professional classes, merchants and Moscow manufacturers, all of which represent in different forms the Liberal elements of the country, appear to have intervened, and rumour has it that Moscow threatened to rebel and call upon the army to go on fighting if Petersburg gave in. The Government was frightened and the crisis passed. The bourgeois and Liberal elements won their victory, which was for 'war and internal reform' against the Court and higher bureaucrats, who were for 'peace and internal reaction'. ... The Duma was summoned in February amid great excitement. For the first time in Russian history the Emperor came to the Duma and opened it, thus giving it a recognition which it has never had before.

The speeches showed a keen determination to continue the war. The extreme Right or Reactionary Party spoke for war, but not with such fervour as the Progressives ... the intellectuals and bourgeois, merchants and capitalists, who constitute the Cadet and kindred parties. They are the most keen for carrying on the war to the end, and the most bitter haters of everything German in the country ... They dislike Germany's economic hold over Russia and want to see Russia develop independently of outside influence. Some of them even said, in speeches in the Duma, that while they welcome

English and French political influence they don't want their economic influence, and want Russia to be economically self-supporting ... These Progressives, or Russian Liberals, while very determined to get all concessions from the Government on internal questions, such as equal rights for small nationalities in the Empire, responsible government etc., are nevertheless on all foreign questions most chauvinist of any party in Russia, and are great believers in war to the last gasp as a means of saving Russia internally. They are the modern representatives of the old Slavophile school: strongly nationalist but more practical and, in internal affairs, liberal. It is safe to say that all the thinking men of Russia are in sympathy with these parties, which now call themselves in the Duma the 'Progressive Bloc'.

But now we come to the Social Democrats who, though a very small party in the Duma and in the country too, are interesting as showing exactly the same sort of split as in the Social Democrats of Germany and England. A part of them, about half, are for war with Germany and so are the Socialist Revolutionaries, because they think that Russia is threatened with German militarism. They seem to be like the English Trade Unionists. The other half, like the ILP in England,[11] have been uncompromisingly against the war from the first and are now. I know their leader but have not seen him for some time.[12] The other day he made a speech in the Duma, which was not reported but which I heard about, calling on the Government to say what the objects of the war were, and declaring most courageously that the masses of Europe were for peace and were only held to war by their rulers. The speech was violently attacked by Miliukov, the leader of the Progressive Bloc, who said that although Russia did not begin the war still she would not end it till she had got Constantinople – a rather naive admission of an appetite for territorial expansion ...

So you see Imperialism and militarism are as deeply rooted in Russia as in Germany, only in Russia it is less effective because it is badly organised. The common people, meanwhile, are getting daily more and more sick of the war. The economic situation is becoming serious. There is little capital in Russia. Loans and Treasury Bonds have a very limited market, so that the war is being financed on paper money, with the inevitable result of currency depreciation and high prices. The cost of living has risen 75 per cent. The wages in industrial centres increase only very slightly and the income of the peasants not at all. The deposits in the banks have been increased by three-and-a-half milliard roubles but this represents profits of contractors and private firms fattening on the war. There is no income tax in Russia so the whole burden is falling on the poor and they are beginning to get pretty restive. I have talked with many common soldiers on my visits to the fronts.

The first thing they ask me is 'when is this war going to end? We want to go home – we have had enough'. That has been said to me not ten or a hundred times but I should think a thousand times these last three months. Even the lower grade of the bourgeois and some of the poorer intellectuals speak in this strain for they feel the economic pressure is becoming so serious. The other day Tiflis was without bread and sugar for three days. Disturbances have also taken place in Baku and Moscow, led by women.

Anyhow the war, with all its suffering for Russia, is certainly doing this much. It is forcing the Government to introduce a direct system of taxation and for the first time in the history of the country an income tax is before the Duma. All the large profits of the war contractors and the huge bribes taken by officials will now be unearthed and made to contribute and, last but not least, the vast estates of the Empire and the Imperial family, representing 35 per cent of the land of European Russia, which up to now has been left undeveloped and simply used as instruments for squeezing out revenue for the Imperial Chest will, if the logical result of this new taxation is followed up, have to contribute too. But before this takes place, there will be some pretty tough struggles and the future is one of absorbing interest. The autocracy and privileged classes will not yield their position easily, but the days of the old regime are numbered. Whether the chauvinism of the Progressive Bloc is likely to be better than the reactionary stagnation of the Court Party seems to me doubtful, but it is one of the changes that are obviously inevitable.

Meanwhile the silent masses suffer, and hardly a murmur breaks the sound of the tramp of Siberian peasant youth going off to kill and be killed by Arabian and Turkish shepherds.

Memorandum to C. P. Trevelyan
Tiflis, 27 September 1916

Perhaps the most acute and dangerous problem in Russia is the land question and the status of the peasants. On this question it is very difficult to generalise, because the conditions are not the same all over the country. Thus where I have been in the government of Kharkov I found most favourable conditions. Landlords have never been very powerful there and most of the land has for a long time past been in the hands of the peasants, who are the descendants of old Cossack colonists, who received their lands free. In the villages I found here only men over 45, boys under 18 and women. The whole of the male population between these ages are at the war and my impression is that Russia has mobilised the whole of her available manhood ... Of course it must be remembered that a very large percentage of Russia's mobilised manhood is non-combatant, infinitely greater than any Western army, because in the cumbersome machinery of the Russian army there is always much leakage of strength. But the astounding thing is that this does not seem to have made any difference to the productiveness of Russian agriculture. Just the same amount of land is tilled and worked as before the war and agricultural production has decreased in the Empire by only a quite infinitesimal amount. I account for this first of all by the absolute sobriety among the peasants that remain in the villages.[13] Before the war in Siberia, when I was there, I remember observing great drunkenness. The state of affairs is absolutely different now. Then again the price of agricultural produce is very high and the peasants are making money at the expense of the taxpayers and the urban population. Their increased wealth they are partly hiding in coin and partly laying out in agricultural machinery, which helps them to get over the labour difficulty. So what with this and sobriety, one Russian peasant produces from the land very much more each year than he produced before the war. In some governments where the landlords have long been poor, the peasants are steadily buying up the land. This is more the case in the south-western governments. Everywhere the principle of peasant proprietorship is growing and with it a feeling of economic independence which will give rise to a stronger political consciousness. In one house I went into with Professor Sobolev we talked first with the old people, an old man and woman. In discussing the war they ended their remarks by saying 'Glory to God; for our Emperor there will still be victory'. They were still living in the psychology of the reign of Nicholas I or Alexander II. Not so however was the younger generation of this household. They read the papers, knew all about Romania's entry into the war, knew about the naval battle of Jutland, wanted to know when the war would end and what Russia, that is the Russian people (not the Tsar), would gain by this war. They were intensely interested but quite calm and free from any bitterness, although it was clear they were in a state of great expectation.

On the other hand Russian friends of mine both here and in Kharkov, who have been in the central and northern governments, tell me that the disposition of the peasants that are left on the land there is very different and much more bitter. A Russian lady who has been about a good deal among the peasants of the government of Moscow tells me that the peasants there are talking most extraordinarily openly and frankly and with an independence that she has never heard before in her life. What most seems to anger them is the fact that the Government is doing nothing to provide after the war for the maimed and disabled soldiers and they say openly what they will do if Petrograd does not bring itself into line with their wishes. In the more central governments of Orel, Kursk, Kaluga and Riazan the land question appears to be acute. Here the remnants of the old aristocracy are strong and there are great estates of Grand Dukes to whom the possession of land is part of a social privilege. This sort of landlordism has weakened a good deal, of recent years, from natural causes. But it remains in these governments and in times like these entrenches itself all the more strongly behind its privileges. Here the peasants, on emancipation from serfdom, received – in spite of all that Alexander II could do – very small land portions, and since then they have increased in numbers, making their position worse. I hear that Petrograd is alarmed at the feeling in these governments, for there is almost certain to be an attempt by some means or other to increase the peasants' land by dividing up the estates after the war. It is too much to expect, with the present regime in Petrograd, that the problem will be handled with statesmanship. On the other hand I doubt a conflagration. The Government is strong and has a large force of military and civil police, which I have heard variously estimated at from one-and-a-half to two millions. They could probably count on bribing a part of the army, and for the rest the soldiers on demobilisation will be so keen to return to their homes, that they will probably throw over any idea of marching on Petrograd out of sheer exhaustion. Besides, as I point out, this particular form of discontent is not found all over the country and in other parts takes other forms.

Memorandum to F. W. Hirst
(published in Common Sense, 9 December 1916)
Kharkov, 30 November 1916

A correct analysis of Russian politics at this moment is very difficult. The one thing certain is that discontent is universal, mainly owing to an extraordinary mismanagement in the distribution of resources. Russia, which up till now was providing practically the greater part of Europe with the surplus of its agricultural products, is more or less faced with a famine. The reckless commandeering of livestock during the first twelve months of the war, by which large quantities of cattle were often driven together without sufficient fodder or attendance, resulted in much fruitless destruction and waste. In most cases no distinction was made as to the quality of the cattle commandeered, so that high-class breeding cattle were slaughtered along with those of inferior quality. Last year's precipitate retreat resulted in the destruction and loss of large stores behind the army lines. The consequence is that at the present moment meat in Russia proper, apart from rising fourfold in price, is practically unobtainable, and supplies, in so far as they can be provided for the three days on which the sale of meat is permitted, have to be drawn largely from Siberia.

Disregard of the actual position and red-tape calculations have brought about similar conditions for all commodities, with a consequent enormous rise in prices ... The rise in prices of manufactured articles has even surpassed that of food supplies. The Russian industry labours under the difficulties of procuring sufficient raw material and labour. Wages have trebled and imports from abroad are practically restricted to articles of immediate war necessity ...

During this war all classes in Russia have since the beginning tried to help the Government to bring the war to a successful end at the cost of great personal sacrifice. The best relief work for the wounded, as well as for the refugees, has been carried out by the two most powerful unions in Russia, the Union of the Town Councils, with the Mayor of Moscow, Tchelnokov, and the Union of the County Councils, with Prince Lvov as the head. The admirable results obtained by these organisations, and the consequent popularity of their respective presidents, has been from the very beginning a cause of dissatisfaction to the authorities in Petrograd. The popularity of the above-mentioned personalities is known to be viewed with great suspicion in bureaucratic circles, which are well aware of the efficient work done by private enterprise during this time and are afraid, with good reason, that in any movement against the present system these personalities are likely to take a leading hand.

Memorandum to F. W. Hirst
(published in Common Sense, 13 January 1917)
Tiflis, 9 December 1916

The most important part of the front in Russia is undoubtedly at the moment the 'rear', for the economic disorganisation in the country will, unless removed, interfere with further military operations. If, as according to some, the war which burst on Europe in August 1914 was made inevitable by the internal condition of the Continent, so now the economic strain caused by war is beginning to make each belligerent State look more closely into its own internal condition. This is as much true of Russia as of any other belligerent ... The lack of railway facilities may be one cause which leads to this result, but perhaps more significant is the unwillingness of the Government to make use of the voluntary efforts of the public bodies like the *Zemstvo*s, the Union of Cities and other popular institutions, which have shown their readiness to work for the common welfare ... Mr Miliukov, the spokesman of the

Progressive Bloc in the Duma, has severely criticised the Government for its attitude towards the *Zemstvo* organisations which have been engaged, for a long time past, in organising the rear of the armies, building roads and hospitals and establishing food distribution centres for refugees. The Government, he said, was secretly accusing these public bodies of revolutionary tendencies and was planning to 'emasculate' them. The same criticism of the Government was expressed by Alexander Guchkov, the president of the 'supply department of *Zemstvo*s, cities and Red Cross' in a conversation with the writer ...

The influences in the country that are said to be working for peace are the least undesirable of Russian public life. It is true, of course, that the Social Democrats have this object also in view, but their numbers are too small to be of any account ... Among what is known as the 'Right' both in the country and the Duma there appears to be a split ... One group is nationalist first and reactionary second and the other group is reactionary first and nationalist second ... It is not correct to assume that the reaction in Russia is a purely German product, although this notion is widespread, even among Russians themselves. Reaction can be a Russian-made product just as it can be a Prussian-made product. The members of the present Cabinet have Russian names and are Russian to the backbone, and if the idea that created and fostered the Holy Alliance[14] is still in existence today it is because the conservative elements of two neighbouring countries naturally see that it is their interest to support each other.

It must not be forgotten, however, that the causes of the economic crisis which has brought all these slumbering political questions again to the fore, have deep roots and these cannot be removed simply by a change in the political orientation of the Government or by constitutional reforms. The plain fact is that Russia, like all belligerent countries, is consuming more than she is producing, and the greater part of her population is employed on unproductive labour.

CHAPTER 2

The Eve of the Revolution

Price arrived in Tiflis (now Tblisi) with letters of introduction to the Commander-in-Chief, who at the time was still the Grand Duke Nicholas. From there he set out with horse and tent for the front against Turkey, which had entered the war on the side of Germany and Austria in October 1914. In the spring of the following year the Turks, in an attempt to outflank the Russian army in the Caucasus, had occupied part of northern Persia. In the course of the summer the Russians turned them out and the retreating Turks devastated the villages of the Armenian populations on the Urumiah plateau who had risen against them in the wake of their advance. By the end of the year there were something like a quarter of a million refugees, Moslem as well as Christian, in the area between the Black Sea and the Caspian.

Price now began to play a double role as War Correspondent and as an agent for the distribution of relief on behalf of the Lord Mayor's Fund in London. He wrote 20 major articles for the Manchester Guardian *about the fighting in this theatre and its strategic implications. Most of these were posted from Tiflis although the Russian army sometimes let him use their wires. Scott did not consider that news from this theatre was of immediate topical importance and treated it rather as background material. In the summer of 1916 Price also spent several weeks in Kharkov with his friend Professor Sobolev, working in the University Library, where he did much of the research for his* Economist *articles.*

During this time the Social Democrats were little in evidence. It has been estimated that in March 1917 both branches of the Social Democrats plus the Socialist Revolutionaries numbered no more than 40,000, many of their leaders still being then in exile abroad or in Siberia. Moreover the Mensheviks themselves were split between the main body of the party and the Left, who were now distinguishable from the Bolsheviks more by disagreement over tactics than by theory. From 1916 the left-wing Mensheviks began to be known as Menshevik Internationalists or Zimmerwaldists, so named after an international peace conference of European socialists held at Zimmerwald in Switzerland in September 1915, which Lenin himself attended. A second conference was held in Kienthal in April 1916. There was general agreement on condemning the war at both conferences, but on little else.

Postcard to Anna Maria Philips (aunt)
Kutais, Caucasus, 16 December 1916

I have returned from a journey in Lazistan (NE Asia Minor) where I have been distributing winter clothing for the Moslems. Have come here to buy more material to send up. Return to Tiflis shortly. Most important events are happening in the internal situation of Russia about which I cannot write. As soon as I can I must go to Petrograd. I have delayed hitherto because in the towns of European Russia one is threatened with starvation. [No sugar, no meat, often no bread]* and when there is any it is sour and black. Food is still to be got in the Caucasus.

Letter to Anna Maria Philips
Tiflis, 1 February 1917

I have been here all the time since I wrote to you last. Mr Backhouse of the Lord Mayor's Fund has just been joined by Mr Catchpool, a young Quaker who has been out in the government of Samara working with the Friends' Unit, who are organising relief for the Polish refugees. We are all three going to start an industry in Erivan, about a day's journey from here, to provide work for the Armenian refugees, of which there are about 200,000 in the Transcaucasus this winter. We want to start them on making by hand cotton clothing for them to wear next summer, when it is hoped they will be able to go back to their homes. I have been busy doing some writing but not as much as I should like, because I want to bring out a book with my diary of my travels in the last two years.[15] I want to get it finished before the spring but I don't know if I shall succeed.

I have not heard a word from Charles [Trevelyan]. When you write to him please find out if he got my long letter in September and my article which I sent him for the *Contemporary Review* in October.[16] It seems very little use to send long articles or descriptive letters home now. The post has been very irregular indeed of late. My *Manchester Guardian*s have been weeks late and many I have not received at all. The postal service between Norway and England seems to have been cut off for some days on account of disagreement about the blockade. Also the state of affairs in this country is becoming so remarkable that it cannot adequately be described in a letter for obvious reasons ... It is no use attempting to make a journey into the interior of European Russia because I should probably never get back here again. In order to travel on the

* The passage in square brackets was blacked out by the Russian censor but remained legible.

railways you have to wait for days at the station, and then fight your way into cattle trucks in which you have to stand, not sit, for anything from a week to ten days. There is nothing to eat anywhere on the way, so that a railway journey now is becoming as dangerous an experience as fighting on the front.

The Liberal parties and the Progressive Bloc in the Duma are accusing the Government of being responsible for the present state of affairs but they don't seem to see that this is the inevitable result of a war of unparalleled destruction that has lasted over two years. The ministerial crisis in England and France seems to me to have been caused by the same dissatisfaction as exists here.[17] In both cases the people are right in being dissatisfied but they are dissatisfied at present for the wrong reason, for they imagine that it could all be made a paradise if the war was prosecuted more vigorously instead of realising that the only thing that will save the civilisation of Europe, if it can be saved at all now, is peace.

Some remarkable events have been taking place in Petrograd and the air is full of weird and uncanny rumours. All one can do is to sit tight and wait till something happens, and before the year is over I expect something is pretty sure to take place, more or less exciting. I can say no more.

I have sent every fortnight or so an article to *The Economist* on the economic situation in this country, from information that I obtain from the various economic journals that I take in. That in itself is no small work, I can tell you, to read every day some ten or twelve Russian papers and journals and extract all the news for an article.

Letter to C. Lee Williams (uncle)
Tiflis, 1 February 1917

... For my part, living as I am on the threshold between east and west, I can look with dispassion on the ruin of European civilisation and I am only surprised at the extraordinarily rapid rate at which it totters to its fall. After all, it took the best part of 500 years for Rome and its civilisation to decay, and even the Ottoman Empire in Europe has taken four centuries to recede. But now, in less than three years the lid has been torn off the whited sepulchre of Europe and within we see—! I and some of those who think with me see however one hope. We fancy we can see a dim light shining in the east in the confines of Asia. 'Ex Oriente lux!' ... I should not be surprised if 1917 may not see the dawn of reason in the mind of man, stimulated by that most valuable of all psychological tonics – hunger.

CHAPTER 3

The March Revolution

During Sturmer's premiership the loss of Poland and much of the railway system in the north-western provinces of the Russian Empire further aggravated the food shortage. When the Duma met in November 1916 the Cadet leader Miliukov made a ferocious attack upon Sturmer's mismanagement of the Government, with the repeated refrain 'Is it incompetence or is it treason?' He succeeded in getting Sturmer dismissed but his successor, the former Minister of Transport, Trepov, did nothing to deal with the causes of growing and now open discontent. Rasputin was murdered at the end of December 1916 by aristocratic members of the Court circle if only because his behaviour was now so notorious as to bring the monarchy itself into disrepute.

When, early in February 1917 a British delegation under Lord Milner arrived in Petrograd to discuss inter-Allied strategy, finance and supply, strenuous efforts were made to keep them from discovering how serious the state of affairs in Russia had become. The President of the Duma, Rodzianko, together with Miliukov and Prince Lvov were among those who succeeded, however, in warning members of the delegation that a revolution was now probably inevitable.

The Russian Revolution did not take place on a particular day or even in a particular month. A whole series of events led, in March 1917, to the abdication of the Tsar and the formation of a series of Provisional Governments. What is called the March Revolution was – apart from the abdication of the Tsar – little more than a series of planned reforms, and the inadequacy of these was the main reason for the November Revolution.

In Tiflis, in February, Price began to hear rumours of strikes, even of the possibility of a general strike. The Duma met on 27 February. The Government chose this moment to order the provincial offices of Zemgor (the alliance of Town and County Councils) to close down. Zemgor was the one organisation that still managed to ensure that some food, at least, was distributed. There were bread riots in Petrograd. The police fired into the crowds but soldiers sent to restore order began to take the side of the people. Ordered to disperse, the Duma refused. On 12 March, it appointed a Provisional Committee under the chairmanship of Rodzianko. On the same day the first meeting took place of a hastily elected Council [Soviet] of Workers' and Soldiers' Deputies: the Petrograd Soviet. Thus a kind of dyarchy was created. The Provisional Committee's appeals to the Tsar

*to appoint a Prime Minister enjoying popular confidence remained
unanswered and the Tsar remained at the Army Headquarters. On 14
March, therefore, a Provisional Government was formed under Prince
Lvov. The Minister of Justice in that government was the populist
[Trudovik] lawyer Alexander Kerensky. Kerensky was also Vice-
President of the Petrograd Soviet. The soviet was willing to give conditional
support to the Provisional Government on the understanding that a
Constituent Assembly based on universal suffrage should be summoned.
The Provisional Government now secured the support of the Army in
demanding the abdication of the Tsar and the formation of a government
responsible to the Duma. On 15 March, the Tsar met a delegation from
the Provisional Government and agreed to abdicate in favour of his brother,
the Grand Duke Michael. But the Grand Duke declined the office and
Russia became,* de facto *at least, a republic.*

*Price heard the news of the Tsar's abdication on 16 March and
attended, two days later in Tiflis, a great gathering of people from every
corner of the Caucasus who had come together to mark the occasion. Later
on the same day he was summoned by the Grand Duke Nicholas, who
wished, he said, to make a statement for the* Manchester Guardian.
*Price wrote an account of the interview and sent it off, together with the
Grand Duke's statement, at once. To the end of his life he was absolutely
certain that he had seen this dispatch in print, in the* Manchester
Guardian, *in the reading room of the British Embassy in Petrograd a
few weeks later. But it is not to be found in any copy of that paper in
the British Newspaper Library. The most likely explanation is that the
newspapers sent to embassies abroad were first editions whereas the
editions deposited in the British Library were later, if not the last,
editions. It was not at all uncommon for censors at the Official Press Bureau
to be instructed to ring up an editor and let him know that if he printed
or continued to print a certain item he might find himself in trouble under
the Defence of the Realm Act. Such an hypothesis would certainly
explain the disappearance of Price's piece from the* Manchester Guardian.
The account which appears below comes from UDC *and was probably
an extract from one of Price's memoranda to Trevelyan, which he sent
by post.*

*The probable reason for its disappearance is instructive, and is an insight
into the instinctive reaction of the British government and the Foreign
Office to the mere fact that the Tsar had abdicated. It is a matter of record
that, on the day of Price's interview with the Grand Duke, the British
Ambassador in Petrograd, Sir George Buchanan, reported to London
that he had been discussing with Miliukov (now Foreign Minister in
the first Provisional Government) the undesirability of Russia becoming
'committed to republicanism'.*[18] *Buchanan added that he could see a
possibility that the Grand Duke Nicholas or another Grand Duke might
be persuaded to accept the role of Tsar 'in a really liberal constitution'.
Almost the Tsar's last act had been to reappoint his uncle Commander-*

in-Chief and the appointment had been confirmed by the Provisional Government. It soon became clear, however, that most members of that government were in fact opposed to the appointment and so were a significant number of officers at the Army Headquarters, who feared that the Grand Duke might indeed do exactly what Buchanan hoped he might be persuaded to do. But the Grand Duke was a disappointment to the British Foreign Office. He refused to become involved in any intrigue and went quietly into exile. Clearly the British government found it difficult to envisage a Russian government without a Tsar.

Despite the attempts to warn the Milner Mission in February, the March Revolution was so little expected in London that the chamber of the House of Commons was almost empty when the news was given, and a group of MPs had twice to prevent it from being counted out. When at last an official statement was made on behalf of the Government, a week later, Lloyd George told the House that the Provisional Government had been formed solely for the purpose of carrying on the war more efficiently. At the Official Press Bureau censors had been instructed to 'pass nothing relating to any internal trouble in Russia'. A large number of telegrams were thus held up for some days. When they were released the censors were told they would have to be 'carefully dressed' and editors were asked to use 'great care and discretion' in the publication of any matter relating to events in Russia.[19] Robert (later Sir Robert) Bruce Lockhart, then still a Vice-Consul in Moscow, sent a message to the Foreign Office saying that most accounts of the March Revolution in the British press, and especially those in The Times, *had 'entirely misunderstood the psychology of the Russian Revolution' and that 'a most unfortunate impression' had been created in Russia.[20]*

Postcard to Anna Maria Philips
Tiflis, 13 March 1917

Just a line to say I am well. Most exciting times. I knew this was coming sooner or later but did not think it would come so quickly. Have been running about the Caucasus for last fortnight attending revolutionary meetings. Interviewed Grand Duke Nicholas last week before he left here and telegraphed his statement to 'M G'. Tomorrow I leave for Moscow and then Petrograd. Will keep you informed of my movements. I am not sure what my address will be till I get there ... Whole country is wild with joy, waving red flags and singing *Marseillaise*. It has surpassed my wildest dreams and I can hardly believe it is true. After two-and-a-half years of mental suffering and darkness I at last begin to see light. Long live Great Russia who has shown the world the road to freedom. May Germany and England follow in her steps.

Manchester Guardian, *27 April 1917*
'How the Revolution Came to the Caucasus'
Tiflis, 19 March 1917

The prorogation of the Duma on March 11 was the signal for revolt. The news reached the Caucasus the following day, and the railwaymen of Tiflis and the oil workers of Baku prepared for a general strike. The rapid developments in Petrograd, however, leading within four days to the abdication of the Emperor and the establishment of the Provisional Government, rendered the general strike in the provinces unnecessary. Complete outward calm prevailed with intense suppressed excitement all over the Caucasus, and as soon as communication was established between the heads of the municipalities, local labour organisations and the Provisional Government preparations were made for a great mass meeting at Tiflis on Sunday, March 18. That morning telegrams had been received at Tiflis ordering the abolition of the secret police, the release of all political prisoners, and the handing over of all civil affairs to the municipalities and rural councils. The Grand Duke Nicholas's appointment as Commander-in-Chief of the Russian army had also been confirmed by the Provisional Government. The Viceroyalty of the Caucasus therefore ceased to exist from March 18, and all authority, except in the zone of the active army in Armenia, passed into the hands of the civil administration.

On the morning of that day I passed down the streets of Tiflis and crossed the bridge over the Kura to the outskirts of the city. The streets were full of silent and serious people walking also in the same direction. They were all going to the mass meeting of the Caucasian people and to welcome a great day in the history of the Empire of which they are all sons. In an open space I saw a vast multitude assembled, and platforms were raised in six places. It reminded me at once of scenes at a general election in England, but it had surpassed my wildest dreams to think that I should witness such a sight in the Caucasus. Here had assembled almost every element in the multi-racial population of this part of the Empire. There were wild mountain tribes, Lesgians, Avars, Chechens and Swanetians in their long black cloaks and sheepskin caps. In the recesses of the Caucasus range, where their homes lie, the eddies of the waves of revolution had swept. Sunk in patriarchal feudalism until recently, many of them did not know whether they were subjects of the Tsar of Russia or of the Sultan of Turkey. Yet they had come walking across miles of mountain tracks to pay their humble tribute to the great Russian Revolution.

There were picturesque peasants of the fair provinces of Georgia who had driven in bullock waggons to the city. The Georgians are politically perhaps the most advanced of all the races of the

Caucasus. Formerly crushed under their corrupt and degenerate aristocracy, they have in the last twenty years developed every form of Western political thought. Marxism, collectivism, internationalist and Socialist Revolutionary movements have all got adherents among them. For years their ears have been turned to Europe, where they have listened patiently for every echo of political conflict. Then there were the Armenian merchants of Tiflis, typical bourgeois and staunch supporters of all progressive movements in Russia. There were the Tartar peasants of the East Caucasus who helped so much to inspire the revolutionary movements in Persia during 1908–9.[21] There were the representatives of the urban proletariat from the railway works at Tiflis and from the oil fields at Baku – the grimy products of Western European industrialism, which is slowly creeping into the East. There was the intellectual Russian student, Georgian poet and Armenian doctor, who up to this day of deliverance have been forced to hide the talent of their brains. Here in this great concourse of Caucasian peoples were standing side by side the most primitive and the most progresssive types of the human race. For years they have been sunk in apathy, fatalism and scepticism and their racial feuds have been purposely fomented by the old Government. Now the flood of their combined intellect and energy had burst forth and broken the rotten banks of privilege and oppression. I felt as I looked on that crowd that I was in the presence of a great psychical phenomenon. The spirit of Demos had suddenly risen out of a multitude of suppressed personalities, and had appeared in the form of that great concourse of mediaeval mountaineers and twentieth century proletariat, all inspired by one idea – brotherhood and freedom.

The scene was indeed a memorable one. First upon the platform mounted the Social Democrat leaders, who until now had held their meetings in secret places. They called upon the people to preserve order, and invited all to join their federations and form branches all over the Caucasus. While they were speaking there marched into the open space one regiment of the Tiflis garrison, headed by the colonel on horseback. He rode up to the platform and took off his hat. 'I have come,' he said, 'to ask in the name of the regiment that I command, to be allowed to take part in this gathering and to put our services unreservedly in the hands of the Provisional Government.' Amid tremendous cheering he mounted the platform and made a speech welcoming the dawn of a new day for their fatherland. 'Long live Great Russia!' he cried. 'Long live the peoples of the Caucasus! Long live the brotherhood between us! Long live all those who take part in this great work!' After him some of his soldiers from the ranks mounted the platform, and one of them said: 'Comrades, let us not forget that over there in Germany we have brothers crushed under that name, tyranny, from which we have just been delivered. May God grant that the hour of their deliverance has also struck.' Other orators among the soldiers also spoke in the same sense. In an automobile there then drove up the Chief of Staff of the Caucasus army, who mounted the platform and read a message from the Grand Duke, in which he stated that he realised the old regime had got to go, but asked the people to preserve quiet and keep the army free from political strife.

Amid deafening cheers there then appeared twenty political prisoners who since 1906 had been pining in the dungeons of the Tiflis prison for their support of the last revolution.[22] They were carried in on the shoulders of comrades and addressed the people with tears of joy in their eyes. Women representatives of the Post Office servants and of the Women's Educational League then spoke. Speeches in Georgian, Armenian, Tartar and the mountain dialects were made by those who, if not united in tongue, were now welded in human sympathy with the great Russian people.

Last, and perhaps most wonderful of all, there marched into the open space another garrison regiment with a brass band which at once struck up the *Marseillaise*. Every head was bared, the mountain tribesman took off his shaggy fur cap, the long hair of the Russian student fluttered in the breeze, and the troops who three days before had sung 'God protect the Tsar' now presented arms to the great French revolutionary hymn. Three times it was played amid frantic cheering. A young officer then got up and said: 'As one who took part in the last revolution and suffered, I know that it failed because the army was not united. Let us make no mistake again. Let us all, officers and men, keeping strictest discipline and the firmest union, stand by the Revolution with our lives.'

The great meeting then quietly dispersed, the mountain tribesmen to their distant valleys, the peasants to their villages, and the townsmen to their homes, and one of the greatest days in the history of the Caucasus had come and passed.

UDC, *July 1917*
'The Background of the Revolution'
Moscow, 11 April 1917

... In the afternoon of that day I received a letter from the military censor saying briefly that the Grand Duke Nicholas would receive me at three o'clock for the purpose of giving me a communication for the *Manchester Guardian*. Knowing the attitude of the Grand Duke toward the Revolution as a member of the Imperial family, and knowing also the fear all over Russia that he was about to put himself at the head of the Caucasus army and march on Petrograd and Moscow to crush the Revolution, I hastened at once to the palace.

I was received by Prince Orlov, the Grand Duke's secretary, who was looking very worried, and he led me into the large hall, where I saw the Grand Duke Nicholas walking up and down with his head down. He looked pale and thin, his hands were shaking, and when he began to speak his voice was so faint that I could scarcely hear what he was saying. He had evidently been living through a great deal those previous three days. He then said to me in Russian: 'I have asked you to come to make you the following statement,' and then he read from a bit of paper what I took down and telegraphed off that evening to the *Manchester Guardian*. He said that he considered it necessary to recognise the new order of things in Russia as the sole salvation of the country, and that as Commander-in-Chief of the Army he would allow no reaction of any kind, for the new state must be founded on a sure basis. I then thanked him for his communication, congratulated him on his appointment, and left. It was thus clear that whatever his intentions may have been on the Friday and Saturday, he had decided by Sunday that the Revolution must be recognised as successful. Hence, no doubt, the reason why he called me to make that statement ... On the last day of his Viceroyalty in the Caucasus he summoned the representatives of the people and bade them preserve order and internal peace for the honour of Russia ... Then the whole of the Cossack bodyguard of the Viceroy went over to the Revolution. On the Tuesday they accompanied the Grand Duke to the railway station waving red flags and singing the *Marseillaise*. Thus ended the last Viceroyalty of the Caucasus.

CHAPTER 4

The Provisional Government, April–August 1917

When Price arrived in Moscow, early in April, he had been in the Caucasus for nearly two years. He had to re-establish all his former contacts and make new ones. He had got to know several prominent Georgian Mensheviks in Tiflis, and as soon as he found them they asked him to get them some Socialist literature from England because they had been cut off from Western Europe for so long. (Price wired to Trevelyan to send him some pamphlets; the wire was intercepted by the Official Press Bureau and only released to Trevelyan when one of the censors realised that he could have found out about it from other sources, and might ask a Parliamentary Question.)

The Bolsheviks had played virtually no part in the March Revolution. Lenin was still in Switzerland. The Petrograd Soviet was composed of Mensheviks and Socialist Revolutionaries. The Provisional Government was almost entirely made up of Liberals and Kerensky was the only link between the two bodies. The Provisional Government accepted a commitment to carry on the war in association with the Western Allies. The Soviet wanted peace but was not prepared actually to pull out of the alliance. Instead it developed a formulation that peace, when it could be achieved, should be made on the basis of 'no annexations, no indemnities and the right of small nations to self-determination'. The Soviet had also declared against the secret treaties which were believed to exist between the Allies, one of which was known to give Constantinople to Russia.

Soon after Price arrived in Moscow he learned that Miliukov had been visiting the city. He got an interview with him, literally on the point of departure, in the train. To his astonishment Miliukov insisted that Russia must control the entrance to the Black Sea and would therefore annex Constantinople. Price telegraphed his account of the interview to the Manchester Guardian *and it was immediately telegraphed back to Petrograd. Miliukov was denounced by the Soviet, who demanded an explanation, and he resigned. This necessitated a reconstruction of the Government and the first Coalition was formed, including a number of Socialist Revolutionaries and Mensheviks. Kerensky was appointed Minister of War.*

A few days before the Miliukov interview Lenin arrived in Petrograd, having accepted an offer from the German government to send him back from Switzerland in a sealed railway carriage. A month later Trotsky arrived. He had been in America when the war began and had been interned in Nova Scotia by the British when he was trying to return to Russia. The Bolsheviks now had a leader, indeed two leaders. Trotsky had been a Menshevik until then, but he now accepted the Bolshevik programme. 'If Lenin was the planner of the Bolshevik Revolution,' wrote Lockhart many years later, 'Trotsky was the organiser.'[23]

Price first saw Lenin at the First All-Russia Congress of Peasants' Deputies in May and he was not impressed. Neither his appearance nor his manner of speaking were prepossessing. To Price he seemed doctrinaire and unrealistic. Lenin tried in vain, on that occasion, to persuade the peasants that the interests of the urban and the rural proletariat were identical. The peasants at that time, however, were only interested in the redistribution of land. By now Soviets of Workers' and Soldiers' Deputies had sprung up throughout Russia and represented an unmistakable alternative source of political power. On 16 June the First All-Russia Congress of Soviets was held in Petrograd.

Price attended most of the sessions of that first Congress and witnessed an historic encounter between Lenin and Kerensky, which he described in detail in a memorandum which was published in Common Sense *and which is reproduced below. He then went off to see what was happening in Finland, where he observed that there was considerable support for the concentration of power in the hands of soviets: 'All Power to the Soviet'. He returned briefly to Petrograd and then went off again, this time to the naval base at Kronstadt, at the mouth of the Neva. In Petrograd rumour had it that the base was in a state of anarchy and he wanted to see for himself. While he was there a period of unrest known as the 'July Days' occurred. Opinion is still divided as to whether this was a premature and unsuccessful Bolshevik* coup *or a spontaneous and unorganised outburst of frustration with a Provisional Government which had not only failed to deliver any of the promised land reforms, but had also just mounted an unsuccessful and costly land offensive against Austria and Germany at the request of the Allies.[24] Whatever the reasons, the result of the July Days was that Lenin had to disguise his appearance and go into hiding. Meanwhile the economic situation continued to deteriorate and no date was set for elections to the Constituent Assembly. On 20 July Prince Lvov resigned the premiership and Kerensky became the head of the third Provisional Government.*

In the late spring and summer of 1917 Price was not the only correspondent for the Manchester Guardian *in Russia. In April David Soskice, formerly a Russian political refugee in England, asked Scott to give him temporary status as Special Correspondent to enable him to return to Russia for the first time since the Revolution. Price thought – with hindsight and quite mistakenly – that Soskice had been sent out because his own work was already showing pro-Bolshevik bias.*

In fact Price at that time was as unimpressed by the Bolsheviks as a party as he had been by Lenin as a man, and it was not until early in 1918 that he began to think of them as the only people capable of ruling Russia. Moreover Scott could hardly have been blamed if he had sent out another correspondent to supplement Price, considering that there was both a war and a revolution to cover, and he quite often had no idea where Price was. The two men came to an agreement about the division of the work. Soskice would concentrate on events in the capital and on the Provisional Government. Price would concentrate on events outside the capital and on the Soviet or soviets. It was an arrangement not without compensations for Price, since it positively encouraged him to travel. One result of this division of labour was that very little appeared over Price's name in the Manchester Guardian *between July and November 1917, since Soskice was dealing with the political events in the capital. Price continued to write to all his correspondents in England, however, although not all his memoranda of that period appear to have survived; some of the ones which did appeared later in* Common Sense. *Soskice became Kerensky's secretary and fled back to England with him after the November Revolution.*

Memorandum to C. P. Scott
Rostov on Don, 31 March 1917

It is not strictly speaking a revolution, meaning by that a sudden political change accompanied by internal conflict, that has taken place in this country during the last three weeks. It is rather a step in the process of evolution which has been slowly going on for many years ...

On March 29th I left Tiflis and by permission travelled in a military train going north to European Russia. On the second day we reached the Cossack steppes, which lie to the north of the main range and here I bought the local papers in order to see what effect the Revolution had had upon the Cossacks. The state of feeling here was probably even more remarkable than anywhere else. At the wayside stations I saw Cossacks who in the last revolution were the bulwarks of the reaction, wearing red ribbons and singing the *Marseillaise*. At one station they had scrawled in chalk on an empty waggon: 'Goodbye, Nicholas. You are tried and found wanting'. I found that in the Terek and Kuban – the two provinces of the Caucasian Cossacks – revolutionary committees had been formed who had arrested the Atamans and other officials appointed over them by the late Government in Petrograd, and had elected their own military commanders and civil governors. In the Mozdok region the Cossacks had passed a resolution dismissing their Ataman because they said he was trying to stir up trouble between them and the Tartar and Circassian natives of the foothills. They then proceeded to elect a committee on which Cossacks and natives were equally represented. At Piatagorsk in the Kuban I found that a great meeting had taken place a few days before in which every '*stanitza*' [village] had sent its representatives. The chief Ataman had gone over unreservedly to the Revolution and, in proposing a resolution of support to the new Government had said; 'We have not forgotten the mistakes we made in 1905, when we were deceived. Now we rejoice with our brothers ...' This is perhaps less striking than appears at first sight. The Cossacks are after all only returning to their original social state, as a free people who fled from the tyranny of Tsars in order to found their own communes and elect their own leaders far from their baneful influence. The use of the Cossacks as an instrument of the Russian government and reaction is only a comparatively modern phenomenon.

Memorandum to C. P. Scott
Moscow, 6 April 1917

As the train in which I was travelling up from the south last week rolled across the great open plain of Central Russia through the governments of Kursk and Orel I saw many strange sights at the wayside stations. The slushy platforms on which the snow was beginning to melt were packed with soldiers waiting for any train that might come along and give them a lift in the corner of an open truck or on the roofs of the carriages. They seemed to be travelling in all directions. Some were going back to the front, which they had quitted in the ecstasy of the first days of the Revolution to celebrate the great event with their families. Others were going to their houses having held themselves in restraint during the first fortnight. In every station were the offices of the 'Alliance of Soldiers' Deputies', a sort of military trades union which like a mushroom has suddenly sprung up in the night, in response to that great Russian tendency for communal councils. Old peasants could be seen at the newspaper stalls eagerly asking for news from Petrograd. The chief thing that seeemed to interest them was the land question and the possibility of new agrarian legislation. Internal reconstruction, not foreign war, was everywhere the topic of the day.

My train pulled up at Moscow in the early hours of the morning. I walked through the streets and soon remarked the change that had taken place since I was here last. Not a single policeman or *gendarme* was to be seen. They had all been arrested and sent off to the front in small detachments. Moscow was without any police and seemed to be getting on quite happily without them. True a number of thieves had escaped when the prisons were opened on that memorable March 14th. In some of the rural districts the new authorities had issued plaintive appeals asking the escaped prisoners to be kind enough to return or else they would have to serve their sentences over again.

My first idea was to get in touch with opinion among the Moscow merchants and to find out how they were reacting towards the Revolution.[25] With this object in view I called upon the head of one of the great cotton manufacturing houses whom I had known for some years, himself a descendant of one of the old Muscovite trading families. Seated between his two sons he received me in one of the houses on the banks of the river commanding a gorgeous view of the great Kremlin.

'The danger to our country is still great,' he began. 'We suffer from three things: Jesuits, Germans and Jews! If we defeat them in the open they appear below the surface and poison our life by secret methods.' He then treated me to a long discourse on the evil influences which had been at work round the late Emperor and which in his opinion had brought the country to its present state ... I asked the sons what were their views on the matter. I found that the young generation of Moscow Merchant, if, as I think, it is well represented by those two gentlemen, had got beyond the stage of 'God, the Tsar and Holy Russia'. They had dropped the Jesuits out of their trio of bugbears, not because they loved them but probably they did not think them of sufficient importance. Germans and Jews however they had no more love for than their father, but for different reasons. With them the jealousy of commercial competition had taken the place of antipathy in race sentiment and religious dogma. If they did not enthusiastically welcome the new government regulation giving equal rights to the Jews, they did not have anything against it.

I then turned the conversation on to the possible system of government in Russia in the future. I found that even the old man, who had been brought up in the tradition of autocracy, was convinced that the only form of government now possible was a republic. Knowing the interest of Moscow merchants in the export trade to the east and across the Black Sea, I asked the opinion of my friends on the question of Constantinople and the Dardanelles. 'If Constantinople were internationalised,' came the reply, 'then I think we should be right in asking for the internationalisation of *all* great centres of that kind. If however these remain as they are, then in fairness we consider that the Dardanelles ... should be in the hands of Russia.'

I then approached the question of the economic crisis in Russia and asked what hopes he could hold out of the new Government being able to cope successfully with the problem. In his opinion the crisis had been brought on by a number of causes. The first concerned transport which, he maintained, the late Government had deliberately disorganised in order to terminate the war in the interests of Germany. They had not done any repairs to the rolling stock since the beginning of the war and as a result a large part of the waggons had gone out of use. I asked, 'Is there a hope that the new regime will be able to restore the country to its normal state as a result of better organisation?' 'There is much that can be done to remedy the present state of affairs,' came the answer, 'but beyond a certain point it is impossible to go, because the disorganisation concerns the general state of war in Europe. In the case of our own cotton mills we have had to reduce our production 15 per cent during the last year and after Easter we shall reduce it by another 30 per cent. This is because firstly the labour at our disposal is decreased and secondly because our fuel supply is inadequate. We own large forests in the north but we cannot get the peasants to go out and cut fuel for us to run our mills. They say to us, "We do not want the paper money that you offer us. Guarantee us food out in the forests and we will go and cut". But how is it possible' said my friend 'to guarantee them food a hundred miles from a station in the depths of the forests, when the Government itself can only with difficulty feed the large towns?'

He concluded by saying that the situation must be handled with courage ... 'for otherwise the economic crisis will be made use of by the reactionaries, working underground, to discredit the new regime and bring themselves back to power ... The partisans of the late Government are still spread about all over the country. Many of them have joined the revolutionary movement and are now wearing red ribbons in the street. They will act as informers and provocateurs. They may entice the supporters of the Revolution to do unwise acts ... They acquiesced in the abdication of Nicholas II because they realised his utter incapacity to lead the country. But if the new regime were to fail to deal with the economic crisis, these persons might quite conceivably try to re-establish the monarchy in the person of some other member of the Romanov family.'

UDC, *July 1917*
'The Background of the Revolution'
Moscow, *11 April 1917*

The most splendid thing for the civilisation of the world and the hopes of peace has been done this last week. The Socialists and revolutionary soldiers have through their committees forced the Provisional Government to declare that it has no intention of annexing territory or demanding indemnities from the Central Powers. I have seen some of the leaders of the Socialists and soldiers and have talked with them about this. They are all firm on this point and are determined to keep their Government up to its declaration. Meanwhile they are ready to prosecute the war energetically, but only, as they tell me, to defend their new-won freedom, and as soon as they can come to an arrangement with the German Socialists to upset the ruling class in Germany and establish an international settlement in Eastern Europe and Western Asia they will force peace ... The Socialist leaders here are very anxious to get in touch with Labour opinion in England and have asked me for papers of the ILP and Trade Union organs.

Great indignation is expressed at the abominable behaviour of the Northcliffe Press in England, especially of its correspondent, Wilton, in Petrograd, whom by the way I know quite well, for spreading provocative reports about the Union of Soldiers and Workers and trying to discredit them in Western Europe. I am doing all I can to tell the soldiers' and workers' leaders here about the nature of the abominable Northcliffe Press in England, how it is the organ of a reactionary syndicate in London which has in the past deceived the English people about Russia and has received money from the reactionary Government which has been for years oppressing them, in return for bolstering it up ... I think the people understand now ... and are determined that whoever Englishmen allow themselves to be governed by, the Russian people will have no truck with it [sic]. I only hope that they will turn *The Times* correspondent out of Petrograd.

Meantime the army, being a peasant army, is intensely interested in the land. The following is typical of why that interest is so acute. In the government of Kamenetsk-Podolsk there are areas where villages of 80 families have only 100 dessatines (250 acres) while all around is the land of the landlords – thousands of acres. On this land they work and receive only 20 kopecks (8d) a day and the produce goes to the landlord. 'If we ask him' said one of the soldiers – the inhabitant of such a village – to me 'to let us rent some of this land at a fair rent we are met with a blank refusal and often worse, for they send the rural police after us. We have decided that when we are demobilised we shall not put down our guns but will go straight home and parcel up that land among ourselves and not pay one kopeck for it, except for improvements like houses, drainage, etc.' It is quite clear that these peasants mean business and they are already beginning to deal with the situation. I believe the large number of desertions that have taken place in the army during the last month are due to peasants who want to get home and have the first pick of the landlords' land.

Manchester Guardian, 26 April 1917
'Russian Control of the Straits'
Moscow, 22 April 1917

... I have just interviewed the Russian Foreign Minister. M. Miliukov received me in a private railway carriage at a station just before his departure last night from Moscow, where he has been on a short visit. I asked the Minister if he had any information about Austrian peace proposals to Russia. He replied: 'We have no official offer which could form the basis of negotiations.' Asked how the declaration of the Provisional Government last week would affect the question of Constantinople and the Straits the Minister replied: 'If neutralisation means freedom for the trade of all nations through the Straits Russia will agree. She must, however, insist on the right to close the Straits to foreign warships, and this is not possible unless she possesses the Straits and fortifies them.'

Manchester Guardian, 21 May 1817
'Free Russia's Peace Formula: Miliukov Repudiated'
Petrograd, 19 May 1917

... One of the chief conditions [upon] which the Council of Workmen's and Soldiers' Delegates [Petrograd Soviet] have agreed to join the Provisional Government, is that the interpretation put upon [their peace] formula by M. Miliukov is definitely removed. M. Miliukov's resignation is taken here as a complete victory for revolutionary democracy in standing for the principle that the Allied governments shall come to an agreement on peace terms and agree to the principle that each nationality in disputed districts shall have the right to choose its own form of government. It is also regarded as a clear indication that the new Coalition Government desires the revision of the secret treaties contracted between the Allies and the late Tsar's government.

There has been as yet no detailed discussion of the formula 'Peace without annexations or indemnities'. The Cadet organ *Rech* today insists that the guilty powers must be held responsible for damage in war areas, but the official organ of the Council of Workmen's and Soldiers' Deputies, in a recent article, suggests that the damage done by the armies in war areas should be assessed by an international commission and made good from funds supplied from all the belligerent powers.

Common Sense, *4 August 1917*
'The Parliament of Russian Labour'
Petrograd, *26 June 1917*

The first week of the Parliament of Russian Labour [First All-Russia Congress of Workers' and Soldiers' Deputies] is over. From the workshops, the trenches and the battlefield over 700 delegates of organised revolutionary democracy have gathered together for the constructive work that lies ahead. Early in the second week in June the corridors and dormitories of the Cadet Corps buildings on the Vassily Ostrov were crowded with delegates arriving from east and west. They came in groups, bearing with them the mark of the regions whence they hailed. One room was filled by a jolly gang of Little Russians, who immediately got their accordion going round with their samovar. In another room there was a group of soldiers from the garrisons in Turkestan, in another some dark-eyed people from the Caucasus. There were bulky soldiers from the ranks and serious-looking officers from the trenches; there were artisans from the Moscow factories and mining representatives from the Don. But it was not long before the raw national materials were worked up into the political finished article. On the next day they began to split up into their party sections – the Socialist Revolutionaries in one room, the Social Democrat Maximalists [Bolsheviks] in another, and the Social Democrat Minimalists [Mensheviks] in another.

On the first day of the great assembly the hall of the Cadet Corps was decked in red bunting. From every corner and ledge hung a gory banner with the words: 'Proletariat of all countries unite! Long live the International!' If the last assembly in April had been one of rejoicing and triumph – the first to be held after the great events of March – this assembly was pre-eminently businesslike. A long programme of work lay before it, and the delegates stood in the hall discussing their party resolutions or preparing their speeches in collaboration with their comrades on the party committees.

It was soon clear that there were to be three main parties in the assembly. On the left of the platform were the Social Democrat Maximalists led by the bullet-headed Lenin and numbering in all 105. This was the 'Cave of Adullam'[26] to which all irreconcilable Marxists, Syndicalists and even Communist-Anarchists came for shelter and comfort. How powerful this group was we did not know at that time. We know that they were bitterly opposed to the Socialist participation in the 'bourgeois' Government and meant to bring this matter to an issue now, but how far they could carry with them the main body of delegates we did not know. In the centre was the great amorphous mass of the Social-Democrat Minimalists led by Tsereteli and Dan ... It was they who had solved the Miliukov crisis by coming into the Provisional Government. Seeing the danger of a full proletariat revolution in an economically undeveloped and unorganised country, they had stood for a policy of temporary conciliation between the masses and the capitalists. The whole of the right side of the hall was filled by the Socialist Revolutionaries, the largest party there, numbering 321. The Socialist Revolutionaries are an essentially Russian political party. Holding aloof from materialist Marxism, they have in the past fought for ideas rather than for things. They are the product of the Russian mind, ever seeking something abstract, something which will relieve the spirit of man in the evil surroundings of the world. The Socialist Revolutionaries are the expression of the Russian revolt against sordid materialism imported from Germany.

It was in these surroundings that the resolution of confidence in the Socialist Ministers of the Provisional Government was moved on 17 June. On behalf of the Executive Committee of the Council [Petrograd Soviet] M. Leber opened the great debate. He began by explaining the circumstances which had led up to the participation of the Council in the government of the country. The Russian Revolution, he said, was like no other revolution in Europe, for in its inception it was an uprising of the masses against their capitalist and landlord rulers. But in trying to solve the class problem by revolution in Russia it had come against the class problem in Western Europe, which was not yet ripe for settlement on these lines. Two problems, therefore, lay before the Russian revolutionary democracy. First in the region of foreign affairs it must bring the war to an end as soon as possible on the basis of an international agreement between all countries. 'There can be no victory of one coalition over another, for in the interests of democracy this war can only end by a victory of the working classes of all countries over the Imperialists and capitalists of all countries.' The second problem was the reorganisation of the whole internal social and political structure of the country ... The bourgeois Provisional Government, left high and dry, had nothing to rest upon. The old regime was gone; the vast masses of workers, soldiers and peasants had no confidence in them and were organising themselves and working out their own programmes.

There now came forward Tsereteli, the Minister of Posts and one of the leaders of the Social Democrat Minimalists. A spare, thin man with the dark complexion and the deep kindly eyes of a Caucasian, he bore upon him the signs of former physical suffering. The Revolution had released him from the foul prisons of Ufa, where he had been with other noble lives rotting to decay ... If Kerensky is the Garibaldi of the Russian Revolution, Tsereteli is the Cavour. Statesman and diplomat in him are combined in one. He is a living example of the marvellous capacity of the Russian people to assimilate themselves to the races of the East. Not a sound was heard in the great hall as in soft Georgian accents he addressed the audience.

'The Russian people,' he began, 'in lifting up the standard of peace for all the world, has had also to take upon itself the burden of a war begun by other governments, the ending of which does not depend upon it alone. Here is the great and fundamental difficulty which faces the Russian Revolution. Until those aims are attained for which the Russian democracy is striving, the conclusion of a world peace on the basis of the exclusion of force, from whatever quarter it comes, is impossible. We know, however, that to secure the safety of the Russian Revolution we must categorically break with the Imperialistic policies of the past. But how is this to be done? Are the old diplomatic channels of any more use? Can the Russian democracy trust its fate to the European Chancelleries that made this war?' The answer was decisive. 'By way of diplomatic negotiations and treaties questions of world importance cannot at this moment be decided. Our problem therefore is to set before the governments and peoples of the world the lessons of the Russian Revolution. We must approach the governments allied to us and above all avoid a breach with them, for a Russia isolated would mean a Russia forced to a separate peace and would mean ruin for the Revolution. Indeed, a separate peace is not only undesirable, but it is impossible, for to come out of one alliance in this war would only mean to go into another.'

Like the threads of a carefully woven carpet, Tsereteli's argument went on: 'If a separate peace is impossible we must convince the Allies of the truth of our ideals. We are calling them to a conference now.[27] We are inviting them to reconsider the terms upon which they would be prepared to make peace. We believe that there is already at work in all countries forces which will bring their peoples to appreciate the ideals of the Russian Revolution. Let us therefore begin with our Allies and let the result of our labours influence our comrades in Germany.' Turning to the question of the Army, he told his hearers that it must be ready to advance in order to defend the principles of the Russian Revolution. 'We are fighting now not for the Tsar's government nor for any other government, but in order to carry the banner of our ideals of brotherhood throughout the world.'

On the conclusion of this great speech the whole of the delegates rose to their feet and gave the orator an ovation which lasted for several minutes. There then rose upon the tribune a man whose name has been on all lips for many weeks past – the leader of the Social Democratic Maximalists, Lenin. He is a short man with a round head, small pig-like eyes and close-cropped hair. The words poured from his mouth, overwhelming all in a flood of oratory. One sat spellbound at his command of language and the passion of his denunciation. But when it was all over one felt inclined to scratch one's head and ask what it was all about. 'Where are we?' he began, stretching out his short arms and looking questioningly at his audience. 'What is this Council of Workers' and Soldiers' Deputies? Is there anything like it in the world? No. Of course there is not. Then let us have one of two things – either a bourgeois Government with its plans for so-called social reform on paper, such as exists in every country now, or let us have that Government which you (pointing to Tsereteli) long for, but which you appear to be frightened of bringing into existence – a Government of the proletariat, which had its historic parallel in 1792 in France. Look at this anarchy which we now have in Russia,' he went on. 'What does it mean? Do you really think that you can create an intermediate stage between Capitalism and Socialism? Can Tsereteli's fine plans for persuading the bourgeois governments of Western Europe to come to our point of view ever succeed? No, it will fail ignominiously, as long as power is out of the hands of the Russian proletariat. That power I and my party are prepared to take at any moment. (Shouts of derisive laughter resounded all over the hall.) Look at what you are doing,' he cried, nothing daunted, and pointing a scornful finger at the Socialist Ministers. 'Capitalists with 800 per cent war profits are walking the country, just as before. Why don't you publish the figures of their profits, arrest some fifty of them and keep them locked up for a bit, even though you may keep them under the same luxurious conditions as you keep Nicholas Romanov? (A yell of delight came from the corner of the hall where the Maximalist delegates sat.) You talk about peace without annexations and contributions,' he continued. 'Put that principle into practice in our own country, in Finland and the Ukraine. You talk to us about an advance on the front. We are not against war on principle. We are only against a capitalist war for capitalist ends, and until you take the Government entirely into your hands and oust the bourgeoisie you are only the tools of those who have brought this disaster on the world.' And with these words the demagogue finished his fiery speech.

There was a hush in the hall as there rose a short, thick-set man with a square face and close-cropped hair. He wore a brown jacket and gaiters, his face was pale with nervous tension, and his eyes blazed like fiery beacons. It was Kerensky, the popular hero of militant revolutionary Russia. Standing bolt upright, with his right arm clasping the button of his breast pocket, he began his speech in quiet, measured tones.

'We have just been given some historical parallels,' he said. 'We have been referred to 1792 as an example of how we should carry out the Revolution of 1917. But how did the French Republic of

1792 end? It turned into a base Imperialism which set back the progress of democracy for many a long year. Our duty is to prevent that very thing from happening, to strengthen our new-won freedom so that our comrades who have come back from exile in Siberia shall not go back there, and so that comrade, who has been living comfortably all this time in Switzerland, shall not have to fly back again. He proposes to us a new and wonderful recipe for our revolution; we are to arrest a handful of Russian capitalists! Comrades, I am not a Marxist, but I think I understand Socialism better than brother Lenin, and I know that Karl Marx never proposed such methods of Oriental despotism. (A hurricane of applause rose from the body of the hall and shouts from the corner of the discomfited Leninites.) I am accused,' he went on, 'of opposing the national aspirations of Finland and the Ukraine and of reducing the principle of peace without annexation to ridicule by my actions. But in the Fourth Duma it was *he*,' he added, turning savagely on Lenin, 'who attacked *me* when I stood up for a federal republic and national autonomy; it was *he* who called my Socialist Revolutionary comrades Utopianists and dreamers. Today I say only one thing. I recognise the rights of the Ukraine and Finland, but cannot agree to their separation until the Constituent Assembly of the Russian people has sanctioned it.'

Turning to the question of fraternising on the front, Kerensky evoked a storm of laughter as he referred in sarcastic terms to those naive people who imagine that friendly meetings between a few parties of Russian and German soldiers can usher in the dawn of Socialism throughout the world. 'Our Maximalist comrades,' he added, 'had better be careful or they may wake up one day and find they are fraternising with the mailed fist of Wilhelm!' His face flushed and his voice became harsher with excitement as he braced himself up for his supreme effort. 'You tell us that you fear reaction,' he almost screamed; 'you say that you want to strengthen our new-won freedom, and yet you propose to lead us the way of France in 1792. Instead of appealing for reconstruction you clamour for further destruction. Out of the fiery chaos that you wish to make will rise, like a Phoenix, a dictator.' He paused and walked slowly across the platform towards the corner where the group surrounding Lenin sat. Not a sound was heard in the great hall, and we waited spellbound for the next sentence. '*I* will not be the dictator that you are trying to make,' and so saying he turned his back scornfully upon Lenin, while the assembled delegates thundered their applause. 'Comrades,' he then concluded, in a quiet, half-apologetic strain 'I am here amongst you not as a Minister but as one of you; as an old revolutionary, to give an account of my stewardship and to tell the truth about all that we are living through in these days. I have disclosed everything to you, my brothers, and I leave you to be my judges.' It was a memorable speech of a fascinating personality, and in its way did much to consolidate the Russian revolutionary democracy assembled in that hall and to disperse the forces of chaos and disorder.

Postcard to Anna Maria Philips
Petrograd, 25 July 1917

I am just back from Finland, where I have been to study the Finnish question. I missed the rebellion here last week or at least only came in for the tail end of it [The July Days]. Things are pretty bad here now both in the rear and at the front. I don't see how Russia can hold out beyond the autumn. The army is breaking up and the country is threatened with famine. I get very little to eat – only three-quarters of a lb. of black bread a day – no meat or sugar. For the rest I have to drink water and imagine I have eaten a dinner! It is essential that people should realise in England the desperate straits in Russia. Thanks for your letters of May and June. I have received some five or six in the last week. Hope you are well. I am well but we never know here what tomorrow will bring us. Tell CPT [Trevelyan] I have his letter of May 5th and will write soon.

New York Tribune, 7 August 1917
'The Kronstadt Commune'
Petrograd, 26 June 1917

Lately Petrograd began to get alarmed about the state of affairs in Kronstadt. Rumours circulated that this important island fortress guarding the sea approaches to the capital was in the hands of the most dangerous type of anarchists, who had destroyed the fortifications, were selling secrets to Germany and were preparing to spread terror and destruction all over Russia.

Knowing there are people in Petrograd who spread rumours for sinister purposes I decided to go down to Kronstadt and investigate for myself.

With some little misgiving I passed by the sentries and asked to see the president of the Council. I was taken into a room where I saw a young student with a red badge on his coat looking through some papers. This was the president of the Council, elected by the revolutionary soldiers and sailors and workers of Kronstadt. His hair was long and his face bore that expression of mingled sympathy and mystery which is so often seen in the Russian student.

'Well,' he said, 'they seem to be very frightened of us in Petrograd, but we are doing nothing more than putting our house in order after the chaos and terror of the Tsar's regime.'

I asked him if the Council recognised the Provisional Government of Russia and he replied, 'Of course we do, if the rest of Russia does. But that does not prevent us from having our own opinions as to what the Government ought to be. We would like to see the whole of the Government in the hands of the All-Russia Council of Workers' and Soldiers' Deputies [Petrograd Soviet].'

I was taken to see the prisons where the agents of the Tsar's tyranny were sitting. In the first prison I found about 100 *gendarmes* and secret police agents. The quarters were very bad and many of the cells had no windows at all. Great hulking men with coarse animal features were lounging about dark and narrow corridors. Some of them still had on the uniform of their former profession. 'I am afraid you must be very uncomfortable here,' I said to one of them. 'Ugh!' he grunted. 'If only they would let us go to the front and fight or work and do something.'

In the next prison I found a number of admirals, generals and naval and military officers of all ranks. They told me stories of how they had been arrested as soon as the news of the events in Petrograd had become known to the revolutionaries in Kronstadt. They all complained that they had been kept for three months without any trial or examination of their cases. But the young sailor who accompanied me chimed in: 'I sat in this very prison, not for three months but for three years, for having been found with a Socialist pamphlet in my possession. All that time I never had a trial of any kind whatever.' I pointed out to the sailor that the prison accommodation was unfit for a human being. He answered, 'Well, I sat here all that time because of these gentlemen and I think that if they had known they were going to sit here they would have made better prisons!' This attitude of the revolutionary Kronstadt sailors, if not justifiable, is explicable. These officers are now being tried by a commission sent from Petrograd.

Revolutionary ideas have always been strong in the Russian navy, and the great naval fortress in the Baltic has been the centre of the force which the Tsar's government created to crush them out. Almost every sailor in Kronstadt has at one time or another been in these government prisons and been lashed with the knout. Several of them that I met that afternoon told me how they had been sent to Siberia for life and had escaped from there in order to come back to Kronstadt, in spite of the terrors of the place, and carry on revolutionary propaganda there. They were always treated like dogs. They were not allowed to walk in the boulevards or go into any public places of amusement, and for the smallest offence they were beaten. On the first day of the Revolution they went to the admiral's house, dragged him out, shot him and tried to burn the body. It was a law of blood and iron that ruled in Kronstadt and I fear during the first days of the Revolution the sailors gave back what had been given to them.

That evening I was taken to the house of Admiral Veren, who had been murdered as I describe. I found the anarchists in possession. In the sumptuous halls where once councils of war were held by medalled officers I now saw unkempt, long-haired revolutionary students and sailors. I was introduced to their leader, a veteran fighter who had taken a prominent part in the mutiny of the *Potemkin* on the Black Sea in 1908. I expected to find the most desperate characters among this lot, but I confess that they turned out very harmless. Their revolutionary ideas did not go beyond the speedy application of Marxism and the class war, while the anarchists I found to be peaceful Tolstoyans, who would refuse to shed blood on principle. As it was already late they invited me to supper and to sleep the night.

Next day I was taken to visit the battleships and training ships in the harbour. I first went to the naval staff. The commander of the fleet I found was now a young lieutenant. He received me very cordially, called me 'Comrade' and took me to his cabin to lunch, which consisted of the same food as that eaten by the sailors. He wore no epaulettes on his uniform, he was not saluted by the sailors, and when they spoke to him they called him 'Comrade'. All the officers of the fleet in Kronstadt are now elected by the crews of the ships on which they serve, and the Council of Sailors' Deputies elects the officer commanding the fleet. My first question was how did this new principle of electing officers affect the work and efficiency of the fleet. The Chief of Staff, although himself an old sailor and not accustomed to this new way of doing things, said that on the whole it worked well. At first there was some difficulty. The sailors elected officers just because they liked them and not because they knew their job. But after a while, he added, the men got to know who were efficient as well as those who were nice to their men.

On the following day I was taken to see some of the factories where war material is made and ships are repaired. I found all the men working busily and the rumours of disorganisation in Petrograd quite unfounded. All the private works and shops are put under the control of the Council and the profits divided with the workers. Most of the private owners, however, left after the Revolution, so that now the works are run by the committees of the men. An eight-hour day is compulsory throughout the island, with three hours' overtime for special and urgent work. Trade unions are being formed among the different grades of artisans. I came across a meeting being held by the Union of Strikers in the ship-repairing yards. The men were discussing a plan of mutual insurance against unemployment and sickness.

CHAPTER 5

The Interregnum, August–November 1917

By August 1917 it was clear to Price that the Provisional Government was failing to justify the hopes of the March Revolution. Politically little had yet been settled and the economic situation had actually deteriorated. The peasants were not waiting for a Constituent Assembly to devise an orderly redistribution of land; in some areas they had seized it for themselves, but had neither the manpower nor the machinery to work it effectively. Industry, too, had been starved of manpower by the demands of the army, and the introduction of the eight-hour day put a further brake on production.

The principal political event in August 1917 was the summoning by Kerensky of an All-Party State Conference in Moscow, away from the uneasy atmosphere of Petrograd. On 25 August over 2,000 delegates met, chosen on an arbitrary basis to 'represent' the political parties and non-party organisations such as Zemstvos, co-operatives, trade unions and soviets. It was, Price thought, 'a supreme attempt to bridge the ever-widening gap between the classes and to find some common "national programme"'.[28] The Bolsheviks boycotted the conference altogether and after only three days it was clear that no common ground existed between the participants and no 'national programme' was available. The Mensheviks and Socialist Revolutionaries then convened their own conference – the 'Democratic Conference' – to meet in the last week of September. This had a somewhat clearer objective: to create a responsible government capable of ending the war and ensuring that elections for a Constituent Assembly should take place and that the Assembly should meet. But again, the Bolsheviks wanted nothing to do with it. Lenin was still in hiding after the 'July Days' but Trotsky led a group of Bolsheviks in to the first meeting, denounced the conference as bourgeois and unrepresentative, and led them out again. Meanwhile Kerensky had created his own executive: a Council of the Republic consisting partly of former members of the Moscow State Conference and partly of his own nominees.

Price attended the Moscow Conference but did not write about it, in accordance with his agreement with Soskice. While there he began to hear rumours of a counter-revolutionary plot in the making. Shortly after he left Moscow to make a fact-finding tour of the Volga provinces he

*learned that General Kornilov, whom Kerensky had appointed
Commander-in-Chief after the failure of the Brusilov offensive [see note
24] and the consequent German counter-offensive, had declared that
Petrograd was now in the front line. He dispatched troops, supposedly
for its defence, on 7 September. Speculation still exists as to whether
Kerensky and Kornilov were in some kind of conspiracy to bring down
the Petrograd Soviet, or whether Kornilov, backed by counter-revolutionary
elements in the army and the country, was trying to bring down the
Provisional Government itself and establish a military dictatorship.
Whatever the truth, he failed, was dismissed, arrested, imprisoned, and
then released to play his part in the forthcoming civil war. But by this
time Price was on the road to Samara.*

*During his seven weeks' travels in the Volga provinces he saw for himself
the catalytic effect of the attempted* coup. *Everywhere he went he saw
how the authority of the local soviets had been enhanced as a result of
their success in keeping order during that period. Moreover, he noticed,
the soviets were becoming increasingly Bolshevik-dominated and the
Mensheviks were becoming more left-wing.*

Common Sense, *8 September 1917*
'Economic Crisis in Russia'
Petrograd, *12 August 1917*

The Russian Revolution is now passing through the gravest of all
its crises. It is not difficult to put economic values upon recent events
in the Russian capital and to trace all to one elementary fact:
material exhaustion resulting from the attempt to carry on a foreign
war and an internal revolution at the same time ... It was war
which destroyed the old Russian Empire, proving once again the
truth of John Bright's remark that 'war destroys the Government
that makes it'. But when it comes to reconstruction the Russian
Revolution is faced with an almost impossible situation. It tries to
rebuild on the ruins of the old, but its neighbours in Western
Europe persist in making it continue to destroy and thereby sap
all its remaining strength. The machine of the old Russian State
has collapsed, but nothing has yet has come in its place because
the whole attention of the country has still to be turned on works
of destruction.

Take for instance the system of State finance in Russia. Its
complete breakdown was probably the chief cause of the produce
crisis, and this in turn led to the spread of revolutionary ideas
throughout the masses ... Up to March 1917, of the 28 milliard
roubles total cost of war expenditure, over nine milliards had to
be found by inflating the currency ... It is true that an income tax
was passed in the summer of 1916 but up to the outbreak of the

Revolution none of it was collected. Meanwhile the great landlords continued to draw their annual toll from the labour of the peasants without any taxation being imposed on them whatever, while the industrial classes carried on a riotous orgy in war profiteering without contributing one kopeck to the State. Here therefore one sees an example of a country trying to carry on a modern war of unparalleled destruction for two-and-a-half years while living all the time under a primitive social system in which the vast proletariat masses are the economic serfs of the privileged few. Of course there could be only one end to it, and that came last March.

As soon as the Russian masses had thrown off the yoke of their century-long slavery, their first instinct was to improve their standard of living. Being without any experience in these matters, and having no trained political organisations ready at hand, they had nothing to restrain their appetites or to keep them within bounds. The country was already in such an exhausted state materially that it could ill afford a large dose of social reform without experiencing complete economic collapse ... At the present moment, before the new harvest is got in, there is roughly 600 millions pounds [sic] of cereals unconsumed. It can only be collected by inducing the peasants to sell ... The peasants are hardly likely to get the manufactures and products which they want in exchange for their corn in order to keep themselves going in the villages. Even if it is possible to secure enough to satisfy them, the next problem is to transport the corn to the consuming centres ... Last year there were 3,387 locomotives unable to work on account of lack of repairing materials, now there are 4,799. Last year there were 23,067 waggons needing repair, this year 42,520. The railway staff is entirely unable to deal even with the goods traffic before the harvest. It is difficult to imagine what will happen when the new harvest comes to be distributed ... Thus we see that the combined dose of war and social reform is threatening one of the richest and fairest regions of this earth with an unspeakable calamity.

Russia's Western Allies and their champions here, the Cadets, led by M. Miliukov, are preaching that she must throw over her social reforms, stifle the developing stages of her Revolution and concentrate upon war for the partition of Austria and die in the last ditch for the annexation of Constantinople. It is not difficult to see why the Western Allies are not popular in some quarters and much as the 'bourgeois' press tries to insinuate that this discontent is connected with German propaganda, they are unable to explain away the deep-seated longing for peace among the masses, who are in no mood to drop their social reform and who feel that famine is slowly gripping them by the throat.

Letter to C. P. Trevelyan
Samara, 22 September 1917

Since I wrote to you last from Moscow describing the National
Assembly last month I have travelled far down the Volga to this
province on the borders of Central Asia. I have visited Yaroslav
and Novgorod, where I saw typical life going on in the northern
provinces, while here in Samara I have come in touch with the rural
life of a great corn-growing territory. I have been in the villages and
stayed there some days, attending the meetings of the rural
communes, studying the development of the tremendous agrarian
revolution which is going on in these parts and which is typical of
what is going on all over Russia. I have just sent off three long articles
to the *Manchester Guardian* which, if published, will tell you all about
the purely domestic aspects of the Revolution in the provinces. I
assume however that you are more interested in the Revolution in
its relation to the war, the prospects of peace and the attitude of
the revolutionary democracy to the Western Allies. Of course the
internal and external aspects of the Revolution are very closely related
to one another, and the struggle going on between the masses and
the classes is to my mind only the outward sign of a much greater
struggle, in which the proletariat and the peasant masses are
consciously or unconsciously trying to join hands with their
comrades in other lands and establish the basis of an international
peace. You will remember when I wrote from Moscow describing
the National Assembly [Moscow State Conference] last month I
called attention to the creation at that Assembly of two great
Blocks, the revolutionary ...

PARAGRAPH CUT OUT OF PAGE BY RUSSIAN CENSOR[29]

They knew that when the Constituent Assembly meets they will
be left in an insignificant minority. They felt however that they had
considerable power in the administrative centre of the Government
and in the brain of the army, the General Staff. Therefore they hoped
by a *coup d'etat* to bring the whole country to a standstill and in
the chaos resulting to establish a military dictatorship, which would
indefinitely postpone the elections for the Constituent Assembly,
would carry on the war in close contact with the Western Allies
and put down all peace talk. Indeed they had to some extent
succeeded in doing this before the Kornilov rebellion, and the
latter's action was only intended to set the seal to the work. One
after another the planks of the revolutionary platform had been torn
up by the reactionary elements round the Provisional Government.
The process began soon after the July disorders when the Council
was weakened by the Petrograd disorders. The land reform
regulations were shelved, thus causing serious unrest among the

peasants in the provinces and only precipitating the agrarian revolution without the directing hand of the Government. The state control of vital industries was put on one side by the Ministry of Commerce in deference to capitalist interests; so also was the proposal for war taxation on capital. The death sentence was re-established at the front, the negotiations with the Allies over the secret treaties were abandoned, the Minister of Foreign Affairs stated openly that no one now was thinking of peace, while an underground intrigue created the impression in London that the Provisional Government was against the Stockholm Conference.

Kerensky, who is either unwilling or unable to stand courageously against these counter-revolutionary plots, appointed as secretary David Soskice, who came out here last June to be – among other things – an agent for certain banks of the Allied Powers!!![30] Now it is plain that all this, coming to the knowledge of the revolutionary democracy in the provinces, has only one effect. It is preparing the ground for a fresh explosion which will be lighted by the masses. Herein lies a very serious danger. Discontent almost amounting to fury is everywhere observed in the provinces through which I have passed. Englishmen are becoming more and more unpopular. In fact if I had not in my possession open letters from the Executive Committee of the Council in Petrograd [Petrograd Soviet] and from the Central Committee of the Socialist Revolutionary Party to all its branches in the provinces, I feel that I should have a very unpleasant time of it. This I find particularly so among the soldiers of the garrisons in the rear, who are becoming more and more ill-disposed to the Allies and more and more convinced that it is only they are who keeping them from an honourable peace. Amongst the urban proletariat of the towns through which I have passed also I find that a dangerous temperament is developing ... I have recently been to meetings of the Trade Union Council for the Samara province where I have heard a number of very violent speeches of an anarchist nature. Lack of confidence in the Provisional Government is everywhere expressed even among the moderate members of the revolutionary democracy. The councils are becoming more and more Maximalist in their composition. Since the Kornilov rebellion they have demanded that all power shall go into their hands and that the new Government shall be formed from their members alone. Whether the councils have men of sufficient experience to form a government is still uncertain. This would be easier if there was a broad radical element among the bourgeoisie. But in this quarter are only to be found the reactionary Cadets who have just been convicted before the bar of public opinion of secret participation in the Kornilov rebellion. In fact no government in the present state of affairs seems possible. The masses in the country won't endure a coalition government which betrays the revolution behind their backs any longer. On the other hand the anarchical elements rising in the councils and the limited number of experienced administrators make it difficult for the latter to form a purely revolutionary government which can firmly rule the country.

The chaotic state of affairs, therefore, which is certain to go on as long as the war lasts, is only preparing public opinion for peace with Germany. I am firmly persuaded that feeling in the last few weeks is more inclined now towards a separate peace than it was a month ago. More than one moderate member of the provincial councils have recently said to me that the time is approaching when the Revolution must energetically push its foreign policy abroad and demand a direct answer from the Allies as to whether they accept the peace platform of the Revolution or not. I always ask what they would do if the Allies decline to give them a straight answer. One influential revolutionary answered me by saying that in that case Russia should consider herself free to approach the German government and the German Socialists with a view to finding a common basis for peace. He then proceeded to point out that the cards in the hands of the Revolution are very important ... The withdrawal of German troops from the Russian to the French front would probably neutralise the effect of America. It is true Japan might make this a pretext to seize Vladivostock but it is doubtful if she could do more than occupy the sea coast of eastern Siberia. The Allies' hopes are the starvation and economic ruin of Germany. The opening of the Russian corn reserves would remove the effect of the Allies' blockade.

I have been surprised to find that many people are now beginning to talk openly in this strain, and this talk is not confined to extreme members of the revolutionary democracy. In short I expect in the near future a serious renewal of the peace campaign and possibly a new departure in the foreign policy of the Revolution. Up to now it has in fact had no foreign policy except abstract phrases. It has left the actual business to the elements in the country which in alliance with Allied diplomacy and capital are hostile to the Revolution and have of course betrayed it. Perhaps by the time I am back in Petrograd a new move will have been made in the direction I indicate.

Manchester Guardian, *4 December 1917*
SERIES: *'THROUGH THE RUSSIAN PROVINCES'*
'The Peasants and their Land Programmes'
Samara, September 1917

The province of Samara may be taken as typical of south-eastern Russia and the Lower Volga. Throughout this region the production and export of corn to the northern and western manufacturing areas is the main industry ... In the last few weeks, with the aid of letters from the Council in Petrograd and from the chief political parties in the revolutionary democracy, I have been able to investigate the development of the Revolution in this part of Russia.

During the July Days, while Petrograd was being convulsed by anarchist and counter-revolutionary plots, and later when Kornilov was raising his rebellion, the Russian Revolution was slowly developing in the provinces. Throughout the summer, at the instigation of peasant soldiers from the neighbouring towns the older villagers summoned their rural communes and elected representatives to the revolutionary committees. This little executive for the commune was called the Council of Peasants' Deputies (CPD). The absence of police and government agents then made it necessary to create some form of authority. So these little political organisations delegated some of their members to act as an executive committee of public safety ... In the course of time these district committees formed into bodies serving larger areas, and these again into those serving provinces. The provincial executive committees elected a commissioner who was confirmed by the Provisional Government in Petrograd and became the figurehead of revolution in the provinces. The urgent need for dealing with the problems facing the Revolution then forced the peasants and the peasant soldiers to go further. The land and food question had to be tackled, and so there grew up automatically in each district a local Land and Produce Committee, the former to control the division and sowing of the land and the latter the distribution of food and necessaries. Here again the members were elected from the local CPD. In the last two months, however, the revolutionary committees have begun to give place to bodies elected upon a legal system of adult suffrage and secret ballot, drawn up by the Provisional Government ... these democratic *Zemstvos* are now taking under their control the local militia and the Land and Produce Committees ...

I find that everywhere in these Lower Volga provinces the burning question is the land. The policy of the CPDs is directed solely with a view to solving this question, and within their ranks can be observed various political tendencies which express the opinions among the peasantry of those regions. But outside the democratic groups which gather round the Council of Peasant's Deputies in the village, small circles of reactionary influence are to be found. They are centred round the local tradesman and retailer, who hates and fears the growing co-operative movement among the peasantry. Co-operation has made enormous strides in recent years and, together with the process of land socialisation, promises to become the pillar upon which Russia's agricultural industry will be based ...

Then there is also the small proprietor who, by favour of the landlord or the agent of the Tsar's government acquired some land.

These two lower-middle-class types, together with similar types in the towns ... have now come into political alliance with the rural landlords and the industrial capitalists of the local Cadet party, and all together form the conservative elements in the provinces which work for a bourgeois reaction. Though small in number the latter are nevertheless rich and not without influence upon the more ignorant of the older generation of peasantry.

Against these underground reactionary influences in the villages, therefore, rural democracy has gathered round the CPDs. In them is included 99 per cent of all the politically conscious peasantry, all the soldiers of the garrisons of the neighbouring towns (themselves the sons of peasants), and a few intellectuals. In the absence of urban factory workers it is clear that Marxist ideas are not widespread in the CPDs. The chief interest of the members is in the expropriation of the landlords and dividing the land. Therefore the Socialist Revolutionary Party is predominant in the CPD. The policy of the latter differs from that of the Marxist Social Democrats [Bolsheviks] in the question of land division. The Marxists stand for State nationalisation, the capitalisation of the agricultural industry and the proletarisation of the peasantry. The Socialist Revolutionaries, on the other hand, see the rich possibilities for social experiment in the Russian peasant, just freed from mediaeval serfdom and untainted with Western industrialism. They hope to utilise his native instinct for creating communal institutions to modernise the latter, and so to lead up to a system in which the land is socialised by the local communes. The peasant, they say, must not be the wage slave even of the State, as the Social Democrats want, nor a proprietor, as the Cadets want, but a member of a social unit with a right to work an area of land and to reap the products of his labour upon it. To the social unit should belong the land, but to the peasant the products of the land. In order to meet the modern necessity for working industries on a large scale, the Socialist Revolutionaries would make use of the agricultural co-operative movement.

But if the Socialist Revolutionaries and the Social Democrats differ on land distribution and the future of the agricultural industry, they are nevertheless united in their determination once and for all to abolish landlordism and the rights of private property. 'The land comes from God and can belong to no one,' is an old Russian saying, and it correctly expresses the spirit of the peasant. The revolutionary democracy therefore, in town and country, presents a solid front to the Cadets, who talk about the sacredness of property and try to represent the Russian peasant as developing into a type like the British farmer or the French small proprietor. With this great mass of revolutionary opinion solid against private ownership it is certain that whatever else may happen the Russian landlord will become a thing of the past.

The question, however, remains whether the landlords ought to be compensated for their land. The Socialist Revolutionaries say that they should not be. They point to the fact that the Russian landlords are not, as in Western Europe, also capitalists who are continually applying capital to the land, and whose rent consists of interest on their own improvements as well as exploitation profits from the needs of the people. In the case of the Russian landlord his rent consists solely of the latter, for he has never, except in the case of the sugar companies, improved or developed it. But simple expropriation without compensation may lead to a disastrous financial crisis, because many landlords have mortgaged their lands to the banks. The Land Bank, specially formed by the Tsar's government to bolster up the landlords, has in many cases advanced money on the land for much more than the land was worth. Therefore the ruin of several banks is probable unless some compensation is afforded. It is interesting to note that at the last conference of the Socialist Revolutionary Party at Samara a resolution was passed that the banks should be compensated for their losses by an extra super-tax upon large incomes. This view also received support in the All-Russia Conference of the Social Democrats recently held in Petrograd.

Manchester Guardian, *6 December 1917*
'The Revolution and its Effects on Rural Life'
Samara, September 1917

Accompanied by a member of the local Council of Peasants' Deputies I arrived one evening in the eastern part of this province. The *'isvoschick'* [driver] drove us wildly down the broad, unpaved street on each side of which the typical wood houses of the Russian peasant stood in two long rows. The street was almost empty. An old peasant – all that was left of the male labourers – was returning home from ploughing. A small boy was trying to direct a huge drove of sheep and cattle back from pasture with the aid of a wooden twig. Some women were digging manure in a back yard. That was all the productive labour that was left in this village. A feeling of depression lay everywhere. It is true that a red flag, flying from the roof of the windmill on the outskirts of the village, was a joyful sign of the great deliverance last March. But on entering the house of my host, an old peasant, I soon felt that the gloom which had temporarily been lifted by the Revolution from the rural hearth was settling down again upon the inmates under the prospects of another winter's war ...

Next day there was a meeting of the rural commune. Outside the common barn, in the middle of the village street, the peasants had gathered. The heads of families and every working hand including sons, if there were any now, were present. I also saw quite a number of women ... Here in fact was the most elementary unit of Russian rural society. It has existed for centuries and is rooted deep in the Middle Ages. It is essentially democratic, for women have equal rights with men. The Revolution when it came had only to make use of this institution ...

The proceedings of this commune, if picturesque, were not exactly businesslike ... Many dogs were walking in and out of the crowd; a ragged beggar suddenly interfered in the middle of a discussion on the land regulations and asked for alms in the name of the Mother of God ... the President of the commune, sitting on a wood box and chewing nuts, would occasionally bawl out 'Comrades, to order – consider the question of the day' and would then relapse again to his nuts. It was only my companion of the Council of Peasants' Deputies who succeeded, after some difficulty, in getting this confused mass together and explaining to them that the provincial Land Committee wanted an inventory of the livestock and seed corn in the commune. After endless conversation something was drawn up.

The following day I set out alone to visit the person who till recently was the local landlord. The farm and about twenty dessiatines of land was all [that was] now left of the 3,000 dessiatines estate. I walked through the overgrown shrubbery up to a wooden two-storied house. Grass was growing on the roof, and in the greenhouse a cow was finishing what remained of the ferns. I found the owner preparing to leave for the Crimea, declaring that he would turn his back on the place for ever ... Referring to the Council of Peasants' Deputies and to my companion whom I had left behind the village, 'these people' he said 'are the ruin of Russia. Everything used to be quiet and everyone so contented. I gave the peasants seed corn and manure when they were in difficulties. No one wanted change. Then people came from the town and stirred it all up. Those stupid Cadets ought to have stopped this rabble long ago in the first days of the Revolution.'

The next day being Sunday, I went to a monastery some twenty versts away to the south ... The abbot was supposed to be a very holy man who had acquired a reputation for working miracles. He had discovered that it was a paying thing to be holy. Land had been given to him by local landlords and he had capitalised his holiness at 100 per cent. I was hoping to have an interview with this important personage, but on my arrival at the gates of the monastery I was told that he had left some days ago. The monks were now in sole possession of the place. What had happened? It was soon explained.

The Revolution had penetrated into the sacred precincts of the monastery; the monks had gone on strike and had turned out the abbot, who had gone off whining to the Holy Synod ... On enquiry into the ideas entertained by the monks for developing their little revolution, I found that they had already entered into an arrangement with the local peasantry. They were to keep enough land for themselves to work, and the rest was to go into the local commune. Thus a new monastic commune was in process of formation.

Manchester Guardian, 5 December 1917
'How the Peasants are Taking Over the Land'
Samara, September 1917

It is generally understood by the peasants and their intellectual leaders in this part of Russia that the establishment of a public law in relation to the land can only be obtained by the All-Russia Constituent Assembly. But on the other hand, it is clearly realised that certain steps must be immediately taken to prepare the way for the general settlement and to prevent reactionary interests from robbing the peasants of the prize they have been waiting for so long. Foremost among these is the measure prohibiting sales of land pending the Constituent Assembly except by permission of the Minister of Agriculture ... The late Minister of Agriculture, Victor Chernov, when he insisted in the Provisional Government on a law temporarily forbidding the sale of land was only expressing the widespread demands of the peasantry. Indeed if this had not been done I am certain, from what I have seen and heard in the last few weeks, that serious agrarian disorders would have broken out and that the feeling of the peasants towards the Western Allies would be even less favourable than it is at present ... Chernov's work, which has aimed at preparing the ground for the great agrarian reform and at establishing temporary regulations for working the land on a democratic basis, met with the most vigorous opposition of the Cadets and the interests allied to them. Everything has been done to delay the reforms and to prevent the preliminary regulations from being carried out. As the result of interminable delays the peasants have begun to lose confidence in the Provisional Government, and in these Lower Volga provinces have taken the law into their own hands. In Samara, Simbirsk, Saratov and Ufa the local Council of Peasants' Deputies and the Land Committees inspired by them have drawn up a temporary land socialisation scheme and have already put this into practice. The land question may be said to be already settled in its main outlines. The expropriation of the landlords and the division of the land on a communal basis has been accomplished and only awaits legal sanction. If this is not given, then all the same the land will remain divided as it is. The peasants, tired of delay, have presented the Goverment with an accomplished fact, and they know that the armed forces of the country, which are their own sons, will be on their side. It makes little difference whether Cadets or Chernov triumph as far as this part of Russia is concerned.

In Samara the provincial Land Committee drew up a series of land regulations this summer which established the following principles: all private purchase and sale of land in the province, before the meeting of the Constituent Assembly, is forbidden; all lands of private owners, banks, the late Tsar and Imperial Family, monasteries and churches pass under the control of the local Land Committees pending settlement at the Constituent Assembly; landowners and small proprietors may retain for their own use that amount of land which they can work themselves by their own labour and with their own livestock; all land which cannot be worked by the owners passes into the public land fund and is freed from liability to [pay] rent; for the season 1917–1918 the land is divided among the local Land Committees or communes; each commune is to draw up a statement of the number of peasant families, their need for land and their capacity to work it, and the provincial Land Committee is to make the distribution, approximating as far as possible to these needs. In actual practice I find that very little change has taken place. Those who formerly rented large areas of the landlords' land still work the same areas, but instead of paying rent for the right to use the land they keep this amount in their pockets ... The change at first sight appears merely a matter of book keeping, but it is fraught with tremendous social and economic consequences.

I find that everywhere the rural commune is not only maintaining its functions but even extending them ... It is clear that the whole country is being covered with a huge network of land communes, all of which are connected with each other in the common purpose of developing the land on a public basis and of removing all traces of private exploitation ... The idea of the more far-sighted Socialist Revolutionaries is to establish a reserve of land in each province under the control of the united Land Committee of All Russia; and to satisfy the needs of the peasantry in the provinces where there is little land, by migration to where there is a surplus. If this is not done it is probable that the peasants of the Lower Volga provinces, where land is plentiful, may develop their own local policy and prevent immigration from the more crowded provinces of the west and the Ukraine. For economic causes the migrations of the Russian peasantry have been going, during many hundred years in an easterly direction, towards the unoccupied spaces of Siberia and the Asiatic borderland. Any attempt artificially to stop this by a development of local patriotism will have undesirable consequences. It is probably the desire for local autonomy in land settlement and fear of immigration from the west which is at the bottom of the Cossacks' movement.[31] The Cadets and other reactionary forces play on this fear for their own ends. It was also without doubt the direct cause of the rebellion and massacre of the nomad Tartars in Russian Central Asia last year.[32]

In European Russia also the tendency of the country to split up into a number of areas, each running its own internal policy, has probably been aggravated by the continuation of the war, which makes the food and produce questions more and more acute. The Lower Volga provinces and the Cossack territories are corn-exporting; the northern and north-western provinces are corn-importing; the Ukraine is sugar-exporting. As food and materials, therefore, get less and less, each area is interested in holding its supplies, preventing exports, and running its own local food and land policies. These demands for autonomy may take a national form, as in the Ukraine, or a semi-national, semi-political form, as with the Cossacks, or may develop in the form of a rapid agrarian revolution without the sanction of the Provisional Government, such as is going on in these Lower Volga provinces and in Central Russia. In the latter case, however, the question assumes a more general character and is connected with the great struggle between classes which is now beginning to overstep the boundaries of race and nationality.

Manchester Guardian, *28 November 1917*
'Asiatic Russia and the Revolution'
Orenburg, *1 October 1917*

To the east of this town lies Asiatic Russia ... There are four zones in this vast area, each of which has its peculiar climate and corresponding human type. There are the Cossacks, living in the long thin strip of black earth steppe running from the Caspian to the Trans-Baikal. North of this comes the 'forest steppe' inhabited by Russian peasant immigrants from European Russia. South and south-east of the Cossack line comes the dry steppe area where the nomad Kirghiz Tartars live together with some Russian immigrants. Further south still, in Turkestan proper, comes the desert, dotted with oases, in which live the settled Moslem population called Sarts.[33] The interesting question now arises: how have the inhabitants of these four zones been influenced by the Russian Revolution?

Let us take the 'forest steppe' of Western Siberia first. The colonists of the black earth lands of Tomsk and Tobolsk and the foothills of the Altai have an enormous reserve of land fit for colonisation still at their doors. Up to now this land has been at the disposal of Petrograd. But the revolutionary organisations which have sprung up all over Siberia in the last six months have now assembled at Tomsk and are engaged in drawing up a scheme of land autonomy in relation to the unoccupied lands of North Asiatic Russia. I understand that the Siberian Council of Peasants' Deputies, together with the Siberian co-operators' alliance, are the most influential of all the revolutionary organisations ... But the predominant element everywhere is the peasant and the co-operator, not the urban worker. Therefore watchwords about the 'dictatorship of the proletariat' are less popular than watchwords like 'Siberian land for the Siberians'. The embryo Siberian Parliament, now sitting at Tomsk, has drawn up a scheme for future land colonisation. The reserve lands are to be placed under the control of a Siberian Land Commission which is to decide how many immigrants from European Russia shall be allowed to come in after the war, and how much is to be reserved for the future needs of the native population ... I have reason to think also that the West Siberian Cossacks are disposed to enter into the Siberian autonomy scheme.

Beyond the Siberian black earth zone come the steppes of the Turgai, Akmolinsk and Semirech, where live the nomad Kirghiz and many hundred thousands of recently arrived Russian peasants. The late Tsar's government adopted the policy of settling this dry steppe region with colonists from the Ukraine ... But this involved ousting the nomad Kirghiz from some of their best grazing lands. This, in fact, was done and the 2,000,000 Kirghiz of these regions were by 1916 reduced to something like half of the territories they possessed ten years ago. When on the top of this the Tsar's government demanded military service in the rear from the Moslems of Asia the camel's back broke. The nomad population of Central Asia rose in rebellion in the summer of 1916 and civil war resulted. About 500,000 were massacred, and something like a million fled into the confines of China at the beginning of the year. While Western Europe has heard about Armenian massacres, the massacre of Central Asian Moslems by the Tsar's agents has been studiously hidden.

After the Russian Revolution the Kirghiz refugees in China tried to return but found that the Russian colonists and Cossacks of the Semirech and Akmolinsk had occupied their remaining lands. So they were driven back to the Chinese borders again, where the Chinese officials refused to allow them to pass. Neither the Provisional Government nor the organs of the revolutionary democracy have been able as yet to control these colonists and Cossacks who refuse to allow the Kirghiz to settle down. At the present moment civil war is still going on in these regions between the nomads and the colonists ... Spasmodically this warfare breaks out every fifty years or so. The Revolution has had nothing to do with it because it broke out last year. But the Revolution has to deal with it amongst all its other difficulties.

On the other hand I find that in the Turgai steppe, to the east of this town, the Revolution has already succeeded in making peace between the Russian colonists and the Kirghiz. The expropriation of the latter has never been carried on to such a degree here as in the regions adjoining the Chinese frontier. When the Revolution came, therefore, the two races living side by side on the steppes elected their revolutionary committees and began to work together. I was present last week at a meeting of the Land Committee of the Turgai province. I found that about three-quarters of the Committee were Kirghiz and the rest Russian peasants. Both races sat side by side on terms of equality, spoke each other's language and had so far forgotten old land quarrels that they were actually engaged in working out a common land programme which will protect their joint interests against future colonists from European Russia ...

The fourth zone is that of the Turkestan oases. How have the native Moslems here been affected by the Revolution? The early days gave great hopes. Under the influence of the Young Sart Party the Emir of Bokhara was forced to declare a Constitution and to abolish corporal and capital punishment. But the forces of progress among the Moslems of Bokhara were not well founded. The enlightened Young Sarts, who had been educated in Russia and had caught the spirit of the age, soon found themselves up against the dense mass of bigotry and superstition which lingers on in the Central Asian oases. The Emir's agents, the mullahs and the landlords began to agitate against the Revolution. The Russian government agent in Bokhara openly supported the Emir against the revolutionaries. Thus the change in Bokhara is only superficial at present.

Very different, however, is the state of affairs in the other parts of the Turkestan oases, in the Sir Darya, Samarkand and Fergana provinces. Here the local Council of Workers' and Soldiers' Delegates formed among the Russian colonists and garrisons continue to work in close contact with the natives. The latter are divided roughly into three political groups. There is a small reactionary society led by the mullahs ... then there is the democratic group organised by the intellectuals and the more progressive merchants of the oases, which is called the Moslem Regional Council ... In close contact with them is the Federalist Party. The leaders of this group are propagating the idea of a Russian Federation in which Turkestan will become one of the units. The idea seems to be having considerable success, for a recent conference of the Moslem Regional Council adopted a resolution favouring this principle of government for Turkestan ... It is interesting to observe that the Revolution has had the effect of developing among the more intelligent Moslem natives a distinctly national feeling. There is as yet little sign of class struggle between native property owners and labourers, and nothing approaching Pan-Islamism, but there is growing a simple Turkestan nationalism.

Outside the educated Moslems, who inspired this national cultural and political movement, there is the great mass of Sart peasantry ... Needless to say they are quite unaffected by the programme of the Russian Socialist Revolutionary Party. 'Land and Liberty' has no meaning for them. No one in Turkestan wants land, because it is all desert. But everyone wants water, and no party has come forward promising 'Water and Liberty' because the water in Turkestan depends not on the political situation in Petrograd but on the snowfall in the Pamir plateau.

But among the cotton workers of the Fergana, on the other hand, trade unions have been formed which work in close contact with the local Russian Council of Workers' and Soldiers' Deputies. The Russian garrisons in Central Asia seem to be very revolutionary in disposition and to be strongly under the influence of Maximalism. Recently, after the Kornilov rebellion, the Tashkent Council arrested the representative of the Provisional Government and established itself as a permanent committee of public safety, claiming sole executive power. But it does not seem to be able to carry the natives along with it in this respect, for the Moslem Regional Council has expressed its readiness to recognise the Provisional Government.

Manchester Guardian, *27 November 1917*
'Equality for All and Cossack Privilege'
Orenburg, *1 October 1917*

The wave of the Russian Revolution, though it swept far and wide in the great days of March, nevertheless soon struck the rocks of ancient tradition and territorial peculiarities in the border regions of Asia. This is well illustrated in the case of the Cossacks. In the early days of the Revolution the latter astounded Russia with their loyalty to the people. They seemed to have forgotten their old role of Tsar's bulldogs and to have united with the proletariat and peasant masses. But as the Revolution passed its infancy and entered the stage where serious work and reconstruction were needed, a change set in, and one of the first of the territorial groups to shown signs of uneasiness at the change were the Cossacks ...

After leaving Samara it was clear that I had passed out of the area where the revolutionary masses were united in [sic] the workers, peasants and soldiers. I had reached, in this gateway into Asia, a region where the Revolution was complicated by other factors, cutting across it and apparently hindering its development. On the day after my arrival I interviewed the Ataman of the Orenburg Cossacks, and the first question I asked him was: what was the attitude of his Cossacks towards the programme of the Russian revolutionary democracy? 'We Cossacks,' he replied, 'are above all things democratic, for we were free when the Russian peasant was a serf. Our ancestors fled out here to escape the Tsar's tyranny, and the Tsar rewarded us with land in return for our services against the Tartars. Our whole institutions are democratic. I, for instance, am elected by the Cossacks of my '*krug*'(the Cossack term for a military area) on an adult suffrage and secret ballot. None of us may own land. Each '*stanitza*' (the Cossack term for a village) has an area of land allotted to it by the '*krug*' and this is divided equally among the families of the '*stanitza*'. Every 25 years the land is redistributed, as is the custom also among the communes of the Russian peasant. Co-operation has made great strides among us. In the last ten years 106 societies have started in the Orenburg district alone.'

'Then why,' I asked, 'is there a feeling that you are not in sympathy with the land programme of the Revolution, seeing that in practice you carry out its ideas?' The Ataman smiled. 'Our lands were bought by the blood of our ancestors; they have been Cossack for centuries. By occupying them we saved Russia from invasion from the east. But Russian peasants are continually wanting to migrate into our territories, and now the Socialist Revolutionary Party tells them that they are equal with us and have a right to the same amount of land as ourselves. We have nothing against those peasants who lived among us for decades. In the *stanitzas* we even admit them on equal terms, but we must have the right to keep fresh immigrants from invading our ancestral territories. What our fathers won we shall not give up.'

The psychology of the Cossack (and this is typical of the majority of them) certainly does not harmonise with that of the revolutionary peasants and soldiery of European Russia. But this is not by any means an accidental phenomenon. It has its roots deep down in history. After the thirteenth century, when the wave of the Tartar invasion in Russia subsided, a European migration eastwards began. The Slavs, gradually developing their economic and political strength, started to invade Asia. The first wave consisted of fur traders, tribute collectors, robbers and soldiers of fortune, who settled down in unoccupied lands and whose descendants became Cossacks. The retreat of the Tartars and the increased safety from raids laid open large tracts behind the Cossack territories to colonisation from European Russia. Gradually the Cossacks began to feel pressure on them. Russian peasants encroached on their lands. Petersburg officials and landlords from the Ukraine, attracted by the richness of the soil, tried to nibble off Cossack land for their serfs. The Tartars, too, were giving up plundering and were settling to stock-raising and oasis cultivation. Thus the Cossacks were now pressed from the west but had no vacant spaces to move into on the east. In self-defence they united to protect their land, which now lay in two thin but almost continuous strips running from the Don to Eastern Siberia.

Numbering only seven millions, the Cossacks have in these strips still great reserves of land, and their average allotment per man is much higher than that of the Russian peasant. The Tsar's government used this privileged position to secure the support of the Cossacks against the Russian people. But their free nature revolted against this moral servitude, and they became at last ardent revolutionaries and republicans. Now, however, when the Revolution sets itself to solve the land question and aims to establish the principle of equal rights for *all* Russian subjects to the land, the traditions of a privileged cast begin to appear again, and as the first occupiers of large Asiatic territories the Cossacks now claim rights of local autonomy to protect their land interests. Thus the revolutionary idea of equality for all and privilege for none meets the Cossack idea of family traditions and territorial rights of ancestors.

On the other hand it must not be thought that the Cossacks are everywhere a united mass ... In many parts of the Cossack territories, where modern industries are beginning to spread, a Cossack bourgeoisie and a proletariat class are gradually being formed. The class struggle, in fact, has commenced on the same lines as the rest of Russia. At the present moment the Council of Workers' and Soldiers' Deputies in Petrograd has a special Cossack section, which draws to it the members of the labouring Cossacks and those with little land. The latter are by instinct in full sympathy with the revolutionary democracy. But they are at present only the minority. The great majority of Cossacks still have large land reserves. Moreover, they have always lived under a strict military discipline and their institutions, if democratic in form, are military in spirit ... Class consciousness has not yet penetrated the bulk of the Cossacks, but with the steadily increasing economic pressure from the West, and especially with the produce difficulties caused by the war, the process of splitting into two antagonistic classes will grow and gradually bring the Cossacks into line with the rest of Russia.

Manchester Guardian, *29 November 1917*
'At a Cossack Provincial Assembly'
Orenburg, *1 October 1917*

Last week I had the opportunity of being present at the gathering
of the Orenburg Cossacks – the first that has been held for 150 years.
On the day of assembly in the square outside the staff headquarters
a squadron of horsemen were drawn up. Their long lances glittered
in a steel line over their heads, their round forage caps were pressed
down on one side and a long lock of hair protruded in the style
always adopted by the Orenburg Cossacks. The deputies from the
stanitzas began to arrive. Officers with blue-striped trousers and
orderlies in attendance on them rode up on shaggy Asiatic ponies.
Heels clicked and salutes were exchanged, a thing rarely seen in
the Russian regular army today. Inside I saw a stately gathering,
but the whole atmosphere was a striking contrast to the revolutionary
meetings of these days. There was no comradeship, no warm
enthusiasm of those working and suffering in a common cause. On
the front benches sat the generals, colonels and Ataman, who all
seemed to suggest that they had come out on parade. On the back
benches the *'ryadovoys'* (Cossacks of the ranks) sat vacantly staring
in front of them, as if they had no souls of their own and were only
waiting for the word of command. Behind the Ataman stood a row
of sentries with drawn swords and on each side of him were fixed
the standards of the Orenburg Cossacks, one with a Russian and
the other with a Tartar inscription upon it (the Orenburg Cossacks
have 50,000 Moslems among their number).

In theory the assembly had been elected democratically on the
basis of universal suffrage and secret ballot. Every 5,000 Cossacks
in the *stanitzas* of the Orenburg *krug* had elected one delegate. Each
Cossack from the ranks had equal rights with his officer. But the
interesting question was whether the spirit of equality in the
assembly hall was or was not in reality influenced by the spirit of
subordination from the parade ground. Here lay the test of a
democratic assembly. The Council of Soldiers' Delegates in the
Russian revolutionary army is guaranteed complete political freedom
and absence of the military spirit because the soldiers elect only
from the ranks. No officers (except a few particularly revolutionary
ones) ever get into the Soldiers' Councils. But here with the
Cossacks I found that at least half the delegates were officers.
That, of course, does not mean that the assembly was necessarily
undemocratic. On the contrary, it might indicate a brotherly
relation between officers and men. But it might also mean a lack
of political consciousness and of initiative among the electors who,
accustomed for generations to being commanded and not to think

for themselves elect by habit those who order them about instead
of those who they think will carry out their desires ...

The initiative for the first two days of the assembly came entirely
from the generals, colonels and officials sitting on the front benches
... The Ataman, a sedate old general, led off with an address of
welcome. The Cossacks, he said, were a free people who loved
democratic institutions. They alone among the Russian people
were inspired by patriotism. The Cossacks realised from the first
that the Revolution was a national one and had no international
significance except in so far as it might be able to make Russia
stronger in a military sense. Therefore, 'away with all talk of a
"democratic peace"! The Cossacks are fighters and not diplomats.
Away with revolutionary councils financed by Jews! They must be
abolished if Russia is to be saved.' And wild applause went up from
the generals and colonels on the front benches. Those sitting on
the back benches sat and looked stolidly in front of them, as if still
waiting for the word of command.

Then amid tremendous enthusiasm, there arrived upon the
scene the representative of the Don Cossacks, sent by General
Kaledin. 'We Cossacks,' he said, 'feel deeply injured by the attitude
towards us of the Provisional Government. It suspects us, sends
people to watch us, refuses us the right to use the telegraph between
the Don and Petrograd except under supervision. It ordered the
arrest of our General Kaledin. But what have we done? We are not
counter-revolutionary. We only stand for discipline, order and
firm power, for the dissolution of the democratic bodies and no
politics in wartime. General Kornilov was the man who knew the
real needs of Russia and he is the man who still inspires the ideas
of us Cossacks.'

Some interesting speeches were made on the second day by
certain officials from the Cossack land organisation ... It was clear
that a strong movement for territorial Home Rule was on foot among
the Orenburg Cossacks. I even heard the word 'federation'
mentioned, but on the other hand some seemed to think that this
went too far, and were content with local autonomy for dealing with
land and other local matters ...

The third day was perhaps the most interesting of all, for it was
only then that the silent mass at the back of the hall began to become
articulate. We heard at last the voice of the labouring Cossacks and
of those from the regiments at the front, which up to now had been
drowned by the trumpet calls of the generals on the front benches.
The spokesman for the Cossacks in the South-western army was
a handsome lad of 25. He came dressed in the simple uniform of
a Cossack horseman. Timidly he rose on the tribune and haltingly
began to speak. Unlike the Russian revolutionary soldier, he was
unused to expressing his thoughts in words. But an impulse seemed

to urge him to bring out an idea that lay within him. He struggled with the words, seemed to fail, began again and pushed through.

'Let not the Cossacks separate themselves from their brothers the Russian soldiers,' he said, 'for we are united in spirit with them. Our soldier comrades are weak but their hearts are sound. If they do wrong things, if they fail sometimes, remember the slavery they have lived in. Blame the Tsar's government for that and not the Revolutionary Councils. Let us help our brother soldiers and not embitter them against us. Let us work with the councils which are trying to teach them self-respect. Only a union between Cossacks and soldiers will save the Russian army. We Cossacks from the South-western army look on the Russian soldier as a brother, failing sometimes through his weakness but in spirit one with us, struggling upwards to the light.'

A dead silence came over the hall as the speaker finished. The generals in the front row were too astounded to utter a sound. Such a speech had never been made by a Cossack ranker in Orenburg before. And he had made it, too, without asking the permission of his superior officer! But before they had time to recover themselves the representative of the Cossack section of the Council of Workers' and Soldiers' Delegates, which contains Cossack workers and labourers from the factories and mines on the Don, rose on the platform and addressed the *krug*. 'We are all agreed,' he said, 'that there should be in Russia a strong Government authority. But some people want to establish that authority by creating confidence and hope in the minds of the masses, and there are those who think they can establish it by the blood and iron of the old regime. We Cossack workers warn you officers against that course. If you try to destroy the Councils you will poison the source whence courage and hope flow to the Russian masses. Start on this mad game if you will, but in that case you leave us behind you.'

That was too much for the front-bench generals. 'Enough! Disgraceful! Insubordination!' was heard on all sides. Since the offender could not be court-martialled in a democratic assembly, the next best thing to do was to exclude him and his associates from the sitting. It was therefore discovered that a number of members had incorrect mandates. By a curious coincidence the incorrect mandates all came from the Cossack rankers at the front who had been 'poisoned' by contact with the revolutionary soldiers, and from the Cossack workers' section of the Council of Workers' and Soldiers' Deputies. These people did not represent the 'free Orenburg Cossacks'. The one had been fighting for three years at the front and the other had been intriguing for revolution in Petrograd. So they were all excluded. Then the front-bench generals and their obedient following of the older generation of ex-service

Cossacks from the *stanitzas* continued their deliberations in peace in the name of the 'free Cossacks'!

Manchester Guardian, *1 December 1917*
'The Russian Tartars and the Revolution'
Kazan, *15 October 1917*

The provinces of the Middle Volga are inhabited by a mixed population of Great Russians and Moslem Tartars. Of the latter there are some eight million, chiefly centred round Kazan and Ufa. Throughout these provinces there is no area inhabited exclusively by one race. It is not possible to separate off certain areas and say that in this or that one the Moslems predominate and have a right to claim territorial autonomy ... The Tsar's government used to the utmost this factor to strengthen its position. By systematic oppression of the Tartars, by withholding all official positions from them, by deliberately hindering the spread of education among them and by attempting to Russify their schools, Tsarism succeeded in making the standard of culture and political consciousness in the Middle Volga provinces considerably lower than in the provinces to the north and south. Moreover the effect is seen also upon the Russian peasants of these regions. I find that in the Kazan government the Russian peasants have, since the Revolution, been much slower and less effective in their organisation of revolutionary committees than elsewhere. It is only in certain places that land committees have been formed for dividing up the landlords' land on a properly worked-out plan. In other districts the peasants have simply seized the land, and in some places agrarian disorders have broken out ... Where the Tsar's government was directed towards turning one race against another or suppressing one of them, the Revolution has developed much more slowly and with greater difficulty than in provinces inhabited by one race only.

On the other hand there are no complicated political problems for the Revolution to solve, arising out of demands for federation and territorial autonomy for this or that race ... In the All-Russia Moslem Conference held in Moscow in May, the speakers for the Volga Tartars openly denounced all plans for political autonomy and even opposed it for their co-religionists further east.[34] At the second All-Russia Moslem Conference, held in Kazan last month, these Tartars passed a resolution in favour of national-cultural autonomy, and then proceeded to establish a Tartar National Council at Ufa to work out a plan for primary education, for a Moslem university in Russia, and for other cultural institutions upon a national Tartar basis ... The Tartars are clearly laying themselves out to become the cultural leaders of the Moslem world in Central and Northern Asia. I find that a large section of the young Tartars here have come under the influences of the *Yeni Turan* movement.[35] This, it may be remembered, began in Turkey a few years before the outbreak of the war, and indeed some of the leaders of the movement in Constantinople were Tartar emigrants from Russia ... Several able young Tartar writers I have met in the last day or two strongly favour the idea of an *entente* between Russia and Turkey, and even hope that the Tartars will become the mediators between the two countries ... It is interesting to observe that the Tartars of this school of thought take no interest at all in their fellow-Moslems in Persia, Arabia, Egypt and India ...

On the other hand I have come across another school here which takes a much wider view of the destinies of the Tartars towards their co-religionists in Asia ... Dissatisfied with the *Yeni Turan* movement, which they regard as a narrow form of nationalism, they see before them the whole world of Asia sunk in mediaeval apathy and superstition, politically enslaved by the ruling classes of Europe and economically exploited by world capital. They note the growth of class consciousness among the urban proletariat of Russia. Feeling instinctively that this psychological wave of class consciousness will not stop on the Russian plain but will surge some day far and wide over Asia, they hope to see the Russian Tartars as the advanced guard of this great movement of cultural renaissance and political awakening in the East ... They denounce all federal systems which will divide one group of Asiatics from another and are against all artificial attempts to create national barriers between the oppressed masses of Asia. Pan-Islamism is to them not a fanatical religious creed nor an idea for establishing a political state or Empire. It is rather a cultural movement for educating the masses of Asia to the consciousness of their condition so that one day they can join hands with their comrade proletariat in Europe in the great international class struggle which is to come.

The Revolution has also brought about most far-reaching changes among the Tartar women. The women's movement here started in the Revolution of 1905, as a result of which women began to go about unveiled. By 1910 a veiled Moslem woman was unknown in Kazan. Directly after the March Revolution the Moslem women in Kazan formed a society and sent their delegates to the first All-Russia Moslem Conference. Here they presented resolutions condemning polygamy and the Moslem inheritance law, according to which female inheritors in a family receive smaller portions than male ... In the elections for the *Zemstvo*s for the Kazan province they are voting along with the men. A separate day is set apart for them to vote on, so as to satisfy the mullahs and the more old-fashioned women ... One only has to walk down the streets in Kazan and go to the Moslem theatre in the evening to see that here, at least, Moslem women are socially the equals of men and have at last shaken off from themselves the shackles of sex tyranny.

Manchester Guardian, *7 December 1917*
'The Voice of the People on the Revolution'
Nijni Novgorod, 21 October 1917

It was getting dark when I reached the quay on the banks of the Volga where the boats discharge and load for Kazan. The barge where the steamer arrives was crowded with every conceivable type of humanity that Russia is capable of producing. In the greasy, chattering throng I saw a large number of peasants with sacks of flour piled up in heaps around them. They had come from the northern governments of Vladimir, Yaroslav and Kostroma to buy flour for their starving families. Their pinched faces and ragged clothes told eloquently of the state to which the war has reduced these forest dwellers of North Russia. In the half-darkness I stumbled over a confused mass of sleeping and squatting humanity and sacks of flour till I reached the ticket office. Here I bought a second class ticket, and on the arrival of the boat settled myself comfortably in one of the cabins for the night.

Presently I heard a commotion, and all at once there burst into the second class compartment a number of 'comrades' – revolutionary soldiers who are now acting as militia on the Volga quays. 'Hey, you bourgeois! Out with you all! Make way for honest folk.' It was no use to explain that although I had a second class ticket I was nevertheless a sympathiser with the Russian Revolution. I wore a black coat and a felt hat and that was enough. I was a bourgeois and I had to clear out – bag and baggage. As I passed out, discomfited, I struggled through a mob of these same peasants whom I had seen on the quay. They had been waiting two days and nights for the steamer to come and take them north to their starving families, and in the faint light I could see a gleam of satisfaction on their thin faces that they were at last one step nearer home. Here on the ship they annexed the first and second class cabins and stacked their sacks in the third class and the hold. The ship sailed away and I was left on the open barge that acts as a quay, to take my luck for the next ship.

It was pitch dark. A cold autumn wind was blowing. The city of Kazan lay five miles distant. There was nothing to do but to 'stick it out' in the open till morning. On the barge I found a number of fellow travellers in the same plight as myself. Several of the hungry peasants with their sacks had not succeeded in getting away. There were also some women from the villages near Kazan who were returning from market; there was a retail trader in skins or, to be more precise in these days, a speculator (*beeshchnik* is the Russian word); two mechanics from cotton factories further up the Volga, a Tartar fisherman, and an officer – the only member of the '*intelligentsia*' present. As comrades in misfortune we all got together. Someone lit a fire, and there was a general atmosphere of companionship around it. Some lay on the sacks, some squatted near the fire. The moon rose and half-lifted the curtain of darkness, while the wavelets lapped rhythmically against the sides of the barge. I lay down and drew my coat over me, but the cold prevented sleep and I listened to the conversation. Every discussion in a public place in Russia now concerns food. It is the essence of politics. It looms larger even than the question of war and peace, for in international politics the stomach seems to be a more influential factor than the brain. Last year food, or rather the absence of it, made the Revolution; this year it seems to be on the verge of destroying it.

'You fellows down here in the south are living in paradise,' said one of the peasants from Vladimir, 'with your flour at 30 kopecks a pood and your eggs at 215 kopecks each. You come up north, my boys, and you'll find no honey that way.' 'There is plenty of corn,' said one of the mechanics, 'but it's hidden in the villages and the speculators have got hold of it. It will be no good until they are searched and made to give it up.' 'We have only just got enough for ourselves,' said a peasant woman from the south. 'In our village each *izbi* (an old Russian term for a collection of families living under one roof) has not more than 50 poods (a pood equals about 36 lb.) each, and what can we sell from that when we don't know what will happen tomorrow? Perhaps next year there will be no machines, no horses, no labour to work. If there is no store in the *ambar* (public village granary) we, too, shall see the kingdom of hunger.' 'Take it from the landlords,' retorted the mechanic; 'they are fat enough. Why don't the councils and the produce committees requisition their granaries?' 'Ah! those committees,' croaked an old woman; 'what do they do but take large salaries and live at our expense?' 'Yes,' said one of the old peasants, 'the Government of Nicholas had little bread to give us but these "comrades" have even less.' 'But don't you see,' suddenly interrupted a young peasant soldier who had joined the company in the meantime, 'the councils and committees are not to blame? They can't get workmen because they are all at the war; they can't make machines for you because the factories won't work; they can't get horses for transport because they are all at the front. Talk about Nicholas if you like, but would he do any better if he came to look after your souls?' 'Anyway,' said an old peasant, 'Nicholas could feed the army but these fellows can't. Only yesterday I had a letter from my son at the front. He wrote imploring us to send them flour to bake bread with.' 'But I replied,' said an old woman, apparently his wife', that if he wants bread he had better come home. What are they fighting about? If the Germans come it could not be worse than it is now.'

There was a general silence and I heard the Tartar snoring on one of the sacks. He was doubtless dreaming about his native steppes away to the east. 'They won't give us any boots or shoes, or cloth for our coats,' persisted the old peasant. 'The workmen in the towns take an eight-hour day and double their wages, but we peasants have to work all day, live on air and clothe ourselves with straw mats; and then they expect us to feed them.'

'Eh, little father,' retorted the mechanic, 'under Nicholas they looked after us well. We had to work all day for 40 roubles a month and if we complained they packed us off to the front and put us in the front trenches to get us killed as quickly as possible. It is time for us to get a little for our work. Ask the capitalists and factory owners why you don't get your boots and shoes. They want to produce small quantities so as to sell them at high prices. They are living nicely off you peasants, if you only knew it. But you don't know it and you go blaming the revolutionary committees.'

'But how are the factory owners to live,' said the leather trader, who had been silent up to now, 'if you workers take all his profits in wages?' 'Fix our wages and his profits and the price of the goods,' replied the mechanic, 'and then these comrades in the villages will get their boots. But that song does not please the gentlemen speculators. The bourgeois want the workers' blood and know how to get it while there is a war going.' 'By the Mother of God,' said an old peasant, 'this is not true. What is a bourgeois? He is a man like you and me. You ought not to call a man bad because he is a bourgeois. It is a sin to say evil things.' 'If a man lives at other people's expense he is a parasite and nothing more,' retorted the mechanic. 'If a bourgeois is a parasite,' replied the old peasant 'then he is bad, but if he is only a bourgeois and nothing more, then he is a comrade like you and me. God forgive us if we say evil things about each other. The war began in the world because the rulers of the people said evil things about the rulers of other people. Now there is war in Russia among her own people because we say evil things about one another.'

There was another silence, broken by the officer who all the time had been intently staring into the fire and puffing a cigarette. 'The real truth is,' he said, 'that Russia is being ruined because her people are dark and ignorant. They have no patriotism or love of their country.' 'Yes,' said the leather merchant, 'we are only fit to be serfs because when we get liberty we don't know what to do with it.' 'Of course we are dark and ignorant,' retorted the mechanic, 'if landlords, speculators and capitalists rule us, because they want us to be so. It serves their interest, just as it did that of Nicholas

Romanov. You say that the Russian people have no patriotism, but what have they got to be patriotic about if they have no land and are wage slaves, and are then told to go and fight for foreign allies who want colonies?'

'Why don't we follow the example of the English and French?' said the officer. 'They are an enlightened and educated people. They have money and they are coming here to put order into the country.' 'And fill their pockets, too,' retorted the mechanic. 'You talk like that,' replied the officer, 'but don't forget that a few years ago we were the slaves of the Germans; now we are only living thanks to the benevolence of our English and French allies. Tomorrow we shall perhaps be the slaves of all three.' 'And that is just what our bourgeois want,' said the young peasant soldier; 'they want us to be slaves. They don't want us to have the land for ourselves; they want us to go on fighting, so that we shall be under the foreign capitalists. Only peace and a union between peasants, labourers, Cossacks and soldiers can stop our sufferings and make us free and independent and give us bread. It was for these things that we made the Revolution.' 'Yes, my son,' said the old peasant; 'you have made it and you have given us neither peace, nor freedom, nor independence, nor bread. You have only brought the black ravens over Russia.' 'Are we to blame for that, little father?' said the young soldier. 'It is bad times now, but don't forget that it was worse before the Revolution. True we had more bread than we have now, but then we had no hope in life. Now we have less bread but more hope.'

The conversation ended, the fire died down, the Tartar continued snoring, and the waves of the Volga still rippled against the sides of the barge. For a long time I lay gazing up at the stars and trying to understand the meaning of the words I had heard uttered that night by the only true voice of Russia.

Manchester Guardian, *8 December 1917*
'How the Maximalists Have Come to Gain Control'
Yaroslav, 24 October 1917

I have now completed my journey through the provinces along the banks of the Volga, and have as a result obtained a general impression of the conditions prevailing in the heart of Russia. Starting from the poorer northern governments I have passed south and south-east to the richer regions bordering Asia. Everywhere I came in contact with the new revolutionary and democratic institutions, and have thus been able to form some idea of the progress of the Revolution in the little-known interior.

At first sight everything seemed to be going well. I found that in every province I visited the revolutionary organisations and political societies had during the summer begun an educational campaign for the enlightenment of the masses. The whole country is now divided up into 'cultural' areas – Moscow, the northern provinces, the Don basin, the central provinces, the Volga, Siberia, Central Asia, the Caucasus and the Ukraine. In every provincial town the political societies that centre round the Council of Workers' and Soldiers' Delegates have libraries from which books on politics, history, literature and economics are lent out to the smaller centres in the surrounding rural districts. There is an immense sale for pamphlets, and the demand is such that it cannot be supplied on account of the paper shortage. The recently elected town councils and *Zemstvos* are organising lectures everywhere to educate the people in the duty of citizenship and the meaning of the Constituent Assembly. I could see, moreover, that a new type of *intelligentsia* is being created. The old *intelligentsia*, such as the professors at the universities, the students, doctors and advocates, have now joined the army of Cadet landlords and bankers. But the new type has sprung more recently from the native mass and is seen in the young men from the villages who, by hard struggle have received a primary education and then by service in the army have travelled and seen the world. To them a helping hand has been lent by the school teachers, co-operators and agronomists. It is this type that is now controlling the provincial democratic bodies and is struggling against terrific odds to spread light where darkness was before.

I found that the revolutionary Councils of Workers', Soldiers' and Peasants' Deputies in the provinces, though still influential, are to a large extent now being replaced by other bodies. Among the most important of these are the professional alliances or trade unions. There are some two million workers in Russia who are now organised in these unions. The railwaymen's alliance alone has 500,000, the metallist union has a paying membership of over 300,000. All these workers, who at the beginning of the Revolution joined the Council of Workers' and Soldiers' Deputies in order to win the political battle over Tsarism, have now regrouped themselves, each in their special trade unions. Thus it would seem that among the Russian proletariat consciousness of the need for political struggle came first and the desire for economic organisation later.

It is the exact reverse of what has taken place in the Labour movement in England. But besides the trade unions there have been set up now in every locality municipalities and rural *Zemstvos* elected on an adult suffrage. These bodies have the advantage of being sanctioned by law, whereas the councils are revolutionary committees, of necessity only temporary, formed for tiding over a critical moment. Much of the work formerly done by the councils has now passed into the hands of these legally elected local authorities. But it need not be thought that the opinions expressed by the councils today are not reflected in the opinions of these new public bodies. On the question of peace and the programme of the Revolution the central executive of the Council of Workers' and Soldiers' Deputies in Petrograd [Petrograd Soviet] expresses the sentiments of thousands of rural *Zemstvo*s scattered all over Russia, while on internal economic policy the trade unions are more advanced than the councils, as was shown in the recent railway strike, which took place against the wishes of the latter. In most cases it would seem that on to the municipalities have been elected the same political leaders that formerly led the councils, if one may judge from the percentage of the political parties represented there. The results of the elections for the 48 provincial towns of European and Asiatic Russia give the following average: Social Democratic and Socialist Revolutionary blocks – 65 per cent of all votes; national groups (standing on the revolutionary peace platform) – 8 per cent; Cadets and bourgeois parties – 12 per cent; non-party – 15 per cent. Everything would therefore seem to point to a gradual deepening and broadening of the Revolution through the country, and the strengthening of the ideas set forth by the councils among the masses.

But on the other hand, it must be observed that factors of disintegration have been at work in the last few months. The terrible havoc caused by the war in the natural economy of the country is reducing the task of the democracy in the provinces to an impossibility. The relations between the social classes that make up the revolutionary democracy are becoming more and more strained. The peasants are dissatisfied with the urban proletariat because the latter have got an eight-hour day and a rise in wages, and buy their bread at a fixed rate, whereas they have to pay speculators' prices for all manufactured commodities of life. The army which, though consisting mainly of peasant youths, has nevertheless a distinct psychology of its own, is discontented with the peasantry in the rear for keeping back food supplies in the villages. The urban proletariat is suffering from a continual shortage of food caused by the breakdown of the transport. With the march of famine each social and economic class is forced to struggle harder for its own existence, and this to a great degree weakens the common revolutionary effort. But on one point all sections of the democracy are united, and that is in the demand for a speedy peace as the only means of saving themselves from economic collapse and famine.

In addition to the increasing antagonism between various sections of the proletariat, there is now also another factor which still further hinders the constructive work of the revolutionary democracy.

Under the stress of food shortage there is an inclination for each district to run its own local policy. Thus I found that in the Upper Volga provinces of Vladimir, Kostroma, Nijni Novgorod and Yaroslav, the peasants are literally starving. Their Produce Committees are making frantic efforts to get corn sent up from the south before the Volga freezes, but the Produce Committees of Samara, Saratov and Kazan, which are controlled by the peasants of those provinces, decline to part with their reserves of corn. In a fortnight the Volga freezes and then there will be nothing left for five million peasants to do but face the winter on roots and herbs from the forest or die of hunger. The Cossacks also are everywhere trying to create local communes and federal republics, the ultimate aim of which is to preserve their lands from immigration from the west and to prevent the local food supplies from being exhausted by the demands of the northern manufacturing towns. Even the councils and the democratic bodies are coming under the influence of local politics through the sheer necessity of saving their own comrades before they attempt to help those in the next province.

As a result of these disintegrating influences, the anarchical spirit has spread at an alarming rate among the masses. The food riots that have broken out in various northern towns in the last month were caused by starving workers who broke into shops and looted bazaars. In nearly every case the local councils and the democratic bodies have taken the most stringent measures to deal with disorder and to quieten the hungry people. In all the towns where famine is threatening I found the revolutionary militia, under the joint control of the councils and local municipal authorities, patrolling the bazaars to prevent pogroms and attacks upon the Jewish shops by the dark forces of the old regime.

Agrarian disorders are also increasing, but the impression I have gathered since my journey is that in those provinces where the revolutionary land organisations have drawn up plans for an equitable distribution of the landlords' land there has been complete quiet. On the other hand, where this has not been done, where the landlords and the local Cadets have succeeded in preventing this work, agrarian disorders have broken out. In some districts also I found that looting of landlords' granaries by mobs with pitchforks was due to the knowledge that stores of grain were being held and were escaping requisition. The anarchy which reigns in the provinces at the present moment is thus the direct result of three things:

1. The incapacity of the towns to supply the peasants with manufactures, leading the latter to hide their corn. This is due to the inability of the Government to control speculators and fix the prices of manufactures; and this in turn is due to the refusal

of the bourgeois elements in the Government to agree to State regulation of industry.

2. The suspicion in the minds of the peasantry that an intrigue is going on in Petrograd behind their backs to rob them of the land for which they made the Revolution.

3. The endless prolongation of the war for objects which – to state the plain fact – nobody understands or cares about, thus undermining confidence in the Government's foreign relations and creating the impression that a citizen had better get for himself what he can, while he can.

During the latter end of the summer the Russian Revolution appears to have reached its second stage, in which the class struggle became the most prominent feature on the political horizon. But now the situation is complicated by the split in the ranks of the democracy on the question of revolutionary tactics. As time goes on this split seems to become wider, and in the third stage of the Revolution the question of revolutionary tactics may temporarily obscure the class struggle. It appears that this stage is being entered upon now. The split in the revolutionary ranks is complete. The moderate Minimalists, who regard this as a bourgeois revolution, are now in alliance with the new democratic *intelligentsia* and co-operators. The Maximalist fanatics, who still dream of the social revolution throughout all Europe, have, according to my observations in the provinces, recently acquired an immense, if amorphous following. The majority of their followers, however, have no idea of what the Maximalist means when he talks of 'all power to the councils'. The soldier of the garrisons in the rear hears the Maximalist's promise of an immediate peace and of course at once goes with him. The peasant, furious with the delay in the land reform, hears promises of immediate seizure of the landlord's land and goes with him. The worker hears talk about State control over the banks and goes with him. Anarchists and secret agents of the Tsar's regime also flock to the Maximalist banner, and thus create a large and very dangerous element widely diffused through the proletariat masses in the country. All the recent provincial elections have given immense majorities to this wing of the revolutionary democracy. There is no sign of any military enthusiasm like that which inspired the French Revolutionaries. There is, on the other hand, a great possibility of a Napoleon – a peace dictator, born out of the three years' sufferings of the people – who will put an end to the war even at the cost of territorial losses to Russia and at the price of the political liberties won by the Revolution. The war and the desire to end it is the one thing which links the confused social mass together in this third stage of the Revolution, and as soon as there is peace it will break up into its component parts and create new combinations and coalitions for the political struggle in the fourth stage.

Memorandum on the State of Russia between August and November 1917 (Probably addressed to C. P. Trevelyan) Petrograd, 2 November 1917

During September the revolutionary democracy had everything their own way. They had shown such splendid union during the Kornilov days that no force could be set up in the country to openly oppose them. But speedily signs of disintegration began to set in. The wound caused by the prolongation of the war became deeper and deeper every week. The economic vitality of the country was slowly and surely ebbing away ... The Democratic Conference at the end of September was the first public event to disclose the real state of affairs in the ranks of the revolutionary democracy.

At its very outset the left wing of the revolutionary parties adopted the most extreme platform. Making use of the Kornilov disclosures to show the bourgeois class in their true light, they demanded their removal from the Government, a dictatorship of the revolutionary councils [soviets] and the immediate conclusion of the war. Another Left section of the Democratic Conference did not go quite so far. The Minimalist Internationalists, as they are called, wanted a government to be formed out of all the democratic elements in the country, that is from the revolutionary councils, the representatives of the Co-operative societies, the recently elected Zemstvos (County Councils), municipalities, and the professional alliances or trade unions. Unfortunately for the union of the revolutionary democracy the right wing of the Council [of the Republic] would not agree to this. They were still afraid of the democracy taking power into their hands, and they allowed themselves to be brow-beaten by the bourgeois class, the banks and the diplomacy of the Allies. The capitalists and the bankers were prepared to declare a strike if the democracy took over the Government. The industrialists would lock out in all the factories and mines, the banks would shut down and the Allies, on the pretext of insufficient security, would cease to send any more war materials and articles needed for the railways, to Russia. I was told on good authority that Kerensky spoke in this sense to the democratic leaders at a secret sitting of the Council. The leaders got frightened, and feeling that they had not sufficient intellectual force at their command to requisition at once all the industries of the country and break the capitalist sabotage, agreed to form a coalition government as before. Thus it may be observed that the struggle for power in Russia at the present time is not decided by numbers only. The democracy has the vast majority on its side but the small body of industrialists and bankers is, with foreign assistance, fighting a stubborn battle for its existence as a class.[36] It is a struggle which knows no quarter. All obstacles to power are to be removed with utter relentlessness. The goose must be cooked even if the house is to be burned in the process. It is the law of clenched fists and the fang and he who gets in first holds on, till life is extinct. That is the class war as we have it now in Russia.

But if the democracy was beaten on the question of power and had to consent to a compromise again, they nevertheless suceeded in gaining one very important point which undoubtedly marks a stage forward in the history of the Revolution – viz., the establishment of a temporary Parliament which is to sit until the Constituent Assembly is elected and before which the Provisional Government is morally responsible [the Pre-Parliament].

This Parliament is now getting to work. It consists of representatives from all the organised political and social groups in the country. The bourgeois class is represented by the Cadets, the Moscow Federation of Industrialists and Traders, the right wing of the Co-operative Societies, the Cossacks and the landowners. The left wing, which has the numerical majority, consists of the Left co-operators, the professional alliances and all the political parties that make up the revolutionary councils in the army and the rear. This Parliament has begun to put questions on State affairs to the Government and to demand answers. Hitherto the great defect of the Revolution has been that round the Provisional Government all sorts of influences, often sinister ones, used to work unseen and there was no legal organ which could demand explanations from the Government and could directly put pressure upon it. The famous Council of Workers' and Soldiers' Deputies [Petrograd Soviet], being only a revolutionary political party, had no legal existence and therefore had to exert its influence indirectly. Unfortunately ... from the very first day the ranks of the democratic wing became hopelessly split. The Maximalist extremists, who are still dreaming of setting alight the social revolution throughout all Europe, declared that they would not sit in a Parliament along with 'bourgeois sharks', [and] demanded that the sole governing authority should be transferred to the Council of Workers' and Soldiers' Deputies. On the refusal of the great majority of the Parliament to listen to such an extreme programme they quitted the sitting and have not appeared since ... The Maximalists have transferred all their activities to the Council of Workers' and Soldiers' Deputies. Sending broadcast their demagogic cries: 'All power to the councils [soviets]', 'an immediate declaration of peace' and 'demobilisation of the army' they have acquired an immense following among the lower strata of the masses ... In addition to this the nervous strain brought on by lack of food tends to make this extreme wing of the revolutionary mass subject to violent outbursts. There is great danger, especially in Petrograd, that the garrison and workers may come out at any moment on the streets, with arms in their hands, and attempt to put down the 'bourgeois Government' as they call it ...

Every week the economic state of the country becomes more and more catastrophic. The industries are simply dying out for lack of raw materials and skilled labour. The Don coal and iron basins have now so decreased their output that they cannot even supply sufficient fuel for the railways, and next week the railways are going to run only one passenger train a day on each line. Half the engines are broken down and cannot be repaired.

It should however be noted that the gradual decline of Russian industry began before the Revolution. Statistics show that outputs have steadily declined since the outbreak of the war. The Revolution only hastened the process, because most of the industries of Russia were founded upon the unsound basis of underpaid labour. When the Revolution came the exploited labourers had all restraint removed from them and began to demand human conditions of life. But this of course only meant that the economically ill-founded industries which had been sickening since the beginning of the war, now began to breathe their last. Under these conditions the peasants in the villages cannot be supplied with clothing against the winter and railways cannot be kept working. That means that the inhabitants of the northern provinces, who live on food imported from the south, cannot be fed. Famine is gripping large areas of the northern governments ... Here in Petrograd we live now on potatoes and nuts. When they are finished we shall have to live on air and comfort ourselves each day with the news that 100 yards more of trenches have been captured in France and that 10,000 more English and Germans have gone to their graves. It is not difficult under these circumstances to see that Russians, in these days, are not enamoured of this twentieth century philosophy from Western Europe ... I cannot help feeling that we are on the brink of one of the most appalling catastrophes than can possibly overcome mankind, viz., the complete collapse of the whole material framework of society ...

And let it be remembered that this cannot be put right, as the people in the West seem to think, by sending a few American engineers to manage the traffic on the Siberian railway or by sending a few cargoes of boots to Archangel. Let it be remembered that we are dealing here with 180 million people covering the greater part of two continents, in which the industrial system of Western Europe has only just begun to exist. Now three years of war has simply destroyed this tender plant and has reduced the country to the economic state of Europe in the Middle Ages. This indeed is a fact.

In my recent journey on the Volga and to the eastern territories of the Cossack and Tartar steppes, I found that each district is running its own local food and land policy without paying any attention to threats from Petrograd or entreaties from the neighbouring provinces ... Russia in fact is splitting up into a number of economic areas in which the inhabitants, seeing the calamity threatening them, cling together for common safety and cannot hear the cries for help from their neighbours in the next areas ... If the war continues much longer a calamity somewhat resembling what happened when the Black Death came to Europe, only on an infinitely greater scale, will take place. Russia, on account of her weaker economic structure, has been the first to snap and thus to disclose the abyss that yawns beneath ... From the picture which I have described above it is not difficult to see that the Russian masses no longer think of the war as something to be fought, and won or lost. The much more terrible war with famine lies before them. The army simply keeps at the front because it can't get away! There are two million deserters in the country and the Government, in order to relieve the commissariat, demobilised four years of reservists recently. What people are really interested in now is how to get something to eat and live through the winter. The anarchy reigning in the country may be ascribed to this simple fact.

And yet *The Times* and other organs of the English oligarchy accuse the revolutionary 'councils' of being responsible for the anarchy and hope for another Kornilov to put them out of existence. I can confidently assert after my recent journey in the interior of Russia in the last two months, that if it were not for the revolutionary councils in the towns, villages and among the soldiers of the garrisons, the anarchy would be fifty times worse ... And yet the English oligarchy, true to its traditions, accuses the Russian people and their revolutionary organisations of all the lowest acts and motives which they themselves are past masters in ... Of course it is plain that the ruling classes of England and their allies, the bourgeois here, must in order to save their class privileges discredit all movements like those which inspire the Russian Revolution. This of course is a perfectly natural phenomenon. Every day makes it more and more clear that the enemies of the Russian Revolution are to be found not only in the propertied classes within the country itself, but also and principally among the powerful financial groups and military oligarchies of Western and Central Europe for whom the Revolution is a deadly danger ... The revolutionary leaders are fully aware of this and, seeing the economic collapse which is threatening the country, they have in the last few weeks embarked upon a really serious peace campaign.

This time they mean business. At no time since the March days have I heard such plain speaking in revolutionary circles about the need for a strong foreign policy and for pressure on the Allies. The revolutionary leaders are at last beginning to realise that Russia is a force in the world still, a force not only moral but material. Even in her present inert condition she holds up over a million Austro-German troops in the East. The mere threat of relieving these to be thrown against the Western front is now recognised as a diplomatic card of no mean value. In all this they will certainly have the great mass of the Russian people with them ... they are all united in one burning desire – to bring the war to an end *at once* and to commence negotiations for an international settlement ... The alternative is that the extreme Maximalist section of the revolutionary democracy ... will attempt some mad scheme for overthrowing the Provisional Government, declaring an immediate peace at any price and establishing a 'Commune' in Petrograd and some of the more revolutionary urban centres ... The constructive side of the Revolution seems to have temporarily come to an end on account of the appalling chaos and economic collapse in the country. But the Revolution has cleared the ground for the new structure which will be built some day ... It will probably succeed in making peace. Whether it makes it constitutionally on the basis of a general international agreement, or chaotically by the communists, who will throw over the Western Allies and make a separate peace, remains to be seen. In the former case the Revolution will be saved; in the latter case it is bound to perish. But in either case there will be peace and the sooner the Western Allies wake up to this fact the better for them.

CHAPTER 6

The November Revolution

Price returned to Petrograd late in October to find yet another notionally democratic assembly in being: the Pre-Parliament. This was made up entirely of the nominees of the different parties, and although it had no constitutional power it was in its way genuinely representative. At least the parties tended to nominate their best men. The Social Democrats – both Bolsheviks and Mensheviks – and the Socialist Revolutionaries were represented in exactly equal numbers but again the Bolsheviks withdrew. The remaining third of the Pre-Parliament consisted of Cadets and members of the Right Wing and Nationalist Parties. The withdrawal of the Bolsheviks was interpreted by some observers as signalling that they were not interested in votes and were preparing, if need be, for barricades, although Lenin was still insisting that a Constituent Assembly must be convened.

On 28 October the Central Executive Committee of the Bolsheviks announced the formation of a Military Revolutionary Committee. Actually the Committee had originally been set up by the Petrograd Soviet as far back as August, to co-ordinate resistance to Kornilov. As reconstituted in October, it contained representatives of the Soviet and of the trade unions and factory committees of Petrograd. On 4 November the Petrograd garrison recognised the Soviet as the supreme political authority and the Military Revolutionary Committee as being in direct command. This was, in effect, the day on which the Provisional Government was overthrown, but Lenin was determined to wait until the Second All-Russia Congress of Workers' and Soldiers' Deputies had assembled in Petrograd, and it was not due to meet until 7 November. On 6 November the Provisional Government ordered the raising of the bridges across the Neva. Red Guards operating under the orders of the Military Revolutionary Committee lowered them again, and the situation was reversed several times on that day. There was no firing, but there was by now a general belief that a coup was either imminent or had already taken place. On 7 November the Second All-Russia Congress assembled in the Smolny Institute and the Military Revolutionary Committee closed down the Pre-Parliament.

Price was unable to send an account of any of these events to the Manchester Guardian *until 17 November because Petrograd was for a time telegraphically cut off from the rest of the world. His first dispatch about the November Revolution was not printed until 20 November and*

*was only 450 words long. By the time the wires were operating freely
again he had more recent events to describe than those of 7–8 November.
His detailed account of the November Revolution appeared only in
1921, in his book entitled* My Reminiscences of the Russian
Revolution.

Manchester Guardian, *20 November 1917*
'Bolshevik Ascendancy: Causes of Kerensky's Downfall'
Petrograd, 17 November 1917

The government of M. Kerensky fell before the Bolshevik insurgents
because it had no supporters in the country. The bourgeois parties
and the generals at the Staff disliked it because it would not
establish a military dictatorship. The revolutionary democracy lost
faith in it because after eight months it had neither given land to
the peasants nor established State control of industries nor advanced
the cause of the Russian peace programme. Instead it brought off
the July advance without any guarantee that the Allies had even
agreed to reconsider war aims.

Ever since the Democratic Conference after the Kornilov rebellion
the cleavage in the ranks of the revolutionary democracy had
widened. The right wing of the Socialists still insisted on a coalition
with the bourgeoisie, fearing that the democracy was unable to stand
alone. The Bolsheviks became bolder and demanded an immediate
break with the bourgeoisie and the beginning of a peace negotiations
programme.

The Bolsheviks acquired great support all over the country. In
my journey in the provinces in September and October I noticed
that every local soviet had been captured by them. The Executive
Committee of the All-Russia Council of Workmen's and Soldiers'
Deputies [Petrograd Soviet] elected last summer clearly did not
represent the feeling of the revolutionary masses in October. The
Bolsheviks therefore insisted on a re-election and the summoning
of a second All-Russia CWSD Congress, the right wing of the
Socialist parties opposing this. After the statement by Mr Bonar
Law that the Paris Conference was only for military purposes they
seem to have decided on armed rebellion.[37]

Though supported by the masses the Bolsheviks now find
themselves isolated from the right wing of the Socialists, who
represent the small bourgeois and intellectuals and control the
Government machinery. The latter are indignant at the Bolshevik
tactics of armed rebellion and terrorism over the bourgeoisie, the
closing of bourgeois newspapers and the wholesale arrests.

The All-Russia Railway Union and the party of Socialist
Internationalists, led by Gorky's paper, the *Novaya Zhizn*, are

making desperate efforts to bring about a reconciliation. Both sides agree on the principle of a coalition Socialist government, a speeding up of reforms and a full land programme, but they cannot come to terms on the details of the composition of the Government. Meanwhile the food shortage becomes more acute.

From M. Philips Price, My Reminiscences of the Russian Revolution, Chapters 9 and 10. [Written in Berlin, published in London, 1921]

At a secret sitting of the Bolshevik Party's Central Committee in the middle of October it was decided to advise the Petrograd workmen, the garrison of the city and the Kronstadt sailors to arrest the government of Kerensky and to declare the coming Second Soviet Congress the supreme authority in the Republic. The die was cast. In the last days of October we heard that a 'Military Revolutionary Committee' had mysteriously appeared in Petrograd and had declared itself 'independent of Kerensky's government'.

On 4 November I was present at the sitting of the Pre-Parliament in the Mariinsky Palace. The Cadets had been attacking the Menshevik Internationalists and the *Novaya Zhizn* group, which ran Maxim Gorky's paper of that name, and were accusing them of Zimmerwald propaganda among the troops. The Cadet Adjemov read out long extracts from the Zimmerwald resolutions, which set forth the tactics for internationalist propaganda in the army. The left wing of the Mensheviks, led by Martov, and the *Novaya Zhizn* group, led by Sukhanov, cheered each clause of the Zimmerwald resolutions and were answered by shouts from the Cadets: 'See what traitors are sitting here!' Presently Kerensky arrived looking very serious, and asked leave to speak. He had news, he said, that a body called the 'Military Revolutionary Committee' had been formed for the purpose of deposing the Government. That Committee was composed of notorious Bolsheviks, who were engaged in traitorous propaganda. The time had come to act. Whereupon loud cheers came from the Cadets and cries: 'So you are beginnng to see that at last!' Warrants were out for the arrest of the Committee, and meanwhile the official organ of the Bolshevik Party, the *Rabochi Put*, was suspended. Then, as if to show that he was still the impartial Kerensky, defending the country and the Revolution from attacks both from the Right and from the Left, he declared that he had ordered *Nashi Rodina*, an organ that was carrying on Monarchist propaganda, to be also suspended. This was Kerensky's last speech in public before his fall. He remained true to himself to the end, spending his time honestly trying to reconcile two irreconcilables, and being finally abandoned by both.

In the lobbies I met a prominent member of the Socialist Revolutionary Party, who told me they had information that the Bolshevik *coup d'etat* was only a matter of days. At the Post and Telegraph Office already Bolshevik Commissioners were appointed, while the sentries were letting all who gave Bolshevik passwords go by, and were scowling on officials of Kerensky's government. A little further on I saw Martov and Sukhanov with grave faces engaged in the most earnest conversation. 'We cannot accept responsibility for such action,' I heard Martov say with a gesture. Evidently the Zimmerwald resolutions which he just applauded half an hour before gave no justification in his mind for a military *coup d'etat*. This was typical of the attitude of the Mensheviks, who were revolutionary only in words. It was then evening, and I repaired to the Smolny Institute, where the Central Executive of the old Menshevik and Socialist Revolutionary Soviet [Petrograd Soviet] had their offices. I found members of the Executive very depressed. Reports from the provinces showed that the Bolshevik agitation for an immediate summoning of a Second Soviet Congress had met with great response. The soviets of the northern provinces and the soldiers' soviets of the north-west front had already elected their delegates, who were arriving. They had done, said the Menshevik Central Executive, everything to prevent the summoning of this Second Soviet Congress because they considered it useless. The National [Constituent] Assembly elections were shortly to take place, and this 'democratic' body, not the Soviet Congress, should have the decisive word. The soviets, they said, from this time forth should withdraw from the front rank and continue only as industrial committees to advise the National [Constituent] Assembly. As I passed out of the Smolny Institute I heard roars of applause issuing from the great hall. The Petrograd Soviet was sitting and Trotsky was making a rousing speech. Delegates for the Second Soviet Congress were arriving. All was bustle and hurry and a look of confidence was on everyone's face.

On the following morning, 7 November, I went again to the Smolny Institute, where the Petrograd Soviet was having a sitting to elect its delegates to the Second Soviet Congress, which was to meet that afternoon. Trotsky was in the chair and on the tribune stood the same short, bald-headed little man that I had seen six months before leading the tiny Bolshevik group in the First Soviet Congress. It was Lenin without his moustache, which he had shaved off in order to change his appearance during his period of forced concealment [after the July Days], now drawing to a close. The Petrograd Soviet was now one solid phalanx of Bolshevik Deputies, and roar after roar of applause swept the hall, as Lenin spoke of the coming Soviet Congress as the only organ which could carry through the Russian workers', soldiers' and peasants' revolutionary programme. Then someone at my side whispered that news had just come that the Military Revolutionary Committee, with the aid of Red Guards from the factories and part of the garrison, had occupied the Winter Palace and arrested all the Ministers with the exception of Kerensky, who had escaped in a motor car. I repaired to the Bolshevik Party bureau on the lower floor. Here I found a sort of improvised revolutionary intelligence department, from which delegates were being dispatched to all parts of the city with instructions, and whither they were returning with news and reports. Upstairs, in the bureau of the old Menshevik and Socialist Revolutionary Executive, the silence of the grave reigned. A few girl typists were sorting papers, and the editor of the *Izvestia*, Rozanov, was still trying to keep a steady countenance.

At three o'clock in the afternoon the great hall was full of delegates from all parts of the country, waiting for the opening of the Second Soviet Congress. The Bolshevik benches were crowded and held fully 50 per cent of the Congress. A good second to them were the Left Socialist Revolutionaries, the coming peasants' party, which, though unrepresented in the lists for the National [Constituent] Assembly through technical hindrances, had by this time captured the bulk of the peasant Soviets of North Russia. Upon the platform mounted the members of the old Executive ... The Menshevik Dan was in the chair.

'We have met,' he began gravely, 'under the most peculiar circumstances. On the eve of the elections for the National Assembly the Government has been arrested by one of the parties in this Congress. As spokesman of the old Executive I declare this action to be unwarrantable. The Executive has done its duty by preparing in the last six months the ground for the democratic Assembly. It now lays down its office and leaves the election of the new Presidium to the Second Soviet Congress.' The delegates thereupon voted, and the Bolshevik Sverdlov became chairman. A member of the Socialist Revolutionary Party now rose on a point of order. 'We live in strange times,' he began. 'Three of our party comrades, members of the Government, are at this very moment besieged in the Winter Palace where they are being bombarded by gunboats manned by supporters of the majority of this Congress. We demand their immediate release!' he roared, thumping his fist upon the table, while derisive shouts arose from the body of the hall. When he had finished up rose Trotsky, cool and ever ready with an answer. 'That sort of speech comes badly from a member of the Socialist Revolutionary Party,' he began, 'for that party has shared joint responsibility for a government which has, during the last four months, kept under arrest a number of *our* party comrades, and has put to watch over the rest of us the members of the old Tsarist secret police!' General sensation and tumult throughout the hall!

Meanwhile the Menshevik and Socialist Revolutionary delegates left the Congress in a body, accompanied by groans and hisses. When they had gone it was possible to see by the empty places that they represented about 20 per cent of the whole Congress. Such, indeed, had been the revolution in opinion since the First Congress.

Upon the platform now rose Lenin. His voice was weak, apparently with excitement, and he spoke with slight indecision. It seemed as if he felt that the issue was still doubtful, and that it was difficult to put forward a programme right here and now. A Council of Peoples' Commissars was being set up, he said, and the list would be submitted to the Congress. The Council would propose to the Congress three resolutions, upon the basis of which three decrees would be issued. The first was that steps should be taken to conclude an immediate armistice on the front, as a preliminary to peace negotiations. The invitation was to go out to the Allies and to the Central Powers, and the answers of each were to be awaited. The second decree would secure for the Land Committees of the peasant communes the right of temporary possession of the landlords' estates, pending the introduction of detailed legislation. The third decree would give the factory workers power of control over all operations of the employers and managers. 'We appeal to our comrades in England, France and Germany to follow our example and make peace with their fellow-workers over the heads of their capitalist governments,' concluded Lenin. 'We believe that our words will be heard by the descendants of the Paris Communards, and that the British people will not forget their inheritance from the Chartists.'

Looking from the platform to the seated delegates, one could not help being struck with the fact that this was a young man's Congress. Whole rows of benches were filled with sturdy, healthy young men from the Baltic Fleet and from the front. The skilled artisans of Moscow and Petrograd, dressed in their collarless black shirts and with fur caps on their heads, were also well to the fore. The peasant delegates were mostly young soldiers who had gone to their villages and had taken the lead in the local communes. There were also a number of intellectual faces, mostly of young men who had during the autumn helped to form the new Left Socialist Revolutionary Party in the villages. Conspicuous by their absence were the middled-aged intellectuals, the old type of peasant with a long beard, and the old Socialist Party leader who had known thirty years of struggle and many prison sentences. Another point of interest was that this Congress showed a preponderance of delegates from the northern and central provinces, the very districts, in fact, where the largest number of poor, half-proletarian peasants were found, where the skilled artisans dominated the towns and the land-hungry soldier deserters dominated the villages. There were relatively fewer delegates from the Ukraine, because the Ukrainian peasants and soldiers were at this time gathering round their National *Rada*, or Council, at Kiev. This Second All-Russia Soviet Congress, therefore, marked the revolt of the workmen and poor peasants of North and Central Russia, with the passive consent of the more prosperous regions of the country, whose populations had not yet felt the pangs of hunger but were simply war-weary.

About ten o'clock at night I passed out of the Smolny Institute. In the street outside a group of workmen and Baltic Fleet sailors were discussing the Congress over a log fire. 'We shall have to get off to the provinces now to work, explain and organise; not one of these delegates should be sitting there a moment longer than necessary,' I overheard one of them say. I passed along the banks of the Neva, already beginning to freeze in the shallows against the wharves ... Opposite the Vassily Ostrov lay the cruiser *Aurora* and a destroyer with guns trained on the Winter Palace. 'Stop,' shouted a voice, and I recognised a cordon of Red Guards across the road. I was near the Winter Palace, which was now the seat of the Military Revolutionary Committee. 'Where are the Ministers of Kerensky?' I asked one of the guards. 'Safe across the river in Petropavlovsk Fortress,' came the laconic answer. 'You can't pass along here,' said another. But before I turned away I looked at a shell hole in the walls of the Palace. It was the mark of the only shot which had been fired by the cruiser, as a sign that the Winter Palace must be evacuated for the new rulers ...

By 9th November it was clear that power in Petrograd was actually in the hands of the Military Revolutionary Committee. This all seemed to me at the time very ridiculous, and I wanted to laugh at what had happened in the previous three days. I was unaccustomed to the atmosphere of Revolution. I tried to imagine a committee of common soldiers and workmen setting themselves up in London and declaring that they were the Government, and that no order from Whitehall was to be obeyed unless it was countersigned by them. I tried to imagine the British Cabinet entering into negotiations with the Committee for the settlement of the dispute, while Buckingham Palace was surrounded by troops and the Sovereign escaped from a side entrance disguised as a washerwoman. And yet something of this sort in Russian surroundings had actually happened. It was almost impossible to realise that the century-old Russian Empire was actually dissolving before one's eyes with such extraordinary lack of dignity.

I went down the Nevsky Prospect on the morning of the 9th. The middle-class press was being sold in the streets as if nothing had happened. At the Chief Telegraph Office I met a man who was connected with banking circles. He was so stunned that he was finding relief by persuading himself that, although the Bolsheviks had temporarily succeeded, they could not possibly hold power for more than a few days. In the Petrograd Telegraph Agency, however, I found a more confident atmosphere. All the old officials were at work as if nothing had happened. I was shown telegrams received from what purported to be soldiers' committees at the front. They promised every assistance in the task of expelling the 'traitors and usurpers'. Couriers were running backwards and forwards to the offices of the Cadet newspapers; leaflets and special anti-Bolshevik bulletins were being printed and distributed broadcast. It was clear that a part at least of the bureaucracy, with the *intelligentsia* at its head, were already mobilising against those who had taken power ... In Sadovaya Street I met an acquaintance who was working with Maxim Gorky on his newspaper, the *Novaya Zhizn*. 'The Bolsheviks have made a great mistake in seizing power by these methods,' he said; 'they cannot possibly hold it unless the moderate democratic parties come to their aid.' This view of a Russian progressive intellectual was very similar to those of outside observers at this time ...

On the following day, however (November 10th), there was a different feeling in the air. It seemed as if there was, for the first time for many months, a political force in the country that knew what it wanted. This was clearly reflected in the common talk in the streets. Outside the Circus Modern a large crowd had assembled for a meeting at which delegates from the Soviet Congress were going to speak ... No word was said about the violent methods by which the Bolsheviks had come into power. The deeds which shocked the tender feelings of the intellectual did not trouble the realist politician of the street. Would they be able to bring food to the towns and make an end to the war? That was the question which was being asked. The Tsar's government could not do it, nor could Kerensky's. 'Give these people a chance' were the words I heard coming from all sides ...

On the following day (10th) [sic][38] I walked over to the Vassily Ostrov and visited the quays where the steamers came in from Kronstadt. At intervals along the embankment little patrols of Red Guards and workmen from the factories, led by sailors with red bands round their arms, were standing round log fires. The sailors of Kronstadt and the Red Guards had made the Baltic Fleet the fortress of the Revolution. They had now come out as the strong arm of the new Government ... For a long time I watched the groups of Red Guards and sailors being interviewed by those who until yesterday, thanks to the propaganda of the bourgeois press, used to look upon the Bolsheviks as monsters, but who now seemed surprised to find that they were, after all, human beings.

Towards evening I went to the Smolny Institute. The Second All-Russia Soviet Congress was just at an end, and the delegates were departing to all parts of Russia. They were being loaded up with large packets of pamphlets, proclamations and appeals, which they were going to distribute in far-off regions, so that the Tartars on the steppes and the fur-hunters in Siberia should have news of the great adventure in Petrograd – the attempt to create the first workmen's government in the world. Upstairs in the office of the official Soviet organ *Izvestia* I found the Bolsheviks already in possession ... Axelrode was trying to put some sort of order into a pile of papers. Someone else was picking with a bradawl at the lock of a drawer from which the keys had evidently been removed by the Mensheviks before they left. Along one side of the room Lenin was walking up and down, sunk in deep thought. I looked on this scene of untidy bustle and wondered: could it last? Was this really the intellectual nucleus of a new ruling power in the world or was it only an amusing incident – a 'fuss in the mud' so to say?...

I left the Smolny about eight o'clock and walked past the Taurida Palace to Sadovaya Street. Here I met the same friend from the *Novaya Zhizn* whom I had met the previous day. 'There are two political bodies in this city and both are pretending to be the supreme authority,' he said. He advised me to go to the *gorodskaya uprava* (municipal council building). It was getting on for ten o'clock but I went. Inside the municipal buildings I found the Menshevik and Socialist Revolutionary delegates of the defunct [Petrograd] Soviet. Apparently, however, they did not in the least degree regard themselves as defunct. The City Council, elected on the geographical franchise some six months before, had agreed to join hands with these Mensheviks and Socialist Revolutionaries of the old Soviet. A joint Committee had been formed – the 'Committee for the Defence of the Country and of Freedom'. 'We have every reason to believe that we shall have the Bolsheviks out of the Smolny in a couple of days,' said a prominent member of this Committee to me. I had formerly known him as a leader-writer on the Socialist Revolutionary Party organ. 'We have got the support of the foreign embassies, who have decided to recognise us as the only authority in Petrograd,' he added. It was clear that the Bolshevik Soviet at the Smolny was now up against the first serious organised resistance. A trial of strength was about to begin in Petrograd between the industrial councils of the organised workers and the institutions elected on the basis of the geographical area ... Both sides were using institutions created by the Revolution to remain in power ...

Round the 'Committee for the Defence of the Country and of Freedom' the upper-middle-class elements of the city were flocking ... Much printed matter was being sent out. I saw one deputation from the Cossacks at the front. Some sort of military action was clearly being planned. The air was full of rumours. Towards midnight I returned to my room. Early next morning (the 11th) I was awakened by the sound of rifle firing. I dressed and went out on to the embankment of the Fontanka Canal ... The dull sound of bullets embedding themselves in the stucco of the building outside which I was standing showed me that it was healthier under cover than in the open. From the safety of the door-keeper's lodge I then surveyed the scene of battle ... In the big red building on the other side of the canal, the Military Academy, a force of Cadets and students had fortified themselves. Machine-gun fire was spurting out of several of the windows, answered by another machine-gun and sporadic rifle fire from Sadovaya Street, and some of the bullets were striking the house where I lived. The besiegers were apparently not strong and presently their firing ceased altogether. In the pause I emerged from my cover and with gingerly steps crept down the side of the Fontanka Canal towards a bridge, which I crossed. When I was opposite the Circus Modern a violent fusillade broke out again from the windows of the Military Academy. I got into a side entrance of a house with a number of other people and waited. Everyone was silent and depressed and trying to hide his inner feelings beneath an outward calm ... During an interval of quiet I crept out. Soldiers with red cockades on their hats and Kronstadt sailors had brought up a field gun. Detachments of Red Guards were arriving. A motor car from the Smolny came along. Someone in a leather overcoat, apparently from the Military Revolutionary Committee, called to one of the soldiers:

'What detachment is this?'

'We are from the Putilov works,' said a young man in civilian clothes with a rifle on his shoulder and a red band on his arm.

'Who is your officer?' asked the Commissar.

'There is none; we are all officers,' said the Red Guard. 'Smolny summoned us by telephone from the works at eight o'clock this morning; we found no one here to give us any orders so we took up these positions.'

Boom! went the field gun and a couple of seconds later a three-inch shell crashed into the red walls of the Military Academy ... Already a dozen Red Guards were lying groaning on the ground at the entrance to the Circus. There was no first aid, although the Smolny had been urgently telephoned. But the Red Cross was working for the 'Committee for the Defence of the Country and of Freedom' ... Soldiers belonging to a regiment supposed to be sympathetic to the Smolny were said to be wavering ... About three o'clock I saw a large detachment of sailors march up from the direction of the Neva. Their arrival was the signal for much bustling, cursing and even kicking. The wavering soldiers on the Mars Field were told to prepare for attack or clear off home if they did not want to face a revolutionary tribunal. Two more field guns were brought up. I was summarily expelled from the point of vantage and safety I had secured under the wall of a small public garden by the canal. There was nothing for me to do but to bolt back to my rooms on the other side of the Fontanka. As I got to the bridge – boom! went the sailors' field gun and a terrific clatter of machine-gun fire came from the Academy. After dodging the bullets by hiding in areas and side entrances when the fusillades commenced, I reached my rooms at last. Shortly after this all was quiet. The sailors had done their work. The Cadets capitulated and were marched off to the Fortress of Peter and Paul, but not before a number of them were selected from the rest and done to death with the butt-end of rifles. Thus ended the ill-starred Cadet rising of 11th November ... The big bourgeoisie and those with the money bags resorted now to the provinces and sought to mobilise the countryside, the 'loyal elements of the front' and the Cossacks against the 'Red bandits' of the capital.

Already on the following day (12th November) it was evident that this new danger was threatening the Smolny Soviet. The Bolshevik *Izvestia* came out with big headlines: 'The counter-revolutionary bourgeoisie is raising its head. The revolutionary proletariat must know how to answer' ... Kerensky, at the head of Cossacks and troops said to be loyal to him, was marching on Petrograd. The force was rumoured to number 20,000 and had already reached Tsarskoye Selo. It was clear that this was the outside force with which the 'Committee for the Defence of the Country and of Freedom' had been in touch from the first. The Cadet rebellion was planned to break out at the moment when Kerensky was nearing Petrograd. It broke out, however, too soon. Nevertheless the Committee had hopes that Kerensky alone could take Petrograd. An enthusiastic member of the Cadet Party, whom I met in the morning, assured me quite positively that Kerensky would be in the city by evening ... The streets on the Vassily Ostrov and on the south side of the Neva were full of armed detachments of Red Guards from the factories, marching in the direction of the Tsarskoye Selo railway station. On passing through the Nevsky Prospect and Sadovaya Street the well-dressed middle-class passers-by would spit and curse under their breath. They were clearly expecting that, in spite of the failure of the Cadet rising on the previous day, this new invasion of Cossacks from the front would bring them deliverance. But the streams of Red Guards pouring out of the factories to the new front completely knocked them off their balance. 'If only the Germans would come and exterminate these vermin!' I heard one of them say ...

It was already clear to me that the Bolshevik Military Revolutionary Committee was not in control of an army in the ordinary sense of the word. The Red Guard detachments were very largely independent of one another, electing their own commanders and removing them whenever the rank and file saw fit ... Hunger and hatred of wage slavery alone bound them together with a band of iron. There was no disciplined Red Army. On the following day (13th November) Smolny announced triumphantly that Kerensky had retreated in disorder from Pulkovo. The Red Guard commanders had evidently persuaded their men to go to their appointed places to defend the Revolution. The leaflet offensive had clearly had an effect upon the Cossacks who, according to communications, were now fraternising with the Red Guards and asking for transport to enable them to get home to the 'quiet Don'. Kerensky was a fugitive, Krasnov a prisoner, to be set free on parole, for the workers were good-hearted, even to the hirelings of their class enemies ...

But what was happening outside Petrograd over the length and breadth of the vast Russian plain? During the next three days news began to trickle through to me. On the evening of the 15th I met an army doctor who had just come up from the south-west front. He had passed Moscow on the night of the 14th by the loop line round the city. Heavy artillery firing could be heard and gun flashes seen in the direction of the Kremlin. The Cadet and Officers' Corps, under the direction of the Right Socialist Revolutionaries, had entrenched themselves in the Kremlin with plenty of ammunition and supplies. The Moscow Soviet, which had for some weeks now a Left majority, sent an ultimatum demanding the disarming of the Cadets. This was refused. The Soviet therefore directed military operations from the old Government House on the Skobolev Square against the Kremlin. As in Petrograd, only a part of the garrison were ready to sustain a heavy sacrifice in defence of the Revolution. The rest wavered and wanted to go home to their villages. But there were no sailors' detachments as in Petrograd to stiffen the revolutionary ranks. The bulk of the work fell on rather inexperienced factory workmen and on the irregular partisan bands hastily organised by the new Left Socialist Revolutionary Party and the Anarchists. The lack of co-ordination of effort was even more felt here than in Petrograd, and it was not till 16th November that we heard that the Cadets and Officer Corps had capitulated to the Moscow Soviet and that the red flag waved on the Bell Tower of Ivan.

In most of the towns of Central Russia the local Workers' and Soldiers' Soviets waited till they received the news that Petrograd was definitely in the hands of the Military Revolutionary Committee before they removed Kerensky's agents and assumed authority openly. In some places, however, the local soviets anticipated Petrograd. This was particularly the case in Kazan and in the Central Asia cities, where the garrison and Red Guards were already in power on 5th November. From all the reports that I received, it was clear that the action of the revolutionaries in Petrograd was only a reflection of what was going on in the rest of Russia in different forms and in different conditions. The Military Revolutionary Committee in Petrograd had not in any way made the November Revolution. The Revolution had arisen out of the need for some sort of order and discipline in the country, which was threatening to dissolve in chaos and anarchy.

CHAPTER 7

November 1917–February 1918

The events of the period between the Bolshevik Revolution in November and the conclusion of peace with Germany in February 1918 cannot be adequately described in chronological order. During this period Price appears frequently to contradict himself. He admired – as did many much more hostile observers than he – the decisiveness of the Bolsheviks. He had himself been preaching the necessity to end the war as soon as possible ever since it began. He appears to have understood Lenin's 'defeatist' theory of war and civil war as necessary prerequisites to world revolution without interpreting it as planned aggression. But on matters of party and domestic policy he was extremely critical of the Bolsheviks. The following attempt to provide a context for some of what Price was then writing will concentrate first on the peace negotiations, then on the fate of the Constituent Assembly, and finally on the origins of the civil war.

Within hours of taking power, the Bolsheviks appealed to all nations and all governments to stop the war. On 21 November Trotsky, as Commissar for Foreign Affairs, sent a note to all the Allied ambassadors in Petrograd officially proposing the immediate opening of negotiations for a general peace. Correctly anticipating that they would not reply, on 23 November he began to try to put pressure on them by publishing the texts of the secret treaties and informal diplomatic understandings made between the Allies for the future carve-up of the territories of the Central Powers (Austria and Germany) and the Ottoman Empire. (Price was given a chance to see and translate these before anyone else, and the Manchester Guardian, *which published the texts in eight instalments between 7 November and 8 February 1918, was credited with a great scoop.)*

On 25 November Russian plenipotentiaries crossed the German lines and a ceasefire was arranged to begin in three days' time, to be followed on 20 December by discussions at Brest-Litovsk for a formal armistice. At this stage Trotsky was still trying to involve the Allies in negotiations for a general peace; he was not contemplating a separate peace. By the time negotiations began, however, it was clear that only Russia and Germany were going to be involved. The Russian peace proposals included the main points of the original formula of the Petrograd Soviet: no annexations, no indemnities, and the right of small nations to self-determination. But with regard to the last point the Germans refused to withdraw from the provinces of the former Russian Empire which they now occupied as the result of the war, insisting that the peoples of those provinces had already opted to belong to Germany. Trotsky broke off the talks and, when they were resumed on 8 January, led the Russian delegation himself. But he was unable to get the Germans even to admit that their occupation of the western provinces amounted to annexation. The Germans had their eye on the food and other resources of the Ukraine and they were in a hurry to get at them. The regional government of the Ukraine, the Rada, had sent its own representatives to the resumed peace talks and was clearly proposing to sign a separate peace (which it did on 9 February). On 18 January the Germans repeated their original terms which Trotsky took back to Petrograd. Lenin himself was prepared to acquiesce in them, arguing that Russia needed a breathing space. But he reluctantly agreed 'for the sake of a good peace with Trotsky' to let him try out first his own original peace formula on the Germans. Russia would not continue to fight but would not sign the German peace: 'No War, No Peace'. On recovering from their astonishment the Germans announced on 16 February that they would renew hostilities in two days' time. Trotsky, having had his chance, now agreed that there was nothing for it but to capitulate and a telegram to that effect was sent. However the Germans not only continued to advance towards Petrograd, but announced new and even harsher terms. On 24 February, at a meeting of the Central Executive Committee of the All-Russia Soviet (which Price attended) the terms were accepted.

By this time the short life of the Constituent Assembly was already over. The proposal that there should be such an assembly, elected by universal suffrage, had been perhaps the one thing upon which all the parties, ever since the formation of the Provisional Government, had been agreed. It was to underwrite all the reforms promised – if not enacted – since March 1917 and it was to be the one authority which could ratify a peace settlement. Electoral lists had been drawn up in the early autumn of 1917 and genuinely free elections were held in the last days of November.

But by now the results of those elections patently did not reflect the state of the parties in public estimation. The Socialist Revolutionaries, numerically the strongest party when the lists were drawn up, had since then split into two completely incompatible wings, Left SRs and Right SRs, which when combined, despite their opposition to each other, held 58 per cent of the seats in the Assembly while the Bolsheviks only had 25 per cent. The Bolsheviks formed an alliance with the Left SRs but they also began to back away from the idea that a Constituent Assembly, based on what they now considered obsolete democratic principles, could any longer be an appropriate body for the running of the country; in future the nucleus of the State would be the soviet. To show their resolve, they dissolved the recently-elected Petrograd Municipal Council and ordered elections for a new Council to be held, run on soviet lines. Moreover they began to arrest all the Cadets elected to the Assembly as soon as these arrived in Petrograd, arguing that they would use the Assembly to incite civil war. The Assembly was allowed to meet on 18 January on condition that it recognised the superior authority of the All-Russia Soviet. Harassed by Red Guards and sailors, and after a day of chaos, the Assembly was dissolved on the same night as it had begun on the grounds that the parliamentary phase of the Revolution was over. The dissolution was confirmed, in order to make the point, at the first meeting of the Third All-Russia Congress of Soviets on 23 January, when the Workers' and Soldiers' Deputies were joined by the Left SR members of the recently-held All-Russia Congress of Peasants.

The third development to take place during the winter of 1917–18 was the unfolding of civil war. Immediately after the November Revolution General Kaledin and General Dutov, respectively the Atamans of the Don and the Orenburg Cossacks, proclaimed their opposition to it. They were joined in due course by a number of Tsarist generals, notably Alexeiv, Kornilov and Denikin. The Cossacks and the Tsarist generals had little in common. The former were chiefly concerned to keep the soviet system out of their areas. The generals, around whom armies of counter-revolutionary volunteers ['White Russians'] began to assemble, wanted to restore an all-Russia government more or less on the lines of the Provisional Government. They also wanted – and got – the recognition of the Western Allies. In November 1917 the British government decided to support 'any responsible body in Russia' which would 'actively' oppose the Bolsheviks.[39] Just after Christmas 1917 the British and French, in what came to be known as the Accord Français-Anglais *agreed on a division of responsibility to achieve this end. France would provide finance and advisers for the 'oppositional forces' in the Ukraine; Britain would do the same for all the others.*

Letter to Anna Maria Philips
Petrograd, 30 November 1917

The miserable government of Kerensky fell like a pack of cards. We had a few days of suspense when Kerensky moved some Cossacks up towards Petrograd but the latter refused to fight against their brother workers and soldiers and the 'siege of Petrograd' soon turned into farce. Then literally began a reign of terror. The [Military] Revolutionary Committee began wholesale arrests of the bourgeoisie and of those connected with the late Government. The Fortress of Peter and Paul was filled with bourgeois officials and Ministers. The Conservative and Liberal middle-class press was closed down, armed Revolutionary Guards searched dwellings. We are all compelled to provide one warm shirt and jacket for the revolutionary troops as a requisition without payment! We have got the dictatorship of the proletariat with a vengeance this time! But I rub my hands and chuckle with glee. May the day soon come when the proletariat of Western Europe does the same.

During all this Revolution I was kept very busy. I don't know if any of my cables get through to England but I have sent a lot to the *Manchester Guardian* in the last ten days. I cabled some of the secret treaties which the Revolutionary Government unearthed when they seized the Foreign Office. They are exceedingly interesting and they only prove all that we have been saying for years. If only Charles could see them, but I don't expect they will get through the censor. Oh! There is such a lot that I want to write and communicate to you but I can't!!

I was up last night till two o'clock in the morning at the Executive Committee of the United Council of Workers' and Soldiers' and Peasants' Deputies' [Central Executive Committee] (I have a press ticket) and heard the communication read direct from the front giving the reply of the German Commander-in-Chief to the Russian Revolutionary Government's offer of an armistice and peace negotiation. The armistice commences at five o'clock on Sunday. Peace is now, I think, assured as far as Russia is concerned, for once there is an armistice, the Russian soldier will never fight again ...

By the way, the Commander-in-Chief of the twelve-million Russian Revolutionary Army is a young lieutenant – Krilenko, a nice young chap. I saw him for the first time yesterday. The elections for the Constituent Assembly have just taken place here. The polling was very high. Every man and woman votes all over this vast territory, even the Lapp in Siberia and the Tartar of Central Asia. Russia is now the greatest and most democratic country in the world. There are several women candidates for the Constituent Assembly and some are said to have a good chance of election. The one thing that troubles us all and hangs like a cloud over our heads is the fear of famine.

It is very cold here now. The snow has fallen and the Neva is fast freezing up. The day dawns at ten and evening comes at five o'clock. Most of the day there is that weird glare – it is not daylight at all – the northern daylight clouded in the mists of the Gulf of Finland. Dostoevsky truly said that Petrograd is the most fantastic city on earth. Perhaps that accounts for its revolutionary spirit, for truly the proletariat of Petrograd are in the front rank of the revolutionaries of the world.

Letter to C. Lee Williams
Petrograd, 30 November 1917

... We are living under the iron heel of the proletariat. The navy is magnificently revolutionary and so is the army at the front. The workmen in the factories also are armed to the teeth. It is a splendid thing to be able to use the armed forces of the country against the landlords and the capitalists. That is what armaments are for!

I have now got the correspondence for three newspapers: the *Manchester Guardian*, the Labour *Herald* and an American paper, the *New York Herald Tribune*. It keeps me pretty well occupied. Evidently my work here is known about in the journalistic world, because I am continually getting letters and cables from editors in England and America, whom I have never known nor met, asking me for an article or for information about this or that subject. I am beginning to demand a price for my information now!! ... We suffered most awfully from hunger about a fortnight ago and I was quite weak and thin. We only got one quarter of a pound of bread in two days and half a pound of potatoes!! But it is better now. They have got some food up from the south and we can carry along

Well, goodbye Tuffet.[40] Don't worry about me and please don't get too downhearted. I am beginning to see the light that will lead us out of all this darkness.

Common Sense, *1 December 1917*
From a Memorandum to F. W. Hirst

['A correspondent, distressed by the distortion of events in Russia which he finds prevalent in the London daily press, writes:']

When will people realise that the misery in Russia is not a result of the recent *coup d'etat* but the cause of it? Chaos and hunger were rampant months even before the March Revolution. When will our press realise that the Bolsheviks are not necessarily blackguards nor Trotsky and Lenin scoundrels (however much certain people on this side may consider their methods unfortunate) and that they really have at heart what they consider is the welfare of the Russian proletariat, who after all do constitute the vast majority of the inhabitants? *Reynolds' Newspaper* today states that 'Lenin, whose real name is Zederblum, was never heard of until the Revolution of March last'. This statement has also occurred in all sorts of newspapers during the past few months. The statement is untrue in both respects, as every Russian Socialist knows, whatever his shade of opinion, and as many British and Continental Socialists know. Ulianov Lenin gave up all his prospects as a member of the Russian aristocracy to devote his life to the cause of the emancipation of the common people. In this he was and is following, although perhaps with more success and by different methods, in the footsteps of Bakunin and Tolstoy, and others less fortunate whose bones lie bleaching in Siberian wastes. He has been known for years in the Russian Socialist world as a stern fighter in the cause of Russian freedom. If we cannot agree with him, do let us at least be fair to him, even though he had to adopt the name Lenin in order to avoid the unpleasant attentions of the Russian Okhrana.

Manchester Guardian, 5 December 1917
'The Russian Class Struggle: Bolshevik Syndicalism Leading'
Petrograd, 1 December 1917

During the last twenty-four hours the extreme section of the Bolsheviks seem again to have gained the upper hand. The Petrograd Municipal Council has been dissolved by order of the Revolutionary Government and new elections ordered. It is difficult to understand the motives for this, except that the Bolsheviks desire to find a pretext to terrorise all opposition in the coming Constituent Assembly.

An article in today's *Pravda* – the organ of the Bolsheviks – contains the following significant passage:

> We are confronted with the question of the relations of the Workers', Soldiers' and Peasants' Councils to the Constituent Assembly, and we consider the councils more truly express the will of the proletariat than any other assembly, for if the councils lose the confidence of the electors they are at once re-elected. The councils must stand on guard over the interests of the proletariat and propose to the Constituent Assembly the permanent constitution of the Russian Republic based on a union of the syndicates or councils from the workers, peasants and soldiers.

This clearly shows the inner character of the Bolshevik movement based on the theory of anarchy and syndicalism preached during the last century by Bakunin. It is not Socialism at all but Syndicalism, and as I stated in a previous telegram, the Bolsheviks consider that the most class-conscious section of the proletariat must lead the country and draw the less conscious peasantry behind it. The economic and social syndicates which they have formed, when backed by bayonets, can offer a formidable resistance to the capitalists and middle classes, who now form a powerful block round the Cossacks and Cadets. Under these circumstances, organised State Socialism, represented by the Moderate Socialist Parties, is swept away and the country becomes the arena of a great class struggle. Nevertheless, the peasants in the main support the Socialist Revolutionary Party and have a moderating influence. The Peasants' Congress at Petrograd has not yet said the last word.

Manchester Guardian, *15 December 1917*
'Bolshevik Terrorism: How the Russian Electors Voted.
The New Dictatorship'
Petrograd, 13 December 1917

Interest in the negotiations commenced yesterday with the Central Powers for a long armistice is overshadowed by the conflict between the Soviet and the Constituent Assembly. The result of the elections for the Constituent Assembly can now be roughly estimated. The small middle-class electors, frightened by Bolshevik terrorism, voted for the large capitalists and the Cadet Party; the urban proletariat and the army and navy went solidly with the Bolsheviks; the poorer peasants of the central provinces supported the Left Socialist Revolutionaries, who are in alliance with the Bolsheviks and have representatives in the Revolutionary Government.

Between these extremes comes the Centre group of the old Socialist Revolutionary Party [Right SRs] which has received the votes of the more well-to-do peasantry of the southern and eastern provinces. These three groups will probably be evenly divided in strength in the Constituent Assembly. Authority will therefore rest with the group which can secure the support of the Centre Party. The leaders of this party, like Chernov, however, are discredited in the army and navy and the urban proletariat on account of their contact with the late Provisional Government, and are accused of having sold the Russian Revolution to the Allied Imperialists. On the other hand, this Centre Party still has a considerable influence among the peasantry and the recently opened Peasant Congress of All Russia showed they had about 35 per cent of all the delegates.

This wholesome brake upon the Bolshevik extremists is evidently frightening the latter, but instead of having a sobering effect it is making them increase the policy of terrorism. The Cadet members of the Constituent Assembly are being arrested and thrown into the St Peter and St Paul Fortress immediately they arrive in Petrograd from the provinces. The apparent object of this is to terrorise all possible opposition to a dictatorship of the proletariat in the Constituent Assembly when the latter commences.

Articles appear in the official Bolshevik organs every day to the effect that the only function of the Constituent Assembly is to serve the will of the proletariat. Even the Left Socialist Revolutionary leaders, who are acting as a brake upon the hot-headed Bolsheviks, say that in transition periods of social reconstruction like the present, authority must rest with the class that made the Revolution. On the other hand they protest against the arrest of Cadets and try to secure the inviolability of members of the Constituent Assembly. But this moderate wing of the Revolutionary Government is powerless to check the mad career of the Anarcho-Syndicalist dictators, who are relying on the bayonets of the army and navy. The soldiers and sailors, both at the front and in the rear, are so embittered by the experiences of the last eight months that they see a dictatorship as the sole form of government which will put an end to the war and crush the capitalist class – which they say made the war – under an iron heel. But they little heed the dangerous precedent which this policy creates. Thus the country becomes every day more sharply divided into two camps – the classes and the masses – and the position of the Moderate Centre, relying on the peasant, becomes increasingly difficult.

Under these circumstances Parliamentary Government becomes an impossibility, and the authority of the Constituent Assembly, which will only reflect these bitter dissensions in a concentrated form, is likely to be small. The soldiers, sailors and workers regard their syndicates or soviets as the sole authority which they will respect, and as long as they have armed forces at their disposal this reign of terror is likely to continue. It is a terrible lesson in what happens when a people, tortured by three years of war, turn on the ruling classes who have exploited and tormented them.

Letter to Anna Maria Philips
Petrograd, 22 December 1917

Today I sent to you, Robin and Uncle Tuffet each a telegram which I hope will reach you in time for Xmas. It said 'Xmas greetings from cold, hungry and peaceful Russia'. It is peaceful in one sense in that the war is at an end, as far as Russia is concerned. There is an armistice on the front, the soldiers are going home in driblets across this vast snow-covered plain, leaving a few Cossacks, Tartars and Poles in the trenches to fraternise with the Germans. But it is not peaceful in another sense, because the class war, which has been hidden up to now, is bursting out with all the violence of a long supressed volcano. An indescribable calamity awaits us here in North Russia unless some compromise can be attained. We shall be doomed to a slow death in darkness, cold and hunger. For the present we have some food, not a lot, but enough to get along with. But the civil war between the northern and southern provinces is cutting us off from the corn supplies and the fuel of the Don Basin. Still, it is possible that at the eleventh hour a way out will be found. It is always the unexpected that happens in this country. I never knew a country which goes so frequently to the brink of absolute destruction and ruin but always manages somehow to escape falling over ...

This last week there have been drunken orgies in various parts of the city. Provocative agents, in order to create disturbances, have broken into cellars and distributed wines and vodka, and the wretched soldiers, after three years' suffering and misery at the front have become half bestialised and of course are easily led into taking part in these orgies. The Revolutionary Red Guards try to put down the disorders but are only partially successful. During these orgies and attempts to stop them there is a good deal of firing. Provocateurs fire revolvers and the Red Guards machine guns. It is a common thing now to hear the crack of bullets over your head as you walk in the streets in the daytime.

We have a house committee here in these flats and every man undertakes to serve as night watchman once a week to prevent strangers getting in at night. We are recognised by the Military Revolutionary Committee, which is now the authority in control. How long it will be in its present position is a question ...

The *Guardian* [has] appointed me telegraphic correspondent as well as special article writer, as I had been up till then. So now I send off regular cables. It means I have to work all day at collecting current information, reading the daily press carefully and interviewing leading people. This gives me no time to do any writing. I was wanting to begin a history of the Revolution and I have an immense amount of material – copies of all the principal Socialist and Soviet newspapers from the beginning of the Revolution. But these are such times that one cannot sit down and write calmly and dispassionately, when all society and civilisation is in a state of liquidation.

Letter to Robin Price
Petrograd, 22 December 1917

... The Maximalist revolutionaries who are ruling here, though they have done very well in destroying the war and I take off my hat to them for it, are nevertheless incapable of constructive work. They are destructive Jacobins who believe that by flaming decrees, passionate speeches, terrorism and the guillotine they can create a worldly paradise. They will have to go and make way for more constructive people.

Manchester Guardian, *26 December 1917*
'Cleavage in Russia: South Against Social Upheaval'
Petrograd, 24 December 1917

The Bolshevik government is apparently not content with social experiments in North Russia, but considers itself a crusader for freedom in all lands ... The first real opposition to this policy comes from the peasant proprietors and small bourgeoisie of the Ukraine. The matter is complicated by the Cossacks, among whom there is a really reactionary element.

The trouble has been brewing for many weeks. After the October [November] Revolution all the Cadet leaders who escaped arrest, and the reactionary general officers, went to the Don regions under the protection of General Kaledin. The latter formed special regiments of reactionary refugees to fight the Bolsheviks, but the actual Cossacks among these forces are few, for the Cossack rankers have no wish to interfere with the Revolution in North Russia, and are only desirous of being left alone in possession of their lands. A fortnight ago, however, General Kaledin, with the reactionary regiments, took the offensive and began arresting leaders of the soviets in the Rostov coal basin in South Russia. His action was directed not only against the Bolsheviks but against all the revolutionary democracy.

The Bolshevik government at Petrograd declared war on General Kaledin and ordered Bolshevik troops to be sent from the front against him. The Ukrainian Rada declined to allow them to pass through their territory on grounds of neutrality. At the same time they allowed Cossacks to cross their territory to the Don. The Bolshevik government declared this a breach of neutrality. The Rada has offered to mediate between the Bolsheviks and General Kaledin.

Meanwhile two parties appear to have risen on the Don. The Moderate Cossacks oppose their generals' taking the offensive against the Don Soviets as long as the latter create no disorder. The position on the Don is still obscure but General Kaledin recently resigned the leadership of the Cossack government.

The class division is not as strong among the well-to-do peasantry of South Russia as amongst the northern proletariat. Hence the Revolution there had not gone beyond the broad democratic idea which aims at uniting all the labouring classes, the peasants, the intellectuals, and the small bourgeoisie in a Constituent Assembly.

On the other hand, the North Russian proletariat dreams of a class dictatorship through the soviets. But the northern Bolshevik leaders are little better than Jacobins and have no capacity for constructive social reform. Their strength lies in the fact that they are the first people who had the courage to see that peace was the first necessity for Russia and to act accordingly. In this they had general support. The Bolsheviks, however, consider peace possible only by a social revolution throughout the whole world. Hence their frantic proclamations scattered broadside.

Letter to Anna Maria Philips
Petrograd, 10 January 1918

Just a line to say I am all right and have managed so far to live through these hard times. I wrote to you and Robin about three weeks ago and described something of what was going on.

Since then our condition has become much worse. The food supply has dwindled to a very small ration – only half a pound of bread for two days and all accessories, such as sausages, at famine prices. To make matters more hopeless still there is a banking crisis. The banks have been engaged in financing sabotage and counter-revolution, so the Revolutionary Government was forced to take them over. They have been shut for a fortnight and I can get no money to buy even the little food that it is possible now to get. I don't know what will happen, I am sure, but we must hope for the best.

Civil war broke out three weeks ago between Revolutionary North Russia and some Cossack forces in the south led by reactionary generals. They were supported by some of the reactionary influences in the Ukraine, where the proletarian revolution has not yet got such a firm hold although it is increasing its strength there every day. But during these conflicts the railways of Central Russia have been torn up and while they are being restored the food trains bound for Petrograd and the North have been plundered by starving peasants. Now consignments of flour and meat have been bought in Siberia but they have not yet arrived because they can get no fuel for the engines on the railways. Still the industries of the country are demobilising and turning gradually from war work to peaceful productive work and the making of implements and goods which will help mankind to fight, not his brother, but famine and pestilence.

But in the meantime we have a terrible time to live through. I don't know, I am sure, if I shall live through to see the spring. I don't know what it is to go to bed feeling I have eaten enough. On Xmas day on my table was a small sausage, a quarter of a pound of black bread and a few sweets that I had bought for about five roubles. But with it all I felt that I was having a happier Xmas than any in the last three years. Physically starving, I was mentally fed with the joyful news that Russia, Red, Revolutionary, triumphant Russia had overthrown her capitalist tyrants, burst her chains and had set out alone on the road to peace. The German government dares not refuse to negotiate with prostrate starving Russia, because it knows that she has the moral force on her side. The rulers of Germany are in terror that the infection of the Russian Revolution is spreading into their army. May it spread further west still.

So on Xmas day I comforted myself with these reflections over my bare table. Then I went out for the afternoon to Tsarskoye Selo, the fine park about 20 versts from Petrograd. The cold was intense and going out there I got my feet numbed and had to spend half an hour rubbing them before a fire to get feeling back into them. Then I walked in the lovely park which once the Emperor of Russia used to call his own. Now he is far away in Siberian steppes. It was beautiful in the crisp snow, covering the pines and firs, and I longed for a pair of skis to run on. But I felt I had no energy to run on them now, as I once had. When one can't get food to eat one has no energy for sport. So I walked quietly round the frozen lake and looked at the fir-clad islands, then came back to Petrograd. Thus I spent my Xmas day.

Manchester Guardian, *31 December 1917*
'The Enemy Peace Offer: Bolshevik Influence Strengthened' Petrograd, 28 December 1917

The unexpected turn in the negotiations at Brest-Litovsk, caused by the recognition of the Central Powers of the first part of the Russian peace programme, undoubtedly raised the prestige of the Bolshevik government and reflected the internal situation. The participation of the Ukrainian Rada in the negotiations proves that the latter agree with the general principles of the foreign policy of the Bolsheviks. This helped to tide over the conflict on internal questions ...

Victor Chernov, who leads the democratic opposition to the Bolshevik government, writes today in the *Dyelo Naroda*:

> The Central Empires divide our peace formula, accepting half but not the other half, thereby rendering the whole useless. But this does not mean we should not continue the negotiations. On the contrary, the refusal of the Allies last year to commence negotiations was a mistake. If they do not come in now we shall not be responsible for the situation created. The Central Empires have shown they want no separate peace.

Chernov ends by advising the immediate summoning of the Constituent Assembly in order to show the Allies Russia's united will.

Manchester Guardian, *8 January 1918*
'Bolshevik Peace Alternatives: the Revolution Against Imperialism' Petrograd, 2 January 1918

The Russian delegates arriving here yesterday from Brest-Litovsk state that the German delegates showed great anxiety to conclude peace and to commence trade relations with Russia. The Bolsheviks seem to expect that ultimately the Allied governments will approach the governments of the Central Powers with a view to finding a common peace formula which will secure the Imperialists of both alliances annexations past and present, in Europe and Africa, in order to defeat the principles of the Russian Revolution. Believing as they do in the possibilities of a Holy Alliance by the Western and Central European oligarchies against the Russian Revolution, the Bolsheviks may soon begin to barter Russian conquests in Asia for German conquests in Europe unless the Allied democracies move in the meantime.

The process of decentralisation in Russia is continuing rapidly, helping the German Imperialists, who hope to separate Ukraine from Great Russia and to conclude a separate peace with each. The Ukraine movement has now become definitely separatist which, added to the stubbornness of the Bolsheviks who still dream of rousing the Ukraine peasants against the Rada, only plays into the hands of the German Imperialists.

The Constituent Assembly is still postponed, but recent indications are that the Bolsheviks are prepared to allow the Assembly if the latter agrees to recognise the authority of the Popular Commissioners [People's Commissars]. An agreement on this basis is hardly likely. The Bolsheviks stand for a dictatorship of the working classes organised in the soviets, while the other parties insist on the authority of all democratic elements, including the small bourgeoisie. It is as if the question was raised: who should rule England, Parliament or the Trade Union Congress?

Manchester Guardian, *22 January 1918*
'Russian Assembly Parties: the Focus of the Class Struggle'
Petrograd, 19 January 1918

The Constituent Assembly, which opened yesterday, showed itself the focus point of the class struggle going on in Russia. One side, representing the small bourgeoisie, the *intelligentsia*, the well-to-do peasantry and the national groups, stood on a national democratic position; the other side, representing the proletariat and the poorer peasantry, stood on the class position. Conspicuous by its absence was the capitalist Cadet Party, squeezed out of existence by recent events.

By the irony of fate the erstwhile inspirer of the Zimmerwald Conference, Victor Chernov, now defends, as leader of the Centre Socialist Revolutionary Party [Right SRs], the Russian national democratic standpoint against the international class position of the Bolsheviks ... A similar situation would be created in England if the Conservatives and Liberal Imperialists ceased to exist and the Radicals and the Labour Party were defending the national idea of British democracy against the Independent Labour Party and the British Socialist Party, standing for the dictatorship of the Trade Union Congress and the international Parliament of labour.

The whole atmosphere of this, the youngest European Parliament, was heated by the conflict of principles which raged in the absence of the sobering traditions and precedents of the Western democracies.

The democratic groups of the Right, standing on the national position, secured a majority and elected M. Chernov as President of the Assembly. The latter's address was a carefully-worded compromise:

> The Constituent Assembly should propose to the Socialist and Democratic parties of Europe an immediate commencement of peace negotiations on the Russian revolutionary programme. The Constituent Assembly should unite all the labouring masses in Russia, the Ukraine party, the labouring Cossacks, the Great Russian proletariat, and let civil war cease from this day. Let the land go to the peasantry, let democratically-elected *Zemstvos*, together with local peasant soviets, distribute the land on the basis of local needs. We can reach Socialism only by slow stages, through gradual social economic development, giving equality of opportunity to all.

The Bolshevik spokesman proposed, in the name of the All-Russia Central Committee of the Soviets, a resolution stating that the authority of the soviet was fundamental, and without it the ideas formulated by Chernov were unrealisable.

> We have already taken steps towards international peace among the working classes, and given land to the peasantry through our soviets, while you spent six months betraying the Revolution to the Cadets. Therefore the only authority that can have the confidence of the proletariat and the peasants is that of the soviet, and the Constituent Assembly can only exist if it recognises proletariat dictatorship and the removal of all the propertied classes from political rights.

Tsereteli then spoke in the name of the Mensheviks, now reduced to a very small group:

> The Constituent Assembly elected by the whole country should be the highest authority in the land; then why send it an ultimatum? Has civil war helped the soviet to realise the revolutionary programme? On the contrary it assists the German militarists to divide the revolutionary front, which should be national, not class. The break-up of the Constituent Assembly will only serve the interest of the bourgeoisie, whom the Bolsheviks profess to be fighting. It alone can save the Revolution.

Tsereteli's speech created a great impression, even on the Bolsheviks, but sounded like an apology for the eight months in which the Russian Revolution wandered in the wilderness under Menshevik guidance. The Bolsheviks and the Left Socialist Revolutionaries moved a resolution demanding recognition of the principle of Russia as a Federal Republic of the Soviets, international peace made by the soldiers over the heads of the bourgeois governments, the abolition of private property, the nationalisation of industry and banks, the disarming of the propertied classes, and the establishment of an army of peasants and labourers. The Revolutionary Right and Centre block demanded all power for the Constituent Assembly, immediate peace negotiations, the land for the peasants, and State control of industry. The point on which the struggle concentrates is the question of authority. Is it to be a national democratic or a class dictatorship?

Manchester Guardian, *22 January 1918*
'The Bolshevik Idea: Lenin's Political Education of Labour'
Petrograd, *20 January 1918*

Last night I heard Lenin move a resolution for the dissolution of the Constituent Assembly in the Central Committee of the Soviet. His speech contained the following passages:

> The Constituent Assembly is a stage in the process of the education of the labouring masses to political consciousness and not an end in itself. When that stage is passed the Constituent Assembly as an institution becomes obsolete. In Russia we have passed quickly through this stage because the growth of class consciousness in the exploited masses has developed with remarkable rapidity. The war, started by the exploiters, has brought untold suffering and enabled the masses, who otherwise would have had to pass through a long schooling in Parliamentary Government, to realise immediately the significance of their class position. What would in normal times have been done by the Constituent Assembly has now been done by the sufferings caused by the war. In all Parliaments there are two elements: exploiters and exploited; the former always manage to maintain class privileges by manoeuvres and compromise. Therefore the Constituent Assembly represents a stage of class coalition.
>
> In the next stage of political consciousness the exploited class realises that only a class institution and not general national institutions can break the power of the exploiters. The soviet, therefore, represents a higher form of political development than the Constituent Assembly. We are passing through chaos and suffering to a new social order in which political power will be concentrated in the hands of the exploited masses. The soviets,

the organs of the exploited masses, become dictators, removing the exploiting elements of the community, absorbing them into the fibre of the new social system.

There is no sign as yet of disaffection among the army over Bolshevik tactics, but the dissolution of the Constituent Assembly will probably widen the breach in the ranks of the peasantry, one side going with Chernov, the other with the Left Socialist Revolutionaries and the Soviets ... The Moderate Social Democrats [Mensheviks] in the Constituent Assembly lost all the confidence of the workers, soldiers, and poorer peasants because, under the guidance of Kerensky last summer, they failed to advance the cause of the Revolution ... The soldiers, longing for an early democratic peace, were forced into the July advance, with all its disastrous consequences, under the pretence that a Stockholm Conference would be called.

The poorer peasants hoped for the satisfaction of their age-long desire for land, but found that Kerensky's government, in coalition with the Cadets and landlords, ruined the prospects of reform. Therefore they now feel that no coalition is possible with the Moderate Democrats, who have been responsible for this policy, and their only hope is to rely on themselves alone and their Soviets.

Thus is created the Russian counterpart of Sinn Fein. The struggle between the Soviet and the Constituent Assembly was the struggle between the idea of a coalition government with the small bourgeoisie and the idea of a dictatorship of the labouring masses.

Manchester Guardian, *31 January 1918*
'Trotsky and the Forced Peace. Enemy and Allies Both Denounced'
Petrograd, 27 January 1918

Last night will be historic in the annals of the Russian Revolution. The third All-Russia Congress of Peasants' Delegates, which opened its sittings yesterday morning, joined the All-Russia Congress of Workers and Soldiers, creating a united assembly of over 1,100 members. By five o'clock as, cold and hungry, I crawled up to the Taurida Palace, I found assembled the greatest Labour Parliament that the Russian Revolution has yet brought forth. Before it lay the momentous decision how to answer the governments of the Central Empires, whether to accept a disgraceful peace or break off negotiations with the Prussian oligarchy. Trotsky struck the keynote of the feeling of the great assembly in a long speech. Reviewing the history of the foreign policy of the Popular Commissioners [People's Commissars] since the October [November] Revolution, he pointed out the unique position of revolutionary Russia.

The Allied Imperialists accuse us of being the agents of Germany. German Imperialists accuse us of being the agents of the Allies. The combined accusations, neutralising each other, prove the hypocrisy of both and our honesty. Hindenburg knows he cannot break the West Front and hopes to strengthen the Prussian oligarchy at the expense of revolutionary Russia. We have disclosed to our German-Austrian comrades the criminality and cynicism of their governments, treacherously pretending to accept peace without annexations. Their representatives, on the second day of the negotiations, refused to agree to the evacuation of the occupied provinces till after the war. On being asked if they would give an undertaking to submit the question of the evacuation of German troops and future government of Poland, Lithuania, Courland and Esthonia to a democratic assembly of natives, they declined to give any undertaking. They think: 'Since Russia wants peace at any cost, and we want peace at Russia's cost, the more we demand the more we get.'

This is not a national and territorial but a class struggle, for the Prussian oligarchy wants to save the German aristocracy of the Baltic provinces from ruin at the hands of the Russian Revolution ... Equally cynical and hypocritical are the Allied Imperialists, who seem ready to agree to a compromise and an annexationist peace at the expense of Russia. For what else did Lloyd George mean when he said Russia could make her own terms with Germany.[41] ... We are not alone. In spite of the censorship the news has filtered into Austria, where the fire of the Revolution is breaking out. As for ourselves, we shall never sign a disgraceful peace with the German tyrants but will carry on a defensive Socialist war against all our class enemies. If we believe in the International, let us join the new Revolutionary Army forming in Petrograd, Moscow, Kharkov, and go forth not to kill our comrades of Central Europe and Allied countries, but to persuade them to join us against the common enemy.

When Trotsky ended his speech the immense assembly of workers and soldiers and peasants rose and, as if at a great religious gathering, solemnly sang the International.

Manchester Guardian, *21 February 1918*
'Russian Restoration: State Machinery Again Working'
Petrograd, 16 February 1918

During the last fortnight the Soviet government of workers, soldiers and peasants has strengthened its position in the provinces. On the new Central Executive Committee elected by the recent [Third]

All-Russia Soviet Congress has now fallen the task of establishing revolutionary order and building up the Socialist foundation of Russian society. Hitherto the weakness of the soviets has lain in the fact that the masses of the remoter districts had not reached the same level of revolutionary consciousness as in the industrial centres.

In the south and east provinces the process of transferring power to the workers' and peasants' soviets and the liquidation of the local Constituent Assemblies and *Zemstvo*s, which represented the idea of a coalition between the proletariat and the propertied classes, took place more slowly than in North Russia. The process was accompanied by conflicts in certain districts where the old Coalition forces held out stubbornly, thus causing civil war ... But the political consciousness of the workers and peasants of south-east Russia is now so developed that the process of clearing out the nests of counter-revolutionary generals, driving the bourgeois agents out of public life and establishing the sole power in the proletarian soviets, is made much easier.

Automatically the railways are beginning to work again and the famine in North Russia is rather less acute. The collapse last week of the Ukrainian Rada and the establishment instead of the All-Ukrainian Soviet shows that the peasants in South Russia realised the danger of falling between the hammer and anvil of the Austro-German oligarchy.

The horizon on the Don is still clouded, for General Alexeiv has now formed a new army of officers and cadets, sons of the propertied classes and counter-revolutionary agents, and is attempting to break northwards to Moscow. It is interesting to observe that the Cossack regiments are not only not supporting him but fighting with the Soviet troops against him.

The North Russia Soviet government was faced last month with the danger of being unable to work the government machinery through the sabotage of bourgeois officials. Now the funds provided for sabotage by the leading capitalists have, since the occupation of the banks by the Soviet troops and the control of banking operations, been stopped. The Bolsheviks, moreover, succeeded in a large measure in creating their own intellectual staffs to work the State machinery ...

It is interesting to note that the Cadet Party applauds the success of Bolshevism, not because it wants to see the principle of the dictatorship of the proletariat established, but because it sees the Soviet government is sufficiently powerful and efficient to develop one day, as it hopes, into an instrument for subjugating Russia once more to the capitalist system.

It is premature to say that the Soviet government has overcome all its difficulties. Alexeiv's counter-revolutionary army is a serious danger, and the country is faced with a flood of paper money and financial collapse. With characteristic originality the Bolsheviks and the Left Socialist Revolutionaries are trying to set up a system of communal economy in which each industry is controlled by workers and exchanges products with other workers' syndicates without the passage of money. A Council of Public Economy[42] is now sitting in Petrograd working out a plan of State control for this new form of National Economy ... All this shows that the Russian people are entering upon an intensely interesting social and economic experiment, and the Soviet government of Petrograd is the instrument created to carry out their desires and aspirations. As such it is the only Government which can guide the destinies of the country.

Manchester Guardian, *23 February 1918*
'Failure of Bolshevik Hopes: A Nation Isolated and Starving'
Petrograd, *20 February 1918*

The decision of the Popular Commissioners to send a telegram to Germany yesterday expressing readiness to sign a separate peace on the basis of the German demands at Brest-Litovsk must not be interpreted as a sudden change of policy, because three weeks ago, before Trotsky left for Brest-Litovsk for the last time, he secured the consent of the All-Russia Soviet Executive to sign a so-called 'unfortunate peace' if all other solutions should fail. Then, as now, two tendencies were running in the Bolshevik and Left Socialist Revolutionary Parties: one for a separate peace if necessary; the other for a refusal to sign and a continuation of the struggle, even if it meant the ruin and destruction of Russia.

During the interval an important event happened, namely the strikes and revolutionary movements in Austria and Germany, which strengthened Trotsky at Brest-Litovsk. However the proletariat movement in Central Europe was apparently too weak to force the hands of their governments, who speedily crushed it, thus strengthening the military oligarchy.

Trotsky was now forced by necessity to abandon hopes of a general democratic peace and to endeavour to obtain the best possible separate terms from the Central Powers. The latter, however, after their victory over the internal revolutionary movement, stiffened their demands. Trotsky therefore tried, as a last chance, the demobilisation of the army and the refusal to sign peace in order to show the German proletariat the sincerity of the Russian Revolution. Now this has failed and the German soldier obeys the orders of the Prussian oligarchy which, terrifed at the revolutionary infection from the east, is now invading Russia not for territorial gains but to crush the hated Revolution. The military party in Berlin is apparently strengthened also by the bourgeois parties, who have hitherto supported the peace resolutions of the Reichstag in July[43] but are now terrified by the Revolution.

The Russian revolutionaries are beginning to see they cannot emancipate mankind from nationalist wars by the development of the class struggle, for Trotsky is forced back to the position he was in before he went to Brest-Litovsk for the last stage of the negotiations, when he received a mandate to sign an 'unfortunate peace'. The Revolution, if allowed to develop unhindered, will strengthen itself internally, and wait till the rest of the world is also ready for internal changes which will make a general democratic peace possible, abandoning all attempts to influence neighbouring countries.

Meanwhile the chance of the Russian Revolution to offer effective resistance to the invaders is very slight. The whole of North Russia is in such a condition of famine and misery that its sole hope is the fear which the Germans must have in occupying such a country. The inhabitants of the towns have nearly all gone to the villages to escape death from starvation. These are conditions which only peace, even a separate one, will repair. On the other hand, there is a section of the Soviet which favours a retreat into the interior of the troops that still remain at the front. This party particularly relies on the newly formed soviets in the Ukraine, and on the possibility of their offering resistance to the enemy. The treachery of the Rada in signing a separate peace behind the back of the Revolution has seriously complicated the political situation there, and given the Central Powers a pretext to interfere in internal affairs not only to prevent the agitation spreading into Central Europe, but also to replenish themselves with Ukrainian corn.

Manchester Guardian, *26 February 1918*
'Russia and the Peace Terms: Strong Opposition to Acceptance'
Petrograd, *24 February 1918*

Last night's meeting of the Central Executive of the All-Russia Soviet was as memorable as it was tragic. It marked the end of one stage of the Russian Revolution and the apparent commencement of a period in which the revolutionary forces will retire underground, as they did during the Stolypin regime after 1906. Yesterday evening was taken up with a party conference of the Bolsheviks and the Left Socialist Revolutionaries. At midnight joint sessions of these two parties were held to consider the German terms.

At this session the Commander-in-Chief, Krilenko, read messages from the front showing that the remnants of the Russian army on the north-west front were declining to fight and were retreating before insignificant German columns ... Nevertheless a member of the Brest-Litovsk Peace Delegation, Radek, made a powerful speech protesting against signing a disgraceful speech, warning his hearers that such a step meant moral bankruptcy for the Russian Revolution in Europe and handing over Eastern Europe to Prussian reaction. Lenin made a long speech, setting forth reasons for coming to terms with Germany now. He warned his hearers not to give themselves over to the influence of phrases but to come to practical considerations.

> It is the plain, naked truth (he said) that Russia can offer no physical resistance, since she is materially exhausted by three years of war. The people may be ready to fight and die in the last ditch in a just cause, but wars today are not won by enthusiasm; they are won by technical skill and efficiency, railways, abundance of food and supplies. The Russian Revolution must sign peace in order to obtain breathing space to recuperate for further struggle.

Lenin's speech had a great effect but did not overcome the strong opposition. A minority of the Bolshevik Party were against signing peace and a large majority of the Left Socialist Revolutionaries supported them ... The leader of the Socialist Revolutionaries, Kamkov, while admitting the correctness of Lenin's thesis that Russia cannot offer resistance, declined on behalf of his party to accept the moral responsibility before Europe of signing a disgraceful peace, and suggested that the Revolutionary Government should evacuate Petrograd, retire to the interior of Russia, and defy the German tyrants to come on. Both sides are agreed that Russia cannot offer resistance, the only difference being on the question whether Russia should make a pretence of bowing before the conquerors or whether she should passively resist and, allowing the Germans to do their worst, retreat to the vast eastern territories, which no enemy can hold down. My impression is that all the educated, intellectual opinion of the Russian Revolution favours the latter course, while Lenin's more practical, if opportunist, policy finds support among the uneducated masses, particularly the peasant soldiers who, since the demobilisation have gone home to the villages in the east and feel no direct interest now in the fate of Poland and Ukraine, but only want to be left alone on their land. Even the factory workers here in Petrograd, who are the most class-conscious of the revolutionary section of the proletariat, are becoming apathetic through famine and are prepared to support Lenin.

I hear that the response to the recent appeal to enlist in the Red Army is very small ... On the other hand the Soviet government has immense power still, since it has become the class organ of the Russian proletariat, leading them in their class struggle. This internal conflict is now the central factor of the Russian Revolution.

It is clear from the terms of the treaty that the Central Powers intend peace with Russia to open for them large economic possibilities which will solve their internal food produce difficulties and break the Allies' blockade. For this reason, if for no other, it is imperative that the Allies should redouble all their efforts to secure the sympathy of the Russian people in their hour of sore trial, and the Allied democracies may rest assured that the reaction against the cynical German peace terms which is bound to seize Russian public opinion, will only work in their favour and make a *rapprochement* between Russia and Western Europe more possible now than ever, provided that the whole policy of the Allies towards Russia is radically revised and made more in sympathy with the new spirit in Russia.

Manchester Guardian, *4 March 1918*
'Russian Revolutionary Tactics: Peace and War Policies with One Object'
Petrograd, 1 March 1918

A member of the Peasant Soviet, Mogiliev, just returned from the front, tells me that the Germans are advancing in small columns composed of Junkers, non-commissioned Prussian officers, Polish National Volunteers and Germans of the Baltic provinces. The opposition offered to these advancing forces is very slight. Most of the Russian soldiers of the old army have gone home; the Red Guards and armed factory workers of the northern towns who have been sent to the front have no training and only inferior equipment. The peasants offer the invaders no resistance, but are peacefully continuing their work ... It is clear that the Germans are following a definite political object – the eradication of revolutionary influence from the regions adjoining the annexed territories ... Yesterday the German movement began to concentrate in the south-west region with the object of clearing Ukraine of the Revolutionary Soviets and re-establishing the Rada ... Ukrainian soviets are receiving support from unexpected quarters. I hear from people arriving from Kiev that among the Ukrainian peasants the Rada is thoroughly discredited. Its fall is due not only to the treacherous separate peace, but primarily to its land policy, which was directed towards compensating the landlords for loss of the lands at the expense of the peasantry ...

The Soviet forces, owing to lack of material resources, are unable to show strong opposition, and are retiring underground wherever the invaders come. Meanwhile resolutions are pouring into Petrograd from the interior of Russia on the question of 'War or Peace' ... It is clear that Lenin, in his policy of acceptance of the German terms, expresses the real desire not only of the soldiers but the peasant masses, as much as other elements of the country.

Here the Tolstoyan spirit of non-resistance to evil is plainly seen expressed in the soul of the peasant – the most truly Russian element in the Revolution – urging him to fight by the aid of moral and not material forces. On the other hand, in the resolutions of the urban soviets one sees the spirit of fiery Marxism from the West insisting on the attainment of social ideals by organised pressure and, in this tragic moment of the Revolution, ready with arms to defend freedom or die. These two psychologies, eastern and western, are at the present moment struggling in the soul of the Russian Revolution. It is characteristic of the present confusion that the Bolshevik Lenin should voice the pacifist feeling of the peasants while the Left Socialist Revolutionaries, hitherto the peasants' party, should stand for the position of the urban proletariat. But the difference between Lenin and his critics is not so much a question of principle as of tactics. The latter want to continue the struggle openly and by material means; the former want to sign peace in order to continue the underground struggle politically and morally.

CHAPTER 8

After Brest-Litovsk, March–August 1918

In March 1918, while the Germans were still advancing towards Petrograd, the decision was taken to move the capital to Moscow. Price was unable to get a seat on any of the official evacuation trains and therefore he went for a few weeks, until the pressure eased, to Vologda, a small town situated at the intersection of the north-south and east-west railway systems. Most of the diplomatic corps had already established itself there, but for Price the most compelling reason was that food could be got in Vologda. He missed the Fourth All-Russia Congress of Soviets which met on 14 March to ratify the Treaty of Brest-Litovsk, so ending the war with Germany. He used his time in Vologda to visit the surrounding villages, and acquired a useful picture of the progress of the Revolution outside the capital. He got to Moscow on 17 April.

While he was in Vologda the Germans occupied Kiev. On 30 April they dissolved the Rada and set up a military dictatorship under their puppet Skoropadsky. When the peasants refused to sell them grain the Germans began to requisition it and fighting broke out – Price called it 'band warfare' – all over the Ukraine. Diplomatic relations with Germany had been resumed and a German ambassador, Count Mirbach, installed in Moscow, but anti-German feeling was widespread. The senior British diplomat in Russia at that time, Lockhart (who had remained in Moscow), believed that given appropriate help the Russian government might have been willing to canalise that feeling into a resumption of hostilities. Throughout the early spring of 1918 Lockhart tried to get the Bolsheviks to invite the Allies to send troops to Russia in order to reopen the front against Germany in a collaborative action. But in London his arguments were dismissed as coming from a young and inexperienced man. The Allies, now including America and Japan, were determined to save the Russians from themselves by landing troops on their own initiative, although they had not yet decided where, when and how.

Rumours about Allied intentions, often remarkably well-informed, were circulating in Moscow. But if Price so much as hinted at them in his dispatches they were cut out by the British censor. By now he was keeping copies of everything he sent so that it is possible to identify the censored passages by comparing the copies with the article as printed. Everything which mentioned the possibility of intervention or Allied complicity in the civil war was cut, although the fact that there was a civil war was allowed. It weakened the Bolsheviks' claim to be the sole government of Russia. Any suggestion that the Allies were missing opportunities for constructive as opposed to obstructive action was cut. Straight reporting on political or foreign policy developments was usually tolerated, that is until 25 June. That was the date of the last dispatch of which any part was allowed to be printed, and it appeared in the Manchester Guardian *of 11 July. He sent off a further 18 pieces before he left Russia in December 1918, some of which are reproduced below. The most important event that Price covered in the last weeks before the Allied landings was the Fifth All-Russia Congress of Soviets, which met in Moscow on 3 July. In the course of this congress a split dramatically opened up between the Bolsheviks and the Left SRs, but not one word of what he wrote about it was passed for publication.*

By now, it is clear from a study of Foreign Office and War Cabinet records that the determination of the Allies to intervene in Russia had crystallised into decisions.

In the spring of 1918 there was in Russia the equivalent of a full Army Corps made up of former deserters and prisoners of war from the Austro-Hungarian army – the Czech Legion – whose only desire was to secure a national homeland out of the ruins of the Austro-Hungarian Empire when the war was over. The Czechs had already agreed to go and fight for the Allies in France if they could be transported there. Early in May some of them had begun to move eastwards with a view to embarking for France at Vladivostock. Others were about to head north-west for embarkation at Archangel or Murmansk. While they were on the move a trainload of Czechs heading eastwards became embroiled in a skirmish at Cheliabinsk with Hungarian prisoners of war going in the opposite direction. The Soviet government, not unnaturally, demanded that they surrender their weapons while they remained on Soviet soil and the Czechs refused. Those already on the Trans-Siberian railway continued on their way to Vladivostock, but as a fighting force now, capturing towns and overthrowing local soviets on their way. The others began to advance up the Volga towards Moscow. For the Allies the opportunity to 'rescue' the Czechs provided the perfect excuse for intervention. In the first half of July the Americans, now persuaded, landed troops in Vladivostock, where they were soon followed by large numbers of Japanese.

In March, during the last stages of the peace negotiations, a small force of British troops had been landed at Murmansk on the pretext of protecting the port and the stores accumulated there for, but unused by, the Tsarist army. In the tense atmosphere surrounding the last phase of the peace negotiations with Germany the Soviet government had only made a token protest. In June these troops were reinforced by French as well as British troops and a virtual protectorate established over the area under the notional control of the Murmansk Soviet. Between 2 and 4 August Allied forces variously estimated as between 1,500 and 6,000 troops, including French and Canadians, landed at Archangel and those already at Murmansk were further reinforced.[44]

Price now abandoned any pretence at objectivity. He knew that nothing he was sending to the Manchester Guardian *was getting past the British censor. He profoundly disagreed with and was ashamed of what the Allies were doing. He could get no money from England, either from the newspaper or from his own bank account. He was offered a job as a translator at the Soviet Foreign Office and took it. Before long he had become one of its leading propagandists in the English language.*

Manchester Guardian, *18 March 1918*
'Russian Revolution and Peace: Gathering Forces for the Future'
Vologda, *12 March 1918*

What happened in Petrograd in October is happening now in the provinces. For instance I find local authority here has come entirely into the hands of the local factory workers and soldiers of the Red Army, to whom are joined various peasant organisations, thus forming a proletarian dictatorship for the locality. Nor is public opinion here different from that of Petrograd. Here exist the same two parties on the question of war and peace, while the majority of the local soviet favours the ratification of the peace treaty as a means of obtaining a respite for the next struggle. Public opinion is hardening to the idea of peace only as a temporary rest during which time preparations must be made not for the Nationalist and Imperialist wars of the past, but for a partisan class war. The Russian proletariat is setting its teeth for that conflict which it believes will inevitably break out in all Europe when the Western countries reach the necessary state of exhaustion ...

I find everywhere the reorganisation of transport and food and industrial problems being seriously taken up, as also recruiting among factory workers for the creation of a small, well-disciplined, effective Revolutionary Red Army which shall first stand on guard against counter-revolutionary agents at home and in time be ready to throw down the glove to any Imperialist government, whether from Western or Central Europe or the Far East ... Every intelligent revolutionary already realises that the cynical violation of justice by the Central Powers and the assault on defenceless, exhausted Russia will one day cost the aggressor dear. The policy of the Bolshevik government will be to wait till the forces making for internal disruption in Germany acquire more impetus than they have at present, and meanwhile to arm to the teeth to assist their comrades in Central Europe against the tyrants who dictated the Brest-Litovsk Treaty at the point of the bayonet.

Manchester Guardian, *2 May 1918*
'Bolshevik Policy: A New Phase'
Vologda, 12 April 1918

The Brest-Litovsk Treaty marked a new phase in the internal development of the Russian Revolution, foreshadowing a change in the attitude of the Bolshevik government to State problems and causing the revolutionary leaders to substitute statesmanship for irresponsible demagogy ... The internal enemy was easily defeated, but when the Russian Revolution entered the period of struggle with Imperialist governments abroad the Bolsheviks realised they were up against a very different problem. They therefore set themselves to create a strong socialist State to act as a centre of revolutionary infection for Europe ...

The official Bolshevik press is full of articles insisting on the necessity of raising the productivity of labour, impressing on the proletariat its responsibilities as well as privileges, and also of the need of a strong revolutionary army for a future war for the liberation of mankind from the yoke of capitalism. It is characteristic of the present state of affairs that the Cadet organ *Rech* – the only bourgeois paper tolerated by the Bolsheviks – has changed its attitude towards the latter, now praising them for adopting energetic measures against anarchy and even suggesting that the Bolsheviks alone can drag Russia out of its present condition. The Menshevik press and Gorky's *Novaya Zhizn*, on the other hand, fearing a proletariat dictatorship will generate a bourgeois dictatorship, denounce the Bolshevik policy.

Meanwhile Lenin's influence on the urban proletariat seems stronger than ever ... The soviet's authority is also spreading everywhere among the peasants. At a conference of the soviets of the northern governments held here recently I saw peasants from distant Arctic regions, who declared that they recognised the soviet as the sole authority in Russia. Everywhere the *Zemstvo*s are being replaced by soviets. The former were elected eight months ago on a suffrage in which the landlords and propertied classes voted while the young peasants and energetic revolutionary elements were still at the front. The latter on return demanded that the authority in the rural districts shall be in the hands of Soviets elected by the labouring peasantry. Thanks to the activities of the young generation of peasant soldiers there is now some hope of saving North Russia from being depopulated. It is reorganising transport and forming a new revolutionary army, and is inspired by the same international ideals. The Bolshevik government seems to be seriously taking these problems in hand.

Manchester Guardian, *18 July 1918* *
'Russia and the Allies: Internal Interference Resented'
Vologda, 14 April 1918

The Imperialists of the Central Empires, by interfering in the internal affairs of the Revolution and supporting the bourgeois Ukrainian Rada against the Ukrainian Soviets, succeeded in overthrowing the latter and drawing south-west Russia into their economic sphere. As the result of this cynical act the hatred of Revolutionary Russia against the Central Empires knows no bounds, and one would have expected that wise diplomacy on the part of the Allies would have made use of it. But this appears beyond the capacity of the statesmen of the Allies, who now, like the Central Empires, must needs interfere in the internal affairs of the Revolution, in this case in Eastern Siberia.

For some months trouble has been brewing between the Siberian Soviets and the reactionary leaders who, hiding behind the so-called Siberian Constituent Assembly, have fled to the border regions of outer China to hatch plots against revolutionary Russia.

Even as far back as last summer Kerensky's government, through the bourgeois Minister Tereschenko, protested against the behaviour of Japan in supplying arms to Russian monarchist bands in Manchuria. The Bolshevik government has just published documents on this matter. The present leaders of these counter-revolutionary bands are General Horvath and Colonel Semenov. The latest information received by the All-Russia Soviet Executive goes to show that 18 heavy guns were supplied to them from Japanese sources. They have now crossed the Manchurian frontier and are invading Trans-Baikal against the Soviet troops in Eastern Siberia.

This policy of the Allies in the Far East in interfering in the internal affairs of the Russian Revolution is an exact counterpart of the policy of the Central Empires in Western Russia. The Russian Revolution is fully alive to the danger from both quarters and is determined to resist with all the forces at its disposal. Recent articles in the official organ of the Central Executive of the Soviet accuse the Allies of deliberately provoking Japan to occupy Eastern Siberia in order to recoup themselves for losses they have sustained in financing the Tsar's government and also to find compensation in Russia in the event of failure against Germany. The Bolshevik press refers in much milder terms to America, whose policy is regarded as being interested, temporarily at any rate, in maintaining Russian integrity and independence. The Bolshevik policy seems to be to utilise the

* Note the interval between the date of dispatch and the date of publication, almost certainly due to the intervention of the Official Press Bureau.

mutual jealousies of the three financial world groups of America, Western Europe and Central Europe, which are jostling each other for economic spheres of influence in the undeveloped regions of the earth. Thereby they hope to obtain a temporary respite to prepare for a future revolutionary war.

Letter to Anna Maria Philips
Moscow, 7 May 1918

I hear there is a post going to England in a day or two and as this is the only chance I have had of communicating with you for many months and heaven knows when I shall get another, I make the best of the opportunity.

When the Germans began to advance towards Petrograd about the middle of February and the foreign Embassies (except the American) and most of the newspaper correspondents began to leave Russia, Ransome and I decided to stick to our guns and sink or swim with the Russian Revolution. So I left Petrograd for Vologda and stayed there in a private house with a Jewish family for about a month. Here I got something to eat for the first time for six months. True there was very little bread but I got quantities of meat, eggs, fish, butter, cream and cheese and I fairly fed up, so that in a fortnight from being a weak skeleton that could hardly crawl across the road I became quite fat. When I had recovered from the effects of starvation I came on to Moscow, where I found the political life of the country centred round the Soviet government in the Kremlin. After a few days I found a room in the family of some very nice people ... friends of the Kropotkins, and I am very comfortable. I am continuing my telegraphic correspondence for the *Manchester Guardian*. Life in Moscow is much better than in Petrograd. Here, although there is little bread, still there are lots of other things, so that if one has money one can get on here. Fortunately the bank crisis has passed and I am able to get the money at last that has been sent out to me from England by the *Manchester Guardian* and from my own private account. So far therefore I am able to keep my head above water ...

I am absolutely without any news from England. A boatload of Russian subjects arrived at the Marmora from England recently and I saw some of them who told me a few things. Otherwise England might be in the moon for all that I know of what goes on there. I shall stick to the Soviet government wherever it goes, and if it is forced to leave Moscow, I suppose it will move eastwards towards the Volga and the Urals.

Letter to Anna Maria Philips
Moscow, 3 June 1918

I have a chance to get another letter through to England so make the most of it. Here life is going on as usual. We have, of course, only one enemy – famine, but so far in Moscow it lays its hands on our shoulder, not yet deciding whether it will grip us by the throat. But it seems to have laid Petrograd to the ground.

I have a room in apartments next door to the German Embassy and I occasionally see Graf Mirbach go off in a motor car. He is, I hear, a harmless old fool who has been sent here to be pleasant to the Bolsheviks in the Kremlin while his real lord and master, the Hindenburg-Ludendorf oligarchy, send their armed bands across the Russian plain, robbing, burning and murdering at will.

Ransome and I keep on hammering away and loading the telegraph wires with our cables, demanding the recognition by the Allied governments of the Soviet government here. I don't know if it has had any effect, but in the last few days I seem to have noticed a slight change of tone in London. The Bolsheviks are the only native Russian element which is capable of reorganising the country and fighting famine. Of course Russia will never take part in Imperialist war such as is being fought still in the West, but is going to wait her time until the inevitable crash comes and the same thing happens there as has happened here. When it comes in the West I fancy it will be accompanied by less confusion than here. Social Revolution in Russia is inevitably accompanied by anarchy because the state apparatus was never here to begin with and had to be created. That is what the Bolsheviks are trying to do here and they will do it, if the German and Allied Imperialists will let them alone.

Manchester Guardian, 2 July 1918
'The Allies and Russia: Intervention Dangers'
Moscow, 11 June 1918*

The last ten days have shown that the task before the Soviet government to maintain order in the country and suppress anarchy is becoming more and more difficult. The so-called Siberian Provisional Government, which was beaten by the Soviet troops in fair fight last winter, has now been able to set itself up as the sole authority in Siberia and has cut off the last corn reserve from starving Muscovite Russia ...

* Due probably to a misprint this was datelined 11 May when printed in the *Manchester Guardian*, but some of the events described in the piece had not yet occurred in May.

If British and American Labour cannot at this eleventh hour prevent the canker of anarchy from rotting the structure of the Russian Revolution, it is well that they should know what will be the future of the country. Russia, which for seven months has been ruled by a pure Labour and peasant government, will become the spoil of foreign Imperialists, and the people, reduced again to slavery, will no longer look to the West for help and moral support. On the other hand, the overthrow of the Soviet government will in the long run only be advantageous to Germany.

We are informed here that the Allies cannot *de facto* or *de jure* recognise the Soviet government because it represents only one class of the community. It is therefore assumed here that the Allied governments will decline *de jure* and *de facto* to recognise a Russian government consisting mainly of landlords, bankers, industrial capitalists and intellectuals who call themselves democrats because they, too, represent only one class. The Allied governments are supposed here to be aiming at creating some form of national Coalition Government including everyone from the landlords to Bolsheviks, to fight against German Imperialism. The fate of Kerensky's government is sufficient proof of the impossibility of this kind of government. It would be like asking the British Socialist Party[45] to enter Lloyd George's War Cabinet or the Independent German Socialists to become colleagues of Hindenburg and Ludendorf.

It should not be imagined that discontent with the Soviet government which has appeared lately among peasants and workers of the northern districts is due to dislike of Socialist legislation. This discontent is purely an elementary outburst due to famine. On the other hand, if the Allies set up in Russia a government of landlords, bankers and property-owners, which does as every government of that sort must do – namely protect the interests of its class – the very workers and peasants who are now discontented with the Soviet government on account of famine will be doubly opposed to the Allies for class reasons. Thus the ground will be prepared for a much more dangerous explosion, and the people looking on the Allied governments as supporters of their oppressors will tend to fall under the influence of pro-German propaganda. Germany will make use of this to occupy Muscovite Russia as far as the Volga. The example of the Ukraine is only a case in point. According to the latest reports Bolshevism, weakening in the north, is spreading like wildfire in the south. The policy of the pro-German Skoropadsky government of liquidating all the conquests of the Revolution, taking the land back from the peasants and reducing labour to economic slavery has at last caused an explosion. It appears that whole districts are held by armed peasants who are murdering landlords, burning farms and ruining crops so that Germany shall not get anything out of the Ukraine. The rising in the Ukraine is not a national but a class rising and the same thing would happen in any district in Russia in which the Allies set up a government of Cadets and landlords, who should proceed to take the land away from the peasants and crush the Labour movement. The days of national coalition governments in Russia are gone, and the capitalist lion can no longer lie down with the proletariat lamb except under one condition – that the lamb is inside ... Those who touch the social reforms of the Russian Revolution are only adding fuel to the Bolshevik flame which, though driven underground will burst out with even more destructive violence later.

Manchester Guardian, *8 July 1918*
'How to Help Russia: Official Soviet View'
Moscow, 20 June 1918

With the object of finding out what form of assistance can be rendered to Russia in her present state I obtained an interview with one of the People's Commissioners [People's Commissars][46] who gave me the view held in official quarters.

> The only practical help the Allies can give is economic and should aim at re-establishing the industrial and agricultural productivity of the country. We know the difficulties of the Allies in respect to tonnage and we cannot expect shipments of food to the starving northern districts, but we expect from them shipments of agricultural machinery, apparatus for repairing our railways, locomotives, waggons, and technical experts to direct our industrial reorganisation. If we can have these things and if the Allies will secure us from danger from the east we shall be able to tide over the next two months till the harvest.
>
> The Soviet government is ready to give compensation for these services by the export of certain raw materials and certain public concessions under specified conditions. We have already made an offer to Germany to treat with us, and to America through Colonel Robins, who is now on his way home. We have not yet made the offer to England simply because we do not feel assured that the words of Mr Lockhart to us represent the views of the British government, or are only his own views.
>
> Nevertheless I may add that the conditions offered to England will not differ in principle from those offered to Germany and the United States. It is necessary, however, to emphasise that we shall in no circumstances allow the workers and peasants of Russia to be made cannon fodder for the Allies, and the first practical step the Allies must take if they wish to help us is recognition of the Soviet government.

The above is the view held in official quarters. My own impression is that if the Allies intend to act they have, as often before in this war, decided too late. The recognition of the Soviet government and the offering of economic assistance two months ago, before the counter-revolutionary *coup d'etat* in the Ukraine and the Don, would have altered the whole political outlook here. At that time the Soviet government had power to unite Great Russia, the Don, North Caucasus and the Asiatic territories in one large neutral territory which, with skilful handling by Allied diplomacy could have been made the barrier against German aggression in Asia. Now the process of disruption has gone very far, and if Muscovy falls under German influence there still remains Siberia, the Urals, and the territories east of the Volga to act as a base for the regeneration of Russia under the banner of the Peasants' and Workers' Government. But here the Czecho-Slovaks are creating indescribable havoc on the railways.

It is my conviction that no greater service could be done to Russia than that the Allies should offer to mediate between the Soviet government and the Czecho-Slovaks with a view to the speedy removal of the latter to France, where they can be much more useful. The Soviet government still demand their disarming, but I have reason to think that a compromise might be obtained under guarantees from the Allies that the Czecho-Slovaks cease interference in the internal affairs of Russia. Thus the first practical help the Allies can afford is to inform all military forces which have raised rebellion against the Soviet government that they cannot count on their support, either material or moral.

I still believe the Soviet government is sufficiently strong to organise Russia, at any rate that part east of the Volga, if given economic assistance, as suggested in the above interview. The only substitute for the Soviet government is foreign occupation, and in order to effect this the Allies must rely on the native Russian bourgeoisie, who require their pound of flesh, namely the liquidation of the land and labour reforms won by the Revolution ... Moreover let the Allies not imagine that the Russian bourgeoisie is ready to fly into their arms. An article by Peter Riss, the well-known Cadet publicist, in yesterday's *Russkoye Slovo* shows too well the new orientation of this class of Russian society. Beginning by recognising the incapacity of Russia to fight in her present condition, he writes:

> We must also abandon blind faith in a peace conference, where we may look for help from England, France and America. There is no more dangerous illusion than the belief that the politics of these countries are swayed by altruism. England and France at the peace conference will consider their own interests ... It remains for us to keep neutral and then, in the limits of

our neutrality, we can enter the peaceful struggle for improving the conditions of the Brest-Litovsk Treaty.

It appears that the lesson of the Ukraine Cadets is being learned by their Moscow colleagues.

Moscow, 29 June 1918 [Stopped by the British Censor]

I hear that the Soviets of the northern provinces are in favour of the landing of Allied troops, providing there is no interference in the internal affairs of these provinces ... Economic ties with the West are strong in the North and the starving inhabitants of these regions are anxious to obtain food from the Allies. On the other hand, the way in which the Allied landing on Murman has been carried out threatens serious complications with the Soviet government.

In Petrograd, where recent elections to the Soviet have given an overwhelming victory to the Bolsheviks, showing that the latter's power is as strong as ever, there appears to be a determination to defend at all costs the neutrality of the territories of the Soviet Republic, and today news has arrived here that Soviet troops have been ordered from Petrograd to Murman.

The Allied governments appear singularly unfortunate in the methods they adopt in relation to Russia and, by their recent action they seem about to create for themselves another Salonika on the Murman.[47] If they had recognised the Soviet government in the spring, and had treated it with ordinary civility, they would be in a position now – with the sanction of the latter – to secure Murman from German aggression and would probably have obtained a dominant economic position in the north and centre of Russia. But now, by recognising the soviets only of the northern provinces they accelerate the process of partition of Russia into spheres of influence and throw Muscovite Russia into the sphere of Germany. Moreover, unless the Allied governments understand that their recognition of the northern Soviets must exclude all attempts to interfere in the internal affairs of the country and to find the so-called 'Real Russia' by overthrowing workers' soviets and by establishing the rule of landlords and the local bourgeoisie as the Germans and Czechs are doing, they will arouse fierce resentment against themselves. It appears that certain people in England are anxious to arouse a so-called 'healthy national feeling' in Russia. But anyone who has lived in Russia during these times knows that a healthy national feeling has been here all along. However it is a nationalism which insists that Russian land shall be given to the Russian peasants who work it, that Russian workmen shall be emancipated from exploitation by uncontrolled foreign capitalism, and that the territories of the Russian Federated Soviet Republic shall be freed from the Imperialist forces of Western and Central Europe which are wandering over its border.

Moscow, 3 July 1918 [Stopped by the British Censor]

... One must follow closely the shifting of parties that has gone on since the Brest-Litovsk Treaty. Last February I reported the fact that, judging from the resolutions of local soviets throughout the country, the urban proletariat were in the main against peace while the peasantry favoured it. The cause of this probably lay in the exhausted condition of the soldiers, who were mostly peasants, while the better-educated urban proletariat more accurately foresaw the probable effects of the Brest-Litovsk Treaty. Lenin, as a matter of fact, never regarded the peace as more than a respite in which to prepare for the next war, and if all the Allies had not hindered the Soviet government by financing rebellion against it, and if they had honestly supported its endeavours to reconstruct the country, Russia would now be in a position to avenge Brest-Litovsk. But even if the period of reconstruction has given no apparent results, Lenin probably feels justified in his insistence upon the signature of peace on the grounds that in these few months the peasant soldiers have gone back to their homes to find that the land is indeed theirs and therefore they now have something to fight for, which they never had under Kerensky. Indeed the signs are not wanting that the peasants and half-proletariat who live in the villages and work in the factories of North Russia are becoming thoroughly aroused against the German tyranny and are slowly drifting towards the idea of an open breach with the dictators of the Brest-Litovsk Treaty. That section of the Bolshevik Party which adopted the policy of no signature of the peace may therefore acquire strength in future if the Allies, by intervention, do not prevent this healthy, normal development.

Another sign of the times is the tremendous growth in the influence of the Left Socialist Revolutionary Party. In the Fifth All-Russia Congress of Soviets which opens today, the Bolsheviks have, according to the latest figures, only a small majority and the Left Socialist Revolutionaries have captured about 200 seats in the villages of Central Russia. It will be remembered that the Left Socialist Revolutionaries broke away from the Right Socialist Revolutionaries last autumn, recognised the programme of the October [November] Revolution, particularly insisting upon the confiscation of the great estates for the peasants, but broke with the Bolsheviks and left the Government on the grounds of the Brest-Litovsk Treaty. The tactic of this party is of war with all the Imperialist governments and under no circumstances to agree to compromise on vital questions of revolutionary principle ... In the Left Socialist Revolutionary Party we find that spirit of uncompromising rebellion against the foreign yoke that overthrew the armies of Napoleon in 1812, and today that rebellion will be raised against all who invade Russia, whether as unblushing counter-revolutionaries like the Germans in the Ukraine, or as lovers or so-called supporters of the so-called real, democratic Russia on the Murman coast or in Siberia. Therefore neither among the Bolsheviks, who represent the revolutionary urban proletariat and poorer peasantry, nor among the Left Socialist Revolutionaries who represent the half-proletariat and rather more well-to-do peasantry, can the Allies hope for any support ... The Allies, therefore, if they intervene, can only rely upon those elements which support the Right Socialist Revolutionary Party ... One is therefore tempted to ask what the Allies intend to do, where and when they decide to intervene, and whether they have any idea of how to deal with the internal social problem in Russia if they set out on their dangerous adventure. The Allies are sowing dragons' teeth in Eastern Europe, which will some day grow into bayonets which may be turned in the direction they least desire.

Moscow, 8 July 1918 [Stopped by the British Censor]

When the Left Socialist Revolutionaries temporarily left the All-Russia Congress of Soviets last Thursday it was generally understood that they meant this only as a protest against the policy of the Soviet government of not breaking with Germany and joining the Ukrainian rebellion. This was confirmed on the second day of the Congress when [they] returned and took part in the debate on the report of the Soviet Central Executive regarding the policy of the Government in the last three months. Nevertheless, even on the second day it was clear that the breach between the Left Socialist Revolutionaries and the Bolsheviks was widening every hour ... In matters concerning the foreign relations of the Soviet Republic, part of the Left Socialist Revolutionary leaders have fallen under the influence of certain terrorist groups. The tactics of the Socialist Revolutionaries, as a matter of fact, have always been distinguished by spasmodic outbursts of terrorism. The present condition of Russia crushed between two armed alliances, produces a feeling of hopelessness and despair which inevitably reacts upon certain unbalanced intellectual minds ... According to documents discovered at [their] premises and published by the Bolshevik press today, the terrorists decided on Friday to assassinate the German ambassador, seize the Government apparatus and denounce the Brest-Litovsk Treaty. On Saturday afternoon part of this programme was accomplished when Count Mirbach was assassinated and the post and telegraph offices were seized for a few hours. But on Sunday the Bolshevik garrison here, among whom the terrorists had acquired no influence, easily succeeded in liquidating the attempted *coup d'etat*. In general the attitude of the Bolshevik majority at the All-Russia Congress of Soviets, which controls the Government, may be seen in a statement issued by Lenin today in which, amongst other things, he states: 'The Revolution, with extraordinary consistency, brings to a logical end every one of its stages, mercilessly exposing the stupidity and criminality of those tactics which are unsuitable to the given moment.' The Bolsheviks, in fact, are standing upon the ground of revolutionary *realpolitik*. They see that the material forces are not at their disposal which would enable them to fight against the military power of the Central Empires with a few guerrilla bands armed with hand grenades, while the governments of Britain and France continue to finance counter-revolutionary organisations in their rear and occupy as much territory of the Republic as they are capable of. Lenin's great speech on Friday was entirely devoted to the need of realising what is and what is not practical for the Russian Revolution, surrounded by the whole world in arms against it. On the other hand, the tragedy of the Left Socialist Revolutionary Party – who apparently have not sufficient balance of mind to resist sacrificing themselves on the altar of terrorism – is much regretted by the Bolsheviks, for the two parties have worked together in more or less close union for many months. Now the Bolsheviks are quite alone, and upon them rests the superhuman task of bearing the cross of the Revolution against the armed camps of Europe until the democracies of other lands awake.

Moscow, 10 July 1918 [Stopped by the British Censor]

... After the liquidation of the attempted *coup d'etat* by the Left Socialist Revolutionaries last weekend Moscow resumed its normal life. Perfect order prevails in the city. The Soviet government's troops prevailed in the crisis with great cool. There were no excesses and civilians were treated with courtesy which exceeds anything known in the days of Tsarism ... Yesterday the All-Russia Congress of Soviets resumed its work ... An important debate took place during which it was shown that, although the condition of central Russia is very serious, a harvest is expected which ought soon to relieve the situation.

Letter to *Anna Maria Philips*
Moscow, 18 July 1918

I have another chance of getting a letter to you so I take the opportunity of letting you know that I am alive and well. I have, as you see, shifted my room and gone to a smaller and cheaper but in many ways more convenient one in the house of Count Sergei Tolstoy, the eldest son of Leo Tolstoy. They are very nice people but rather reactionary. Curiously enough, on account of my good relations with the Bolsheviks they expect me to protect them from the latter ... So far I have enough money but when it gives out I don't know how I shall get any more because telegraphic communication with England is cut off on account of the British occupation of the Murman. The Allies apparently want to complete the iron circle which is enclosing this unhappy land and reduce it to a state of misery indescribable in the history of man. When I am at my last gasp and can do no more work for the *Manchester Guardian* I shall enter the Red Army as a volunteer and be killed fighting for the Revolution.[48]

We had most exciting times here when the German Ambassador was assassinated. The Embassy is near here and I heard the explosion. Now the Bolsheviks seem to have suppressed the terrorists and remain as before the only really effective power in the country. They cannot be overthrown except by foreign bayonets, and that is why the bourgeoisie are longing for the Germans or the Allies to invade Russia. Lenin's policy on the other hand is very able. He plays off one of the great Alliances against the other, knowing their hatred for each other and the fact that they are slowly bleeding each other to death. His whole policy rests on the assumption that the war will continue for many years and end in the complete collapse of the present economic and social system in Europe. I think he is probably right. At any rate he is the most courageous statesman in Europe at present and history will, I believe, put him as one of the greatest brains of the period.

CHAPTER 9

The Allied Intervention, August 1918

Price began work at the Soviet Foreign Office on 1 August 1918 and the Allied landing at Archangel took place next day. His response to it is not to be found in any attempt to get a message to the Manchester Guardian. *As he wrote in his* Reminiscences:

> *I sat down during the second week of August and wrote off as fast as my pen would permit me a pamphlet entitled 'The Truth About the Allied Intervention in Russia' and signed my name to it so that every Englishman should know that there was at least one of his countrymen who would not be silent.*

Some of the first work he did was probably the translation of pamphlets written by Lenin and Tchicherin, appealing to the Allied soldiers not to fight but to go home. He soon began writing similar material himself for Sovprop, the Department of International Propaganda. In September he helped to form what came to be known as the Group of English-Speaking Communists, that is to say English-speaking sympathisers, mainly former refugees returned from America, who were now in Moscow. He contributed to, and perhaps for a while edited, an English-language weekly newspaper, The Call, *which was produced for the same purpose and distributed in the same way as the pamphlets and leaflets.*

At the same time he continued to go through the motions of a foreign correspondent. He read the papers, attended meetings, whether factory meetings or meetings of the Central Executive Committee of the Soviet, interviewed politicians and wrote articles which he tried to send off by wireless in the course of the autumn. By then an attempt had been made on Lenin's life; the Chief of Police, Uritsky, had been assassinated; the British naval attaché Captain Cromie had been killed defending the former British Embassy buildings in Petrograd against intruders, Lockhart was shut up in the Kremlin, the Red Terror was in full force, and Britain had threatened to get Russia declared outlaw by the entire international community. On 13 September Price hopefully dispatched three articles: one mainly about the food and raw materials situation in Russia; one about counter-revolutionary plots (he meant the Red Terror although he did not use the words); and one about the civil war. As he was writing the Czechs were advancing along the Trans-Siberian Railway, the Japanese and Americans were in Siberia, Denikin with his Volunteer Army controlled a considerable amount of territory between the Black

Sea and the Caspian, the Don Cossacks had captured Kazan and Samara and the other Czech force was advancing northwards up the Volga. At the end of August only a narrow strip of land lay between them all. Price later recalled that he could hardly bring himself to look at the maps displayed in Mocow shop windows showing the situation on all the fronts for fear he would lose hope; also how keenly he felt a sense of isolation.

But he had thrown in his lot with the Soviet government and he decided, as he put it, to sink or swim with it. He was appalled by the Red Terror and said so with his voice, but he defended it with his pen.[49] He continued to try to send dispatches well into October, the last of which appears on p. 150. Later he was to write of this particular one that 'while what I wrote somewhat exaggerated the situation in Moscow, it was a healthy antidote to the kind of rubbish that was being circulated throughout the world about conditions in Russia at that time'.[50]

The high point of his life during these months was his interview with Lenin, who attached great importance to propaganda and took a personal interest in everything that was being published under that heading.

It is not certain exactly when this meeting took place. Price put it down in his 1918 diary for 1 November but with a question mark after it, as if he had written it down later, from memory. In his books and in articles which he wrote for the fiftieth anniversary of the Revolution he put it in August or early September. But the conversation he recorded would have made no sense contextually in August, and in early September Lenin was seriously ill and partially paralysed after the attempt on his life. Price records that Lenin assured him that he was recovering well. But as to content, all the accounts of the interview agree. It is the last one that he wrote which appears below.

The fact that Lenin referred to the slow progress of the social revolution in Europe and the danger that Allied troops might soon be released from other fronts to be thrown against Russia, suggests that the meeting did in fact take place more or less when Price entered it in his diary. The war was not quite over; the German 'revolution' had not quite begun. He was present at the meeting of the Central Executive Committee at which the appointment of Prince Max as peacemaker Chancellor was announced.[51] He sat up all night translating the Soviet government's Note to President Wilson commenting on this development and pointing out that a general peace was precisely what they – the Russians – had proposed a year earlier. When the Kaiser abdicated and a Republic was proclaimed in Germany, Price was invited to the party at the Kremlin at which the event was celebrated with dancing and coffee, nothing stronger being available. Privately he thought the celebration was premature, and he noted that Lenin did not attend the party.

The Allied troops were withdrawn from North Russia little over a year later, to avoid a second winter. Nothing had been achieved, either militarily or politically, by the intervention unless the aggravation of the *climate of mutual suspicion and hostility which already existed between Soviet Russia and the Western Allies, and which would culminate in the Cold War, can be called an achievement.*

Moscow, Undated* [Stopped by the British Censor]

During the last fortnight the food shortage in central Russia has considerably abated. Several trainloads of food have arrived in Moscow. The whole population of the city is carefully registered and put on a system of class rations, each grade receiving food according to the amount and character of public work performed. While underground speculation still continues among the more parasitical elements of society, it is clear that the nationalisation of all key industries has at last brought production under State control and cut the ground from under the feet of profiteers.

Trade unions and shop stewards' committees of the Moscow and Petrograd industrial areas have for some time now been organising food expeditions to the provinces. Each industrial union takes a province and sends some of its workmen to conduct trainloads of manufactured goods to the peasants and to receive in return food for the working population of the towns. The peasants readily part with their produce under these conditions and this process of natural exchange has the effect of reducing the issue of fresh currency. The workmen's food expeditions are also organising so-called Committees of Poor Peasants in the villages, to requisition stocks from rural speculators.[52] Last week I was in a rural district of a neighbouring province and found that these committees are almost entirely controlling the peasant soviets and organising village schools where there had been none before, as well as lectures, reading rooms and public restaurants in provincial towns.

In some places I found interesting experiments in the creation of agricultural communes among urban workmen recently returned to the villages. Land is worked in common and produce divided equally among the members. The Soviet government gives loans to them for the development of scientific agriculture through the utilisation of modern machinery and manures, but the scarcity of the latter greatly hinders successful development. Most of these communes are founded on the domains of the now dispossessed landlords.

---

* From the nature of its contents, it seems likely that this dispatch was sent before the Allied invasion on 2 August.

THE TRUTH ABOUT THE ALLIED INTERVENTION IN RUSSIA
BY
M. PHILIPS PRICE
CORRESPONDENT IN RUSSIA OF THE
MANCHESTER GUARDIAN
MOSCOW, AUGUST 1918

One of the most deadly weapons wielded by the ruling classes of all countries is their power to censor the press; for thereby they are able to create under the pretext of military necessity an artificial public opinion with the object of hiding their fell designs. Never was this fact more clearly demonstrated than at the present moment; never was it more obvious that the governments of the Central Powers and the Allies, in order to suppress the workers' and peasants' Revolution in Russia, must hide from their own people the truth about this Revolution, must represent it to the proletariat of the West as the work of a gang of robbers. Just as a criminal or weak-minded man, after having committed some offence against public law, tries to shift the blame on to any person he finds handy, so the ruling classes of Europe, after butchering their people in a cruel four-year war, now in terror before the judgement of humanity and the inner prickings of conscience try to create for themselves pleasant illusions and find convenient scapegoats on which to vent their wrath.

One cannot be surprised, of course, that the governments of England, France and Germany should through the official agencies and their press censors endeavour to blacken the work of the Russian Revolution. Living here in the besieged castle of the Russian Workers' and Peasants' Soviets, surrounded by the armed hosts of the European warlords, I am in a position to see more clearly than those outside this iron ring the power possessed by the ruling classes, whose fell designs include the strangling of this youngest of the governments of the toiling masses. For this is what I have to face day after day. Telegrams to my newspaper are suppressed or if passed by the British censor are decapitated, so that no sense is left in them; postal communication is severed; provocative rumours about what is happening here are spread in London and Paris, and my attempts to deny them are frustrated. All the technical apparatus of the capitalist states of Western Europe is set in motion against those whose duty it is to tell the truth about the Russian Revolution and to convey to the West the cry of the Russian people for help. But let not the governments of England and France forget that 'foul deeds will rise, though all the earth o'erwhelm them to men's eyes'. Those who suppress the truth create forces that bring the truth into the light of day, but by methods which they least expect.

Knowing therefore the love of freedom and the sense of justice of the British working man, I am in these few lines appealing to him to understand the facts that I have here set before me – facts which I have obtained after four years' residence in Russia. When he has read them he will be able to judge for himself whether the policy of the British government towards the Russian Revolution is a policy of which he approves.

I begin from the beginning. The Russian Revolution in March 1917 was nothing less than the first practical step taken by the working classes of a European country to protest against the indefinite dragging on of the war for objects hidden in the Chancelleries of secret European diplomacy. There is no better proof of this than in the fact that the first act of the first All-Russia Soviet conference in May 1917 was an appeal to the workers of the world to lay down their arms and make peace with each other over the heads of their governments. The Russian workers and peasants were brought to this conviction by their intense sufferings during the previous two-and-a-half years. The war in fact had brought their economically poorly developed country to ruin, the industries were at a standstill, famine was raging in the towns and the villages were filled with maimed soldiers. Long before the March Revolution one could see that the Russian army was no longer capable of the offensive, even if it had the inspiration to effect one, and meanwhile all the towns in the interior of Russia were, even in 1916, filled with deserters.

The next fact I wish to set forth is that the governments of the Allies, by refusing to allow the Stockholm Conference to take place in the autumn of 1917, destroyed the belief of the Russian peasants and workers in the sincerity of the Allied cause, weakened the hands of those in Germany who were working for peace, played into the hands of the Prussian war party and made the calamitous Brest-Litovsk peace inevitable.

The 'Bolshevik' Revolution of October 1917 was the second protest of the Russian workers and peasants against the continuation of a war which they had not the physical strength to carry on, nor the moral justification to support. It seemed better for them to risk the dangers of making peace single-handed with the Prussian warlords than be ruined by being dragged along in a war for objects which were disclosed in the secret treaties between the Allies. The October Revolution differed from the March one. For the first time in the history of the world a people realised that only by radically altering the whole form of human government was it possible to put down war. Declining all ideas of a compromise peace between the rulers of the countries at war (a solution which would only have led to another war) the workers and peasants of Russia dared to create a government which, by putting an end to the political and

economic power of landlords and financial syndicates, definitely
rooted out that poison in human society which alone is the cause
of war. For the Russian people under Tsarism saw more clearly
perhaps than the workers of England and Germany that the
competition between the great banking and industrial trusts of
London, Paris, Berlin and New York for spheres of influence,
mining, and railway concessions in undeveloped countries like
their own, was the root cause of all modern wars and that therefore,
to put an end to war, the social and political system which breeds
the exploiting trust must be once and for all overthrown.

From this it follows that the workers and peasants of Russia, after
the October Revolution, were forced to undertake a task which the
weak Kerensky government (controlled, as it was, mainly by
landlords and bankers) could not even attempt to solve, namely
to take directly under its authority the principle means of production,
distribution and exchange. For this reason the railways, waterways
and mines were declared State property and the banks taken under
Government control. But Russia was bankrupt. Exhausted by the
cruel war through which Tsarism had dragged her for three tortuous
years, her economic power was completely broken down. Food and
the raw materials of industry in the country were reduced to a
minimum and the land flooded with valueless paper money. To
repay the bankers of London and Paris the war debts of Tsarism,
the Russian workers and peasants would have to export annually
for many years to come, in gold or raw material, a sum not less
than one milliard roubles (30,000,000 pounds sterling) without
obtaining any return. To bear this burden in addition to others
brought about by the ruin of the industries, the collapse of the
railways and famine, was impossible without reducing the people
to slavery. The Russian workers and peasants therefore could no
longer admit the principle that they should pay tribute to foreign
bankers for the doubtful honour of serving as their cannon fodder.
So the repudiation of the debts of Tsarism and the nationalisation
of all the natural resources of the Russian Republic to serve the
interests of the people was the first and most essential of the
principles of the October Revolution. But no sooner was this done
than the governments of England and France began to plot for the
overthrow of the Russian Soviet government. In November 1917
the French government paid a large sum of money to the Ukrainian
Rada in order that it should raise rebellion against the workers' and
peasants' government. On the Don, General Kaledin received
arms and ammunition from the Allied military missions, in order
that his Cossacks should join in the attack. But the peasants of the
Ukraine and labouring Cossacks refused to be the tool of the Paris
and London Stock Exchanges, threw off the yoke of the Rada and
of General Kaledin and created their own revolutionary soviets in

federal union with the Soviet government of Great Russia. Then followed the tragi-comedy of Kiev, when the Ukrainian Rada, which had been bought by Allied gold, finding itself threatened by its indignant revolutionary peasantry, sold itself to the German warlords and invited the armed forces of the Central Powers to protect its class interests.

Foiled in their attempts to use the Ukrainian Rada, the Allied governments began to spread rumours that the leaders of the Russian workers' and peasants' government were agents of Germany and had betrayed the working classes of England and France because they had brought Russia out of the war. Against these slanders may be set the following facts. The necessity for Russia to obtain peace was dictated firstly by the impossibility of undertaking the work of social reconstruction at home, if a foreign war was draining the country of its material resources; and secondly by the desire of the workers and peasants of Russia to maintain a neutral position between the armed camps of Europe, and to show to the workers of other lands that they had no partiality to any of the warring governments. The best proof that the Soviet government was sincere in its desire to make peace not with the German government but with the German people, was seen in the course of the Brest-Litovsk negotiations. The Soviet government not only showed no desire to bring the negotiations to a speedy conclusion but did everything possible to cause them to drag on indefinitely, so as to expose to the German people the rapacity and cynicism of the German government. By these tactics they were largely responsible for the great strike in Germany during January.

This was the first real protest of the German people against the war and the policy of their government, and it was brought about by the tactics of the leaders of the Russian Revolution. Contrast this with the tactics of the Allied governments who, in spite of their loud assertions that by armed force alone can Prussian militarism be crushed have, after four years battering away at the Western front at the cost of thousands of the noblest lives, failed to call forth a single demonstration in Germany against the war. Trotsky succeeded in the Council Chambers of Brest-Litovsk in creating that spirit of rebellion among the German people which all the heavy guns and armoured tanks of Field Marshal Haig had failed to create in the course of the whole campaign. But the strike in Germany failed and the German government was left free to crush the Russian Revolution. Why did the strike fail?

Because Hindenburg and the Prussian Junkers were able to appeal to the more uneducated and less class-conscious among the German people to say to them 'Don't withdraw your support from us, because if you do, the Allied governments will ruin Germany and reduce you to slavery'. They were able to point to the secret treaties, published by the Soviet government, which showed that the Allies had been fighting to annex Germany up to the left bank of the Rhine, and that their governments had not repudiated these treaties. They were able to point to the fact that although the workers' and peasants' government of Russia had invited the Allies to take part in the Brest-Litovsk negotiations, had waited in fact a fortnight for them to make up their minds, the Allied governments had refused. Thus the Prussian warlords were able to tell their people that the Allies would not hear of peace and that therefore a strike at this time would be treachery to their country. It was only when the Soviet government saw that the Russian Revolution was deserted by the Allied democracies and betrayed by the German proletariat that they reluctantly were compelled to sign the cruel Brest-Litovsk peace. And the very fact that the Kaiser and his hirelings imposed such onerous conditions shows how much he feared the Russian Workers' and Peasants' Revolution and how abominable is the slander that the Bolsheviks are the agents of the German government. It was not the Russian peasants and workers that deserted the Allies but the Allies, yes, and I fear the working classes in the Allied countries, who deserted the Russian peasants and workers in the hour of their distress.

Now what was the policy of the Soviet government of Russia after the Brest-Litovsk Treaty? I submit that it was a policy which aimed at maintaining the strictest neutrality between the two great fighting camps. Yet the governments of Germany and the Allies did everything to make the maintenance of neutrality impossible, because they looked upon the Russian workers and peasants either as objects for economic exploitation or as cannon fodder to be used by them. The Soviet government was forced to give up the Black Sea fleet to Germany (as a matter of fact a great part of the fleet was blown up to prevent it falling into German hands) and was forced to accept the principle of individual exchange of war prisoners, whereby hundreds of thousands of Russian workers and peasants were left to work in Germany in slavery under the Kaiser. And why had the ultimatums which were showered upon the Soviet government from Berlin to be accepted? They had to be accepted because the Russsian army had been ruined. Why was it ruined? Because the Allies had tried all through the spring and summer of 1917 to force the Russian workers and peasants to fight for the objects which were disclosed by the Bolsheviks in the secret treaties. Whenever the Russian people, either through the Soviet or through the more progressive members of the Provisional Government asked the Allies to define their war aims, they were met by platitudes about liberty and justice. Meanwhile the peasants and workers were starving and had no prospect before them but endless war for the undefined aims of foreign governments. Was it likely that a twelve million army could be kept together under those conditions? Was it possible for the Bolshevik government, deserted by the Allies, to do anything else but sign the Brest-Litovsk peace and bow to every ultimatum which the tyrants in Berlin chose to send them? The Allied governments all through last winter acted as if they feared the Soviet government of the Russian Workers and Peasants a great deal more than they feared the Imperialist government of Germany.

But in spite of its isolation the Soviet government in the spring of this year commenced a programme of social reconstruction. In order to succeed in this sphere it was necessary to receive help from economically more advanced countries. The railways were in a state of collapse; technical appliances were needed to repair the locomotives and waggons. The mines were flooded and broken down. Instructors and engineers were required to undertake the difficult task of restoring their working capacity. Agricultural machinery was required to help the peasant to till the soil which as a result of the war had in large areas fallen out of cultivation. The Soviet government asked the governments of Europe to help it in this great task. To each of the countries of the great alliances an offer was made to treat with Russia, to supply her with these material and technical needs, in return for which the Soviet government offered certain raw materials of export and certain railway and mining concessions. These concessions of course were to be kept under strict public control, so as to ensure that, while the foreign capitalists should have a fair return for their undertakings, the workers and peasants should not be subjected to the exploitation which they had experienced under Tsarism. The offer was made to Germany and negotiations proceeded all summer in Berlin.

It was also made to the United States through the medium of one of the most sympathetic representatives in Moscow, who personally took the proposals with him to America.[53] But what was the attitude of the official diplomatic representatives of the Allies? They buried themselves in the provincial town of Vologda, refused to come to Moscow and one of their number last April made a cynical statement to the press that the governments of the Allies could not recognise a government which was not either in fact or in law a representative of the 'true' Russia. More than this; the Allied ambassadors became in Vologda the centre of every counter-revolutionary intrigue in the country and when the Soviet government, seeing what was going on, courteously requested them to come to Moscow, the seat of the Government to which they were supposed to be accredited, otherwise it could not be held responsible for their safety, they left the territories of the Republic on the grounds that they had been insulted!! The Soviet government insisted in putting control on them, if they remained in Vologda, in order to prevent counter-revolutionary elements in the country from getting at them. To what extent this action was justified may be seen from the following facts. On the basis of documents discovered on the premises of the Czecho-Slovak National Council in Moscow in July, the fact was established that at the end of February this year an agreement was reached between certain British and French military agents in Russia and the Czecho-Slovak National Council. This Council had taken under its control the Czecho-Slovak prisoners and deserters from the Austrian army and had formed them into a separate legion to fight against Austria. This had already been done during Tsarism and after Brest-Litovsk the question was raised of sending them to the French front. To this the Soviet government agreed. But it appears that the British and French governments had other work for the Czecho-Slovak soldiers to perform, and were by no means anxious that they should go to France. For between March and May 1918 the French Consul in Moscow paid to two persons on the Czecho-Slovak National Council the sum of nine million roubles and the British Consul in Moscow paid 80,000 pounds to the same people. Directly after these payments the Czecho-Slovak forces, which were scattered all along the Siberian and Eastern railways, rose in rebellion, occupied most important strategic posts in East Russia, thus cutting off central and northern Russia from the corn producing districts and condemning the workers and peasants of Muscovy to famine and the industries to destruction. The legend circulated in Western Europe that the Soviet government was preparing to hand the Czecho-Slovaks to the Austrian government is false, for the former had only too readily accepted the proposal the Czecho-Slovaks themselves made, before the interference by the Allied governments, that they should be sent to France.

But even after the seizure of the Siberian railway and the opening of the road to Vladivostock the commanders of the Czecho-Slovaks not only made no attempt to move their troops out of Russia, but began to advance west towards Moscow, clearly showing they were carrying out the pre-arranged plan for which they had received these payments.

At every town where they arrived they united with counter-revolutionary forces organised by the local landlords and bosses, and began to break up the soviets, shoot the leading revolutionary leaders and re-establish a military dictatorship of the propertied classes. Up to this time every counter-revolutionary rebellion which had been raised against the Soviet government had been suppressed by the Red Army, thus showing that the Soviet government had sufficient authority and support among the massses to put it down. It was only when hired bands of foreign Imperialists raised rebellion and supported the local counter-revolutionary forces, which had been defeated in square fight, that the position of the Soviet government began to be in danger. Thus the Allied governments in East Russia, like the German government in the Ukraine, endeavoured by financing counter-revolution and anarchy to make the work of social reconstruction and the feeding of the starving people impossible for the Soviet government.

The governments of England and France, in order to recoup themselves for the losses of the London and Paris bankers incurred by the Russian Revolution, are now trying to overthrow the Soviet government and re-establish a government with the aid of armed hirelings, which will impose again the milliard tribute of the loans of Tsarism upon the backs of the Russian workers and peasants. They are also trying to force the Russian people to fight in the war against Germany against their will, to use them as cannon fodder, although one of the main motives of the Workers' and Peasants' Revolution was to free themselves from the war, which was ruining them and condemning them to starvation. To impose fresh tribute upon the Russian people, to force them to fight against their will, to still further increase their misery, indescribable as it is at present, that is the task which the British government asks the British soldier to perform when he fights on the Murman; that is the object for which the British munition worker is toiling when he makes shells which are to be fired upon his Russian comrades.

As one who has lived in Russia for four years, has seen the sufferings of her people and their heroic efforts to free themselves, I categorically assert that the anarchy and famine now raging in Russia is the deliberate work of the Imperialist governments of Europe, and in this respect the governments of the Allies and of Germany behave like vultures of the same brood. For what Germany has done in the Ukraine the Allied governments have done in Siberia and the territories east of the Volga.

And yet the British working man is told that in Russia there is chaos and anarchy and that the British government, out of sympathy for the Russian people, is sending expeditions to help them, and to bring a rule of law and order. Where is the law which finances rebellion against a government of the workers and poorest peasantry in order to force it to pay an intolerable tribute and reduce it to industrial slavery? Where is the order which brings war to a land that is already exhausted by the three years' slaughter of the European Imperial butchers? The Soviet government of Russia asked peace and the governments of England and France are trying to give it a sword. It asked for help in its work of social reconstruction and it has been given the serpent of anarchy. It is just because the workers and peasants of Russia are trying to establish new order in their country that the governments of Europe are trembling and are trying by their treacherous attacks on Russia to destroy this new order and in its place to establish the old. For if the Soviet government succeeds it will for ever put an end to exploitation by social parasites and will sweep away the profiteers that fatten out of war.

The 'financial capital' of London and Paris is trying to save the 'real' Russia but it is really forging for it new chains. By a Judas kiss it is trying to hide the shekels of silver for which it has sold the Russian people. But let the workers of England know the truth about this great crime; let them say to the British government 'Hands off! Let none dare to touch the Russian Revolution, the noblest product of these four years of blood and tears.'

I know how firm in the memory of British working men is the tradition of freedom with which they have for generations been associated. When the ruling classes of England acted as suppressors of movements for freedom in America, when they interfered to bolster up privilege and reaction on the continent of Europe, the British workers raised their voices in protest. At the end of the eighteenth century the landlords of England declined to treat with the ambassadors of the free French Republic and declared war upon a people who had cast off a feudal tyranny. Today the banking oligarchies in London try to strangle by isolation and spread of famine the great movement for freedom that had sprung up in Eastern Europe. They will not succeed now just as they did not succeed then, and the conquests of the Russian Revolution will endure as did the conquests of the French Revolution last century. But to bring this about the workers of England must know the truth and, knowing it, must dare to act.

Moscow, 13 September 1918 [Stopped by the British Censor]

While the agrarian problem is in the process of solution the Soviet government is undertaking a campaign against internal counter-revolutionary elements which are composed mainly of officers and servants of the old regime whose organisation would long ago have become extinct if they had not received continuous assistance from abroad. It is now established beyond doubt that White Guard officers and Right Socialist Revolutionaries have had dealings with counter-revolutionary objects, with agents of the British and French governments. Only last week Moscow was startled by a sensational story published by the Government Commission for the fight against counter-revolution, in which Mr Lockhart, the British unofficial agent, was implicated ... More serious, however, is an organisation which has been discovered for blowing up bridges and wrecking food trains in which, according to Zinoviev ... Allied

agents are also implicated.[54] The outcome of these plots has been
to increase measures of repression against the Russian bourgeoisie
and former officers. The principle of taking hostages has been
adopted and in most of the big towns a certain number of the
members of this class have been arrested as security against attempts
on the lives of revolutionary leaders. This action has also in part
been taken as a reply to the arrest of certain Bolshevist leaders by
the Czecho-Slovaks in the Volga territories. As for Allied subjects,
a few wealthy British and French subjects have been arrested on
suspicion of financing counter-revolution and also as hostages for
the safety of Russian subjects in England and France. As soon as
the latter, together with Russian subjects in the Allied armies, are
released, the British and French subjects here will be allowed to
leave Russia.

Moscow, 19 October 1918 [Stopped by the British Censor]

After reading the English papers which have arrived here, I am at
a loss to decide whether the persons giving information on Russia
are deliberately fabricating news for political ends or whether they
are merely the victims of chronic nervous breakdowns. I therefore
feel it to be my duty to communicate a few facts about conditions
prevailing here.

It is safe to say that never since the commencement of the war
has there been more order and tranquillity in Moscow and Petrograd
than at present. Everyone is working in some public department
either in the new Red Army or in one of the numerous economic
councils which are everywhere growing up and transforming the
former anarchical system of speculation and private profiteering
into one in which production and distribution are organised on a
public basis in the interest of the working class population. One
no longer hears shooting in the streets at night; there are no more
wastrels walking about the streets with rifles and beggars have
almost disappeared. Not only is there no unemployment but there
is a shortage of labour, especially of skilled workmen. Last month
only eight to ten waggons of food used to arrive in Moscow each
day; now we get never less than a hundred and sometimes three
hundred waggons of flour alone each day. Food distribution is
carefully worked out. The whole population is classified and receives
rations according to the amount and intensity of work performed.
Everyone is guaranteed with a minimum and former propertied
classes can receive the same food ration and pay as working classes
if they agree to work or enter public service. The whole economic
life of the country is controlled by a powerful body called the

Supreme Council of Public Economy. An American businessman who arrived here recently from a tour in the provinces has described it as a more publicly useful and efficient body than any of the great capitalist trusts in America. It is divided into departments headed by a commissioner appointed by the Central Soviet Executive. Each department controls a public service like rail transport, water transport, nationalised iron, coal, cotton, leather or oil industries, also food distribution and State finance.

In the sphere of public education a new constructive programme is being introduced. Primary schools opened for the winter season last week. Pupils are taught to introduce discipline into schools themselves without its being imposed from above. The whole theory of children's education is that the State is the property of those who work by muscle and brain and only they have the right to citizenship. Theatres are in full swing and crowded. The principal theatres are nationalised and the price of seats lowered to give equal access to all. Each sort of drama and school of art is given its day from classical to modernist. Occasionally there are incongruities. For instance last week I witnessed Lohengrin staged with post-Impressionist scenery.

As regards the Red Terror the real facts are that no one is in danger of political arrest unless he is under suspicion of being connected with counter-revolutionary work. The persons executed have all been convicted of conspiracy against the Revolution: as provocative agents of the old regime, officials misappropriating State funds, or of breaking revolutionary discipline in the Red Army.

In rural districts too, exemplary revolutionary order is being introduced. A large percentage of the urban proletariat from the Petrograd and Moscow industrial areas have gone to the villages and are uniting with poorer elements of the peasantry to form so-called Poor Peasants' Committees. The latter are largely controlling rural soviets carrying out the equitable distribution of land and food requisitions. Each peasant is allowed his share of the harvest for his family and the rest is requisitioned and sent to urban centres to form large grain reserves. Peasants are paid at fixed prices, half in money and half in manufactured goods. It is noteworthy that in the Ukraine the economic process is reversed. There speculation is rampant. Landlords and the bourgeoisie are ruling with the aid of foreign bayonets and the peasants are all the time in armed revolt. More and more land is going out of cultivation and the Don coal basin, which before the German invasion came produced coal at the rate of 60 per cent of production before the war now turns out only at the rate of 20 per cent. German garrisons are everywhere joining the revolted peasantry and in Kharkov recently the garrison arrested its officers, raised the red flag and elected a revolutionary soviet.

Meanwhile the number and strength of the Red Army is increasing every day and discipline is becoming very severe. Trotsky makes periodical journeys to different fronts accompanied by his Supreme Military Council. I may here state that strict orders have been issued to the commanders on the northern fronts that all common soldiers from the ranks of the Allied armies who are taken prisoner are to be well treated. Recently a number were brought to Vologda, where they are now comfortably housed. The situation in Germany is watched here with intense interest and enthusiasm. Lenin in his recent letter to the All-Russia Central Soviet Executive stated that the Russian proletariat must be prepared to help the German proletariat in its struggle against its own and foreign imperialists. He foreshadowed large increases in the Red Army and the creation in central Russia of large grain reserves to help the German revolutionaries as soon as they take over the power in Germany. The contents of this letter have been suppressed by the censor in Germany and recently we hear that the frontier at Orsha has been closed. An article in the *Kreuz Zeitung*[55] stating that the fight with Bolshevism is a bridge across which the Allies and Germany can unite to protect their culture, is looked upon here as an attempt to create a twentieth century form of Holy Alliance.

> [Towards the end of his life Price was asked several times by the correspondents in London of Russian newspapers to write accounts for them of his interview with Lenin. As already stated, the substance of all of them is identical. What follows is part of a piece he wrote for *Izvestia* in April 1967. It is not known when or even whether it was published.]

Tchicherin arranged that I should see Lenin in his room in the Kremlin. It is the same room that one can now see and looks very much as it was then. After my enquiries about his health, we talked about the general situation and I soon began to notice a cautious realism in his conversation, which I had seen in his speeches ever since the Bolsheviks had come into power. It was quite clear to me from this conversation with him, that he did not share the prevailing optimism since the Red Army had recaptured Kazan and had beaten back the Czecho-Slovak troops on the Volga. Nor had he any illusions about the imminence of world revolution. The previous autumn it was he who had insisted on the seizure of power in spite of the opposition of some of his colleagues, but to hear him speak now, it seemed that he had come more and more to the opinion that many obstacles lay in the way of the Revolution and of any world movement which might support it. I had noticed this during his great fight in favour of accepting the German-dictated peace at Brest-Litovsk and later when he had criticised his own followers for being 'slaves to phrases' and impractical people. In answer to questions I put to him, he seemed to think that if the German Imperial system broke down in Central Europe, the Soviet Republic might be exposed to new and greater dangers. His eyes were clearly fixed on the shores of the Black Sea where he seemed clearly to discern Allied naval forces passing through an open Dardanelles and landing well-trained armies equipped with tanks on the coast of southern Russia. 'What can we put against this, if they really send them,' he said, 'and if the Allied soldiers really obey their rulers and march? And,' he added in a thoughtful vein, 'I fear that the social revolution in Central Europe is developing too slowly to provide us with any assistance from that quarter.'

When I first saw Lenin at the Peasant Congress in Petrograd in April of the previous year he had not impressed me greatly. He seemed to have an inelastic mind and was fanatically devoted to a fixed idea. That may have been true at the time, when the Russian revolutionary movement was emerging from underground and when ideological discipline was needed. But when I met him in the Kremlin some fifteen months later, he was becoming a world statesman. He had had to compromise and to force his followers to do likewise in order to save the Revolution in Russia. It was not what he wanted, but he had the wisdom to realise what was possible and what was not.

His whole life had been devoted to the idea of world revolution. It was a religion to him. He did not at first see that other countries had a different history and traditions to Russia, but when I met him he was clearly beginning to see this. If world revolution did not come now it would come some day, and meanwhile the Russian Revolution must be saved. This was how his mind seemed to be working. When I asked him if he thought he had convinced his followers of the need for this temporary compromise he smiled and said nothing. He was not going to give away his inmost thoughts to me. Yet I think he was glad to see me, especially as I was British, and he knew there were few sympathisers in Britain for his Revolution at that time. I suspected while I was with him that, with his realistic outlook, he did not expect changes to come in Britain in the same way as they came in Russia, but of course he would not say anything definite to me. I could see that his main interest now was to save the Russian Revolution. What happened in other countries was for the moment less important.

I left him feeling that, with the philosophy he had, he must have been not only a humble but a happy man. He was humble because as a good Marxist he felt that his personality did not count very much. There of course he was wrong. He mattered very much, not least to Russia. He was a happy man because he clearly enjoyed, in spite of its dangers, directing a great movement so long as fate allowed him to do so.

Epilogue

The Armistice with Germany was signed probably only days after Price's interview with Lenin, and the end of the war clearly affected his position as a man and as a journalist. As already noted, he appeared to think that he could communicate a better account of the situation in Russia from Berlin than he could do from Moscow. He was also, of course, curious to see what was happening in Germany and whether there really had been a revolution. On 21 November he applied by radiotelegram to the Foreign Minister of the German Provisional Government for permission to visit Berlin and report on the situation there for the Manchester Guardian, and on 27 November permission arrived.

It is inconceivable that Price had made this application entirely in isolation, given that he had, for the past three-and-a-half months been in a way working for the Soviet government. Indeed, in an account of this period found among his private papers he wrote that it was Radek's idea that he should go. He certainly discussed the timing and method of his departure with Tchicherin and Radek. The mere fact that he continued to write propaganda material defending or describing the Soviet government from Berlin suggests that he continued to feel personally involved in its fate for a long time. He left Russia, as he wrote in his last book My Three Revolutions 'with a heavy heart. Russia had been my home for so long that I felt it had become part of me and I almost part of it.'

He arrived in Berlin in December 1918 and for the next five years wrote extensively about Germany for the Daily Herald and several of the British left-wing journals, for example Forward and Labour Monthly. On a brief visit to England in 1922 – his first for eight years – he actually did join the Communist Party of Great Britain, but his faith was already being eroded by the policies of the Communist International, and he left the Party in 1924. But that is another story. In Germany, he documented the Spartacist rising in Berlin in January 1919 which resulted in the deaths of Rosa Luxemburg and Karl Liebknecht;[56] the founding of the Weimar Republic, the effects of the Treaty of Versailles, the disarray of the newly-founded German Communist Party, the French Occupation of the Ruhr, and the rise of Hitler in Bavaria, to name only a few of the momentous events which he personally observed.

For the rest of his life he was never quite free, as author of 'The Truth About the Allied Intervention in Russia', of the imputation that he had *behaved treasonably. Several attempts were made to have him charged under the Defence of the Realm Act, but the Home Office legal advisers found that the Act had no extra-territorial application, and the offence – if such it was – had been committed on Russian soil. Nonetheless the British army on the Rhine arranged for the German police to arrest him in July 1919, and he spent ten days in the Moabit prison before it was admitted that there was nothing to charge him with.[57] But he remained an object of suspicion in British official circles.*

Back in Britain he contested Gloucester as a Labour candidate and lost, in the elections of 1922, 1923 and 1924. In 1935 he won the Forest of Dean – Dilke's old seat – and held it until he retired in 1959. During the Second World War he was suddenly seen as an authority on Russia, and in 1946 and 1959 revisited the country as Special Correspondent for the Guardian. *His intellectual honesty made him incapable of mindlessly accepting or attempting to defend everything that had happened in the intervening years, but he never ceased to try to understand and explain. Only a few weeks before he died (in 1973), he was asked to write a new preface for a Russian translation of his* Reminiscences of the Russian Revolution. *The translation was probably made but it was never published. His preface would have included the words:*

> *Naturally I see things more in perspective today [but] I do not in the least belittle what I saw and wrote then. I still regard the Russian Revolution as the most important thing that had happened at that period of time.*

Biographical Notes

ALEXEIV, Mikhail Vasil'evich (1857–1918)
A professional soldier, Alexeiv was a Corps Commander by 1912 and Chief of Staff at the Russian Army GHQ from August 1915 to March 1917. He was appointed Supreme Commander-in-Chief and adviser to the Provisional Government from March to May 1917. After the Bolshevik Revolution he fled to Novocherkassk and began to form the counter-revolutionary Volunteer Army in the spring of 1918. He was Supreme Commander in Denikin's *de facto* government.

AXELRODE, Pavel Borisovich (1850–1928)
A member of several revolutionary groups, Axelrode was for a while editor of the Marxist journal *Iskra*. In 1903 he took the Menshevik side when the Social Democrats split. He was a member of the Petrograd Soviet in 1917 and supported the Provisional Government. After the Bolshevik Revolution he emigrated and died in Berlin.

BUCHANAN, Sir George William, Baronet (1854–1924)
A career diplomat and a royalist, Buchanan was British Ambassador in Russia from 1910 to 1918. He attained a position of great influence with the Tsar and on at least one occasion tried to persuade him to think more constitutionally. Later he strongly advocated Allied intervention in Russia.

BURNS, John Elliott (1858–1943)
Burns, a radical trade union agitator, was one of the leaders of the London dock strike of 1889. He was also active as a Liberal in both local and national politics. As President of the Board of Trade in Asquith's government he resigned from the Cabinet in August 1914 in protest against Britain's entry into the war.

CARRUTHERS, Alexander Douglas Mitchell (1882–1962)
Explorer, naturalist, climatologist, author and map maker, Carruthers' main expeditions were in Syria, the Congo, Russian Turkestan, North-west Arabia, Mongolia and Central Asia.

CHERNOV, Viktor Mikhailovich (1873–1952)
A prominent Socialist Revolutionary theoretician, Chernov returned from political exile in 1917 to become Minister of Agriculture in the Provisional Government. He was elected Chairman of the short-lived Constituent Assembly but continued to play an active part in Socialist Revolutionary politics until he emigrated in 1920.

DAN, Fedor Il'ich (1871–1947)
Dan was a physician by profession. He joined the Social Democrats in 1894 and in 1903 aligned himself with the Mensheviks. He was a member of the Executive Committee of the Petrograd Soviet and of the Presidium of the Central Executive Committee at its first meeting, but he did not support the Bolsheviks. He went into exile in 1922 and published an anti-Soviet journal, *Novi Put*, the organ of Menshevik emigres in the USA.

DENIKIN, Anton Ivanovich (1872–1947)
A professional soldier, Denikin was Chief of Staff to the Supreme Commander-in-Chief for the first few months of the Provisional Government. He was involved in the attempted Kornilov *coup* and fled with Kornilov in December 1917 to take part in the creation of the Volunteer Army. After its final defeat in March 1920 he left Russia for Constantinople. He remained sympathetic to the Cadets. In 1941 he appealed to White emigres in France not to support Germany against Russia.

DORE, Harold (1878–1943)
Beginning in 1904 as a 'learner' with the *Manchester Guardian*, Dore became its highly-esteemed Lobby Correspondent in London in 1914.

DUTOV, Alexander Il'ich (1879–1921)
Elected chairman of the All-Russia Union of Cossack Hosts, in June 1917 Dutov then became head of the counter-revolutionary All-Russia Cossack Congress and was involved in the Kornilov *coup*. In September 1917 he was elected Ataman of the Orenburg Cossack Host and in 1918–19 commanded the detached Orenburg Army under Kolchak. At the end of the civil war he fled to China, where he was killed.

GOREMYKIN, Ivan Logginovich (1839–1917)
Minister of the Interior 1895–9, Council member 1899, Chairman of the Council of Ministers in 1906 and again from 1914 to 1916, Goremykin was hostile to the Duma, to the Progressive Bloc in the Duma, and to democratic reform of any kind.

GORKY, Maxim (1868–1936)
Best known as a writer, Gorky was also politically active, was involved in the strikes of 1905, imprisoned and then exiled. He lived in Italy until 1914. His newspaper *Novaya Zhizn* (*New Times*) supported the Revolution and he was the first President of the Soviet Writers' Union.

GUCHKOV, Alexander Ivanovich (1862–1936)
Member of a Moscow merchant family, Guchkov became leader of the Octobrists and an elected representative of trade and industrial interests in the State Council in May 1907. He was President of the Duma from March 1910 to March 1911, Chairman of the War Industries Committee from 1915 to 1917, and a member of the Progressive Bloc. He was Minister of War and the Navy in the first Provisional Government but emigrated to Berlin in 1918.

HIRST, Francis Wrigley (1872–1953)
Editor of *The Economist* (1907–1916) and of *Common Sense* (1916–1921), he subsequently wrote lives of Thomas Jefferson (1926), John Morley (1927) and Gladstone. He completed only the first volume of an autobiography, *In the Golden Days* (1947), and an account of him by his friends (*F. W. Hirst by his Friends* (Oxford 1958)) does not touch on political activities.

HORVATH, Dmitri Leonidovich (1858–1937)
After a distinguished record in railway building, Horvath became General Manager of the Chinese Eastern Railway in 1902 and virtual governor of the railway zone. He worked in collaboration with the Provisional Government in 1917 but became a focal point of White resistance in the east after the Bolshevik Revolution. He proclaimed himself Provisional Ruler of Russia and established himself in Vladivostock in August 1918. He continued to run the railway until, after Kolchak's death and the end of the civil war, the Chinese forced him to resign. He died in Peking, one of the leading White Russian exiles in the Far East.

KALEDIN, Alexei Maximovich (1861–1918)
A Cossack officer, Kaledin became Commander of the Russian 8th Army in 1916 and initially supported the Provisional Government. He was elected Ataman of the Don Cossacks and did not welcome the intrusion on his territory of the Tsarist Generals Alexeiv and Denikin when they arrived in the Don after the Bolshevik Revolution. When the Red Army began to recapture the Don area early in 1918 he resigned as Ataman and shot himself.

KAMKOV, Boris Davidovich (1885–1938)
Kamkov was an active Socialist Revolutionary from an early age, and returned from exile after the March Revolution. He was elected to the Central Executive Committee of the Soviet government after the Bolshevik Revolution. Like many other SRs, he opposed the Treaty of Brest-Litovsk and was involved in the attempted SR *coup* in July 1918. After three years in prison he remained in the Soviet Union working as a statistician for the rest of his life.

KERENSKY, Alexander Fedorovich (1891–1970)
A lawyer well-known for his work as a defender of socialists in political trials, Kerensky was a prominent member of the Trudoviks in the Duma between 1912 and 1917, when he joined the Socialist Revolutionaries. He became successively Minister of Justice, Minister for the Army and Navy and Minister President of the Provisional Government in the course of 1917. He escaped from the Winter Palace on the night the Bolsheviks assumed power and attempted to organise a counter-stroke with the aid of the Cossack commander Krasnov. After its failure he fled to the Don, then emigrated to France, and died in New York.

KORNILOV, Lavr Georgievich (1870–1918)
The son of a Cossack officer, Kornilov served in the Far East before being given command of a division of the 8th Army on the South Western front in August 1914. He acquired a reputation for daring to the point of insubordination. Kerensky appointed him Supreme Commander in July 1917. After the failure of his attempt to overthrow the Provisional Government in August 1917 he was imprisoned, but escaped to join Alexeiv and Kaledin in the Don. In the Volunteer Army's retreat in February 1918 he was killed at Ekaterinodar.

KRASNOV, Peter Nikolaevich (1869–1947)
As a professional soldier, Krasnov commanded successively a Cossack Brigade, a Division and a Cavalry Corps in the First World War. Appointed by Kerensky to defeat the Bolsheviks on the outskirts of Petrograd, he was taken prisoner, released, and fled to the Don where he was made Ataman of the Don Cossacks after the death of Kaledin. He accepted German support in the civil war and eventually emigrated to Germany. He continued his anti-Soviet activities during the Second World War, was captured by Soviet troops and hanged.

KRILENKO, Nikolai Vasil'evich (1885–1938)
As a very young and highly educated Social Democrat, Krilenko was active in Petrograd and Moscow during and after the 1905

Revolution. He was a member of the Bolshevik faction in the Duma in 1913, emigrated to Switzerland at the outbreak of war but returned in 1915, when he was arrested and sent into the army. In 1917 he was elected a delegate to the first All-Russia Congress of Soviets and later became a member of the first Council of People's Commissars. On 9 November 1917 he was appointed Supreme Commander-in-Chief. After Brest-Litovsk he worked in various Soviet judicial bodies, becoming People's Commissar of Justice in 1931. His many honours included the Order of Lenin.

LIEBKNECHT, Karl (1871–1919)
A Social Democrat member of the Reichstag from 1912 to 1916, Liebknecht was imprisoned for his opposition to the First World War. With Rosa Luxemburg he was a founder member of the German Communist Party and one of the leaders of the premature rising in Berlin in January 1919, in the course of which he was murdered.

LOCKHART, Sir Robert Hamilton Bruce (1887–1970)
A career diplomat, Lockhart was Acting Consul General in Moscow from 1912 to 1918, when he was appointed special British Agent in Petrograd, the British not having formally recognised the Soviet government. He sincerely tried to avert a war of intervention in the early months of 1918 but was briefly imprisoned in the Kremlin in September 1918. He left the foreign service in 1922 but was recalled in 1941 to become Director General of the Political Warfare Executive of the Political Intelligence Department of the Foreign Office.

LUXEMBURG, Rosa (1871–1919)
Born in Poland and, like Radek, active in the Polish revolutionary underground movement, Rosa Luxemburg became the outstanding German theorist of the Left. A friend of Karl Liebknecht, she was also imprisoned for her opposition to the war and like him, she was murdered during the abortive rising in Berlin in January 1919.

LVOV, Prince Georgi Evgen'evich (1861–1925)
A lawyer by education, Lvov was involved in *Zemstvo* activities from 1902. He joined the Cadets and was elected to the first Duma. He became Chairman of the All-Russia *Zemstvo* League and one of the leaders of *Zemgor*. A highly respected man, he was head of the first two Provisional Governments, but emigrated to France after the Bolshevik Revolution.

MARTOV, I (pseudonym) (1873–1923)
While still a student, Martov joined revolutionary circles and was exiled more than once. In 1901 he emigrated and became one of

the editors, with Lenin and Plekhanov, of the Marxist journal *Iskra*. At the Second Congress of the Social Democratic Party (1903) he voted with the Mensheviks on proposals for the reorganisation of the party. He returned to Russia to be a member of the Petrograd Soviet in 1905 but emigrated again in 1907 and took part in the Zimmerwald and Kienthal conferences. On his return in 1917 he was identified with the Left (or Zimmerwald) Mensheviks. He was elected a member of the Central Executive Committee of the Supreme Soviet in 1919 but emigrated again in 1920 and died in Berlin.

MILIUKOV, Pavel (1859–1943)
A historian turned politician, Miliukov was obliged to spend much of his early life in voluntary exile. In 1905 he was a founder member of the Constitutional Democratic Party (Cadets) and was elected to the Duma in 1907. He became unofficial leader of the Progressive Bloc in 1915 and appeared briefly to be the voice of reform. His term of office as Minister of Foreign Affairs in the Provisional Government was not a success and he eventually threw in his lot with the counter-revolution.

MILNER, Alfred, Viscount (1854–1925)
Having made his reputation as an administrator in Egypt, Milner was appointed Administrator of the Orange River Colony and the Transvaal during the Boer War. After leaving South Africa he became steadily more influential in public affairs in Britain. He was a member of Lloyd George's War Cabinet and, after the war, Secretary of State for the Colonies in the Coalition government until his retirement in 1921.

MORLEY, John, Viscount Morley of Blackburn (1838–1923)
After a distinguished career as a liberal journalist and biographer, including classic accounts of both Cobden and Gladstone, Morley turned to politics. His sympathy for the cause of Home Rule for Ireland led to his appointment by Gladstone as Chief Secretary for Ireland in 1885. In the Liberal government of 1905 he was made Secretary of State for India and although he went to the Lords in 1908 he remained in the Cabinet as Lord Privy Seal. He resigned in protest against Britain's entry into the war.

PAQUET, Alfons (1881–1944)
A liberal-minded German journalist, writer and poet, Paquet was sent to Russia as Press Attache when diplomatic relations were resumed after the Treaty of Brest-Litovsk. He published several books giving lively and sympathetic accounts of his experiences and his impressions of Russia after his return to Germany.

RADEK, Karl Bergardovich (1885–1939)
A member of the Polish and the German revolutionary underground movements before the First World War, Radek worked with both Rosa Luxemburg and Lenin in Switzerland. An extremely able writer and propagandist, he joined the Bolsheviks after his return to Russia in 1917 and was made Head of the Central European Department in the Ministry of Foreign Affairs and later of Sovprop, the Ministry's propaganda organisation. In December 1918 he arrived secretly in Berlin as a delegate to the Berlin Soviet and was present at the foundation meeting of the German Communist Party. He was arrested and spent nearly a year in the Moabit prison, where he conducted a kind of political *salon*. On his return to Russia he at first took a more realistic view of the prospects for world revolution than his colleagues in the Third International, but later conformed to the Party line. However he was no longer trusted, and became one of the victims of the treason trials in the 1930s.

RASPUTIN, Grigorii Efimovich (1864–1916)
Pretending to be a monk, Rasputin acquired a reputation as a prophet and holy man, was patronised by the Russian aristocracy and in 1907 invited to the palace. He persuaded Nicholas II and the Tsarina that he alone could save the life of their haemophiliac son and heir, and ensure divine support for the Tsar. He came to exert almost unlimited influence in court circles, and was murdered more to save the reputation of the monarchy than for any more altruistic reason.

REED, John (1886–1920)
Born in Oregon, Reed was already a much-travelled left-wing journalist before he arrived in Russia for the second time in September 1917. After the Bolshevik Revolution he returned to the USA in February 1919 and later the same year wrote his book, *Ten Days that Shook the World* in a matter of weeks. He was in Russia again in November 1919 and March 1920, representing the Communist Labor Party of America at the first and second meetings of the Third International. He contracted typhus and died in Moscow. His ashes are buried in the Kremlin Wall.

RHYS WILLIAMS, Albert (1883–1962)
An American Non-Conformist Minister with an interest in socialism, Rhys Williams happened to be in Europe in August 1914 and began to work as a journalist. He was in Russia from June 1917 until September 1918 and like John Reed wrote, for the Bureau of International Revolutionary Propaganda under Radek, material mainly for German consumption. After his return to America he

continued to speak out against the intervention. He visited Soviet Russia several times and wrote a number of books about Russia.

ROBINS, Raymond (1878–1951)
A lawyer and social worker by profession, Robins was appointed a member of the American Red Cross mission to Russia by President Wilson and was soon put in sole charge of it. He worked to promote recognition of the Soviet government and acted as an unofficial intermediary between it and the American government at a time when the American Ambassador had already aligned himself with the other Allied Ambassadors favouring a policy of intervention.

RODZIANKO, Mikhail Vladimirovich (1859–1924)
As Chairman of the Duma in 1917 Rodzianko played a key, if formal, role in the March Revolution. A landowner and leader of the Octobrist Party, he was nominated to the Council of State in 1906 and 1907, a member of the Duma from 1907 to 1917, Chairman of the Duma from 1911, and a member of the Progressive Bloc. He became Head of the Provisional Committee of the Duma during the period of the formation of the Provisional Government. Later he served with Denikin and in 1920 emigrated to Yugoslavia.

SCOTT, Charles Prestwich (1846–1932)
At the age of 25 Scott was offered a post on the *Manchester Guardian* on the strength of some essays he had written while still an undergraduate at Oxford. Within eleven months he had become its editor. He was also Liberal MP for the Leigh Division of Lancashire from 1895 to 1906, when he formed a lasting, but not uncritical, relationship with Lloyd George. He was permanently open to new ideas and moved steadily to the Left in politics. Although he worked behind the scenes for Liberal reunion in the 1920s he also urged the party to support the Labour governments of 1924 and 1929. He wrote many of the *Manchester Guardian*'s leading articles himself, and transformed it from a provincial paper to one of the most highly respected journals in the world.

SEMONOV, Grigorii Mikhailovich (1890–1946)
Appointed Commissar for Transbaikal by the Provisional Government in July 1917, Semonov led an unsuccessful revolt againt the Soviet government in November 1917, fled to Manchuria, then returned to Transbaikal after the Czechs began to take over the railway, and set up his own regime. After Kolchak's death he became effectively the leader of the counter-revolution in the Far East until driven out by the Red Army. He lived in Korea, Japan and North China, was captured by Soviet troops in Manchuria in 1945, and hanged.

SOBOLEV, Mikhail Nicolaevich (1869–?)
An academic economist, Sobelev was appointed Professor of
Political Economy and Statistics at the University of Tomsk in 1899
and at some later date to a Professorship at Kharkov. Price met
him somewhere on his travels in 1910–11 and kept in touch with
him. In 1915–16 Price became much indebted to Sobolev for
opportunities to study and for information and advice on material
for his articles for *The Economist*.

SOSKICE, David Vladimirovich (1866–1941)
A Socialist Revolutionary while still at school, Soskice graduated
in law despite police harassment but spent three years in various
prisons before leaving Russia in 1893 and settling in England in
1898. He joined the foreign organisation of the SRs in London and
worked with the Society of Friends of Russian Freedom and with
the British Parliamentary Russia Committee. He returned to Russia
in 1905 as correspondent for a succession of newspapers, and in
1917 for the *Manchester Guardian*. While in Russia he became
Kerensky's Secretary, fled with him, and was for a while an advocate
of the Allied intervention. He died in England.

STURMER, Boris Vladimirovich (1848–1917)
One of the most hated figures of Tsarist political circles, he became
a member of the State Council in 1904, Minister for Internal
Affairs in 1907, Chairman of the State Council and briefly Minister
for Foreign Affairs in November 1916. He was arrested by the
Provisional Government and died in prison.

SUKHANOV, N (pseudonym) (1882–1940)
In 1903 Sukhanov was a Socialist Revolutionary but from 1907
onwards he sided with the Mensheviks. As an economist and
publicist he contributed to the most reputable journals, trying to
combine Narodnik with Marxist philosophies. He became a
Menshevik Internationalist member of the Executive Committee
of the Petrograd Soviet in 1917. He continued to work for Soviet
economic institutions until 1931, when he was convicted for
belonging to an underground Menshevik organisation and died in
a concentration camp. His account of the Russian Revolution – one
of the most lively ever written and based entirely on his personal
experience – was published in England after his death. (See
Bibliography below.)

SUKHOMLINOV, Vladimir Alexandrovich (1848–1926)
After a career in the army, Sukhomlinov became Chief of the
General Staff in 1908 and Minister for War in 1909. He was
dismissed in 1915 when his incompetence in providing for the army
had become too flagrant to be ignored. He was arrested in March

1916 on charges coneected with the conviction for espionage of some of his associates. He was imprisoned but released on grounds of age in May 1918. He emigrated to Finland and died in Germany.

SVERDLOV, Yakov Mikhailovich (1885–1919)
A Bolshevik agitator and underground organiser, Sverdlov ran the Party Secretariat between the March and November Revolutions, and as a member of the Military Revolutionary Committee he was the main link between it and the Central Committee of the Party. He supported Lenin over the Treaty of Brest-Litovsk. He was responsible for setting up a system of provincial Secretariats to reinforce the apparatus of centralised Party control.

TCHICHERIN, Georgii Vasil'evich (1872–1936)
Born into a noble family with a tradition of diplomatic service, Tchicherin became an archivist in the Ministry for Foreign Affairs in 1896. He joined the Mensheviks after the party split in 1903. He was in England in August 1914 as Secretary of the Committee of Delegates of Socialist Groups in London. Strongly opposed to the war, he was imprisoned in Brixton jail in August 1917 for his activities in support of Russian political emigres threatened with deportation or conscription into the British army. Shortly after his release and return to Russia he was appointed Minister for Foreign Affairs by the Bolsheviks. He secured widespread recognition for the Soviet government in European conferences between 1921 and 1924. When Lenin died he lost his principal support and he resigned in 1927. Though without influence, he did not become one of Stalin's victims and he died in retirement.

TERESCHENKO, Mikhail Ivanovich (1886–1956)
Landowner and sugar manufacturer, Tereschenko was elected to the fourth Duma and became a member of the Progressive Bloc in 1915. He organised Red Cross Hospitals during the war and was Chairman of the Kiev Regional War Industries Committee. After the March Revolution he was briefly Minister of Finance in the Provisional Government, and from May to November Minister for Foreign Affairs. After the Bolshevik Revolution he was arrested, but escaped and died in Monaco.

TREPOV, Alexander Fedorovich (1862–1928)
After a career in state service: Senator in 1906, member of the Council of State in 1914, and of the Special Conference on Defence set up in August 1915 after a succession of defeats, Trepov went on to become Minister of Transport in 1916, in which year he was also briefly Chairman of the Council of Ministers. He emigrated after the Bolshevik Revolution.

TREVELYAN, Charles Philips, Third Baronet (1870–1958)
Trevelyan's father, Sir George Otto Trevelyan, was the historian of the American Revolutionary War as well as a distinguished radical Liberal politician. Charles Trevelyan entered Parliament as a Liberal in 1899. In 1908 he was made Parliamentary Secretary to the Board of Education. In 1914 he resigned in protest against Britain's entry into the war and was a founder member of the Union of Democratic Control. He was one of the small group of MPs who opposed the British intervention in Russia. After the war he joined the ILP. In the Labour governments of 1924 and 1929 he was President of the Board of Education but again resigned, this time because of cuts in proposed government expenditure on education. He lost his seat in 1931 and did not stand for Parliament again, but remained a force to be reckoned with on the Left of the Labour Party.

TSERETELI, Iraklii Georgievich (1881–1959)
A Georgian social democrat but not a nationalist, Tsereteli had already been in exile once before returning to lead the Social Democrat faction in the 1907 Duma. The whole faction was then exiled until the March Revolution. Tsereteli was Minister of Posts and Telegraphs in the first Coalition of the Provisional Government and chief spokesman of the Menshevik Defensists. He did not support the soviet principle of government, believing in co-operation between classes and parties, and retired from active politics in 1929. He died in New York.

ZINOVIEV, Grigorii Evseevich (1883–193?)
An active revolutionary since his schooldays, Zinoviev met Lenin in 1903 while a student at Berne University. He was a member of the Bolshevik Petrograd Committee of the Social Democrats from 1906 to 1908 and editor of two Bolshevik newspapers. He was arrested in 1908, released, emigrated, but remained co-editor of several Bolshevik publications. He worked closely with Lenin in exile, returned to Russia after the March Revolution and became co-editor of *Pravda*. He was President of the Third International in 1919 but expelled from the Politbureau in 1926. As a principal exponent of Leninism, he was arrested and tried in 1935. The exact date of his death is not known.

Notes and References

1. Price, M. Philips, *My Reminiscences of the Russian Revolution* (1921), p. 1.
2. The only letters from Price to members of his family which have survived were written to his aunt (his mother's sister) Anna Maria Philips, his brother Robin, and his uncle by marriage, Charles Lee Williams.
3. While he was MP for Chelsea Dilke had been named in a petition for divorce by the Liberal MP Donald Crawford. Technically acquitted, he then became the object of a smear campaign by the *Pall Mall Gazette*. In the hope of clearing his name he offered a retrial but it did not succeed in doing so. In the next General Election he lost his seat, but re-entered Parliament as MP for the Forest of Dean in 1902.
4. Price, M. Philips, *Siberia* (1912).
5. The Union of Democratic Control (UDC) was a pressure group set up in the first weeks of the war by a number of prominent people, including several MPs, who believed that the war was largely the result of secret diplomacy. Its objects were 'to secure control over their foreign policy by the British people and for the promotion of international understanding'.
6. Price, M. Philips, *Diplomatic History of the War* (1914).
7. The Defence of the Realm Act was passed on 7 August 1914. Supplementary Regulations were added to it at intervals throughout the war. The original objects of the Act were to prevent communication with, or assistance to, the enemy; to secure the safety of troops, ships and military installations; and to prevent any activity likely to cause disaffection or to prejudice His Majesty's relations with foreign powers. By the end of February 1917 there were 400 pages of consolidated Regulations and almost any area of public activity could be deemed to be covered by one or another of them. Several of them directly affected the press and were the ultimate sanction of the Official Press Bureau. The Act remained in force until 1920 and was not formally repealed until 1927.
8. Price, M. Philips, *War and Revolution in Asiatic Russia* (1918), author's preface.
9. Pares, Sir Bernard, *The Fall of the Russian Monarchy* (1939), p. 332.
10. What Price called the United Provincial Councils of Empire, which was also sometimes confusingly called the Civil Red Cross, was probably *Zemgor*: a union in more than name of the elected County Councils (*Zemstvo*s) and Town Councils (the Russian word for town being *gorod*). Formed in the first month of the war *Zemgor* effectively organised the food supply both for the army and for civilians in front

line areas and provided beds and medical facilities for the wounded in the rear. *Zemgor* also worked in close collaboration with the unofficial network of War Industry Committees set up by Alexander Guchkov, the head of the Russian Red Cross.

11. The Independent Labour Party (ILP) was founded in 1893 as a radical but not Marxist socialist party. It strongly opposed both the Boer War and the First World War. Many of its members were at different times also members of the official Labour Party. It had ceased to function as an independent party organisation before the Second World War.

12. Price did not identify this man. He was probably one of the Menshevik Duma deputies, and a Georgian, since Price's main political contacts in 1915–16 were with Georgians.

13. All manufacture and sale of alcohol throughout the Russian Empire was prohibited by an Imperial Decree of 4 September 1914.

14. The Holy Alliance was more a phrase than a reality, loosely employed to describe the informal association and repressive policies of the rulers of Russia, Prussia and Persia beween the end of the Napoleonic Wars and the year of revolutions in Europe, 1848.

15. Price, M. Philips, *War and Revolution in Asiatic Russia*.

16. Nothing that Price wrote was printed in the *Contemporary Review* between 1914 and 1918.

17. In the autumn of 1916 dissatisfaction with the conduct and progress of the war under Asquith as Prime Minister was vocal and widespread. Proposals for improving the direction of the war and the efficiency of the War Cabinet were rejected by Asquith in December 1916. He resigned as Prime Minister but remained Leader of the Liberal Party. He was succeeded by Lloyd George in what was perceived by some of those faithful to Asquith to have been a virtual *coup*.

18. Public Record Office. Foreign Office archives, FO 371.2998.

19. Public Record Office. Cabinet Minutes, CAB 232.4 and FO 371.2995.

20. The *Times* correspondent in Russia, Robert Wilton, gave most of the credit for the March Revolution to the Tsar, for having had the sense to abdicate. He was profoundly anti-Semitic and lost no opportunity to prefix the word 'Jew' to the name of any Socialist or otherwise to suggest that he was in some way un-Russian. During this period the leading articles in *The Times* harped on the danger to the Allies from 'extremists' with 'fanciful notions' of universal peace.

21. In June 1908 conflict between the Shah and the newly established Persian Parliament (Majlis) escalated into civil war. Early in 1909 Russian troops were stationed near Tabriz, ready to intervene on behalf of the Parliament if called upon, but they were not asked. In July 1909 a combined force of pro-Parliament (Nationalist) troops and Bakhtiari tribesmen from the north entered Teheran. The Shah fled and a new Majlis was opened by his son.

22. In January 1905 a demonstration in St Petersburg bearing a petition to the Tsar requesting basic civil liberties and reforms was fired upon by troops. Over 100 people were killed and several hundred wounded. Strikes and unrest on a great scale followed across the country and involving all classes. In St Petersburg the first Soviet (council) of Workers' Deputies, initially formed as a strike committee, was set up

with Trotsky in the chair. In October 1905 the Tsar issued a manifesto promising an elected legislature and other democratic measures. This had the effect of splitting many of the groups which had united in opposition to the Government. In December 1905 most of the members of the Petrograd Soviet were arrested. The 1905 Revolution did, however, have the effect of forcing the Tsar to summon the first Russian Parliament, or Duma.

23. Lockhart, Sir Robert Bruce, *The Two Revolutions* (1967), p. 89.

24. In the late spring of 1917 the Allies appealed to the Provisional Government urgently to open an offensive against the Central Powers. On 4 June Brusilov attacked the Austrians in Galicia with such success that the Germans were forced to mount a counter-offensive in which the Russian losses were colossal. When Romania came in to the war on the side of the Allies in August 1917 the Brusilov offensive no longer served any purpose and was abandoned. This costly and in the end pointless exercise was much resented.

25. Price did not know many people in Moscow at that time, and may have been acquainted with this family from a previous visit to Russia. On the other hand, many Moscow merchants had been actively involved in the Progressist group in the Duma, and he could have thought their views were worth seeking in any case. See Notes on Party Organisations above.

26. The 'Cave of Adullam' was the name given to a group of reactionary Whigs who joined the Tories in 1866 to defeat Gladstone's moderate Bill to enlarge the franchise. The comparison works only in terms of the tactics used by the Bolsheviks, not in terms of their objectives in this instance.

27. In May 1917 two peace initiatives in Europe more or less coincided. The Scandinavian Socialists proposed a conference at Stockholm for the Socialist parties of all the belligerents. At the same time the Petrograd Soviet wanted a discussion of its own peace formula. The conference never took place due in part to the sabotage of the Russian Charge d'Affaires in London, who succeeded in convincing the British government that the Provisional Government did not want it to take place. Tsereteli, at that time Minister of Posts in the Provisional Government, asked Price to send a telegram to Trevelyan denying that this was the case, but the telegram was held up in London by the Official Press Bureau until the conference had been abandoned.

28. Price, M. Philips, *My Reminiscences of the Russian Revolution* (1921)

29. Price gave up trying to report the war on Russia's Western Front because of the Russian censors, and encountered the same difficulty when he tried to write about the political situation in 1915. There are only two visible signs of their work among his surviving papers, but he constantly remarked in letters to his family that previous letters had not, apparently, got through to them at a time when he had not yet begun to attract the attention of the British censors. In the case of the words cut out in his letter to Trevelyan of 22 September 1917 it would appear that they had related to the Kornilov *coup*,

incidentally suggesting that the Provisional Government was censoring outgoing letters no less than the Tsar's government had done.

30. There is no evidence for this statement and it is a regrettable illustration of Price's resentment of Soskice's presence on what he had clearly come to regard as his territory. It was, however, true that after the Bolshevik Revolution the British succeeded in secretly getting control of several Russian banks, including the Bank of Siberia, partly to finance the Cossacks and the Volunteer Army and partly in the hope of pre-empting German control over raw materials and other resources in areas which were or might come under German control. But Soskice had arrived in London before any of this happened. See Kettle, Michael, *The Allies and the Russian Collapse* (1981), pp. 176–219 and 242–7.

31. See p. 66, *Manchester Guardian*, 27 November 1917: 'Equality for all and Cossack Privilege'.

32. See p. 63, *Manchester Guardian*, 28 November 1917: 'Asiatic Russia and the Revolution'.

33. The word 'Sart' has no ethnic meaning and properly employed serves only to distinguish merchants from nomads. It was used by Europeans out of ignorance. A Young Bukhariot movement had sprung up in the early years of the century, drawn from the better-educated and better-off families, with the object of trying to persuade the Emir of Bokhara to grant some measure of constitutional reform.

34. The first All-Russia Moslem Congress met in May 1917 and could not agree whether autonomy should take a political or a purely cultural form. A second Congress in July briefly toyed with Pan-Turanian ideas. A Commissariat for internal Moslem affairs was created in January 1918.

35. The Pan-Turanian movement originated with people of Turkic origin who remained in the Trans-Caucasus after the Mongols had retreated, and who felt that they had historical, cultural and linguistic links with Turkey. In this they were encouraged by some of the Young Turk leaders before the war.

36. What Price meant by 'foreign assistance' here, at this date, is not clear. He was probably aware that the British diplomatic and business communities in Russia were less than enthusiastic about the political situation, and he clearly had some idea that an attempt was being made to get control of some of the Russian banks (see his letter to Trevelyan of 22 September, p. 55, and note 29). But he cannot have been anticipating Allied military intervention at the time of writing (2 November 1917) as the Allies themselves did not begin to discuss such a possibility until after the November Revolution. He seems to have been prompted to write this largely by instinct.

37. A whole series of Inter-Allied conferences were due to be held in Paris from the end of November 1917. Former members of Kerensky's government had tried to get one of these conferences to discuss and formulate new and liberal war aims with a view to bringing the war to a speedy conclusion. Trotsky's proposal for a general peace was never discussed in Paris. The most that the Allies could agree on was that individual Ambassadors should let it be known to the Russians

that they were ready individually to discuss war aims. They therefore disappointed everybody. It is difficult, however, to see how Price managed to make a cause-and-effect connection here, since the Bolsheviks' decision to assume power at the Second All-Russia Congress of Soviets had been taken more than a month earlier.

38. On p.148 of his *Reminiscences*, and again on p.149, Price used the words 'On the following day November 10th' when he was clearly referring to two separate, successive days. It is almost impossible to check or correct this, as very few eyewitness observers at that time exactly corroborated one another. The calendar changes in 1918 created further confusion. The discrepancy does not, however, invalidate the account.

39. Public Record Office. CAB 286.24.43.

40. Charles Lee Williams, Price's uncle by marriage, lived in Tuffley, on the outskirts of Gloucester, and was known by his family as Tuffet of Tuffley. While Price was away he managed all his affairs in Gloucestershire.

41. At the Inter-Allied Conference in Paris which began on 30 November, Lloyd George originally put forward a proposal, on the advice of Sir George Buchanan, that in view of conditions in Russia the Allies 'should release Russia from the engagement entered into in the Pact of London not to make a separate peace, and that they should tell the Russian people that, realising the extent to which they are worn by the war and the effects of the disorganisation resulting from a great revolution, they would leave them to decide for themselves whether to obtain peace on Germany's terms or fight on with their Allies who were determined not to lay down their arms until they had obtained guarantees for the world's peace'. This was not, however, what either Kerenky's envoys or Trotsky had been been hoping to hear. (Lloyd George, *War Memoirs* (1936), pp. 2570–71.)

42. The Supreme Council of Public Economy (*Vesenkha*) was created in January 1918, initially to reconcile the conflicts of interest which had emerged in the management of the Russian economy as between the Factory and Shop Stewards' Committees, the Workmen's Councils and the Professional Alliances (trade unions). For a time thereafter it was even thought possible that such a body might be held superior to and more democratic than the elected Soviet, and take on wider executive and legislative functions.

43. On 19 July 1917 the leader of the German Centre Party, Mathias Erzberger, succeeded by 214 votes to 116 in getting a Resolution through the Reichstag which included the words 'The Reichstag desires a peace of conciliation and a lasting reconciliation of all peoples'. Strenuous efforts were made in Britain to keep this news out of the daily press. Erzberger eventually led the German delegation to the Armistice talks in November 1918. He was murdered in 1921.

44. The lower figure appeared in the Supplement to the London *Gazette* on 6 April 1920, p. 4109. The higher figure appears in Chamberlain, William Henry, *The Russian Revolution 1917–1921* (New York, 1935) Vol. 2, p. 400. Both are quoted in footnotes on pp. 14–15 of Strakhovsky, Leonid I., *Intervention at Archangel* (Princeton, 1944).

45. The British Socialist Party, founded in 1911, was a rigidly doctrinaire Marxist party with a membership of less than 15,000 in 1914, further diminished when the party split along pro- and anti-war lines in 1916.

46. The Commissar whom Price interviewed on this occasion was Tchicherin.

47. Salonika was captured by the Greeks from the Turks during the Balkan wars of 1912, but the Bulgarians also laid claim to it. During the First World War Bulgaria joined the Central Powers and Serbia joined the Western Allies and Russia. In October 1915 it became clear that the Central Powers and Bulgaria were about to mount an offensive against Serbia, and the French and British landed troops at Salonika, which they retained as a base for the rest of the war.

48. Price briefly considered taking up arms shortly after the attempt on Lenin's life, when he thought the Soviet experiment was doomed. He went to the headquarters of the International Legion of the Red Army which had been formed in February 1918 by the sympathetic American journalist Albert Rhys Williams. But in September 1917 Price found it so disorganised and – he suspected – riddled with counter-revolutionary agents that he decided he would be more use to the Soviet government by continuing as a writer.

49. Price did not so much defend as try to explain the Red Terror. In February 1919 he wrote an article for the Norwegian paper, *Social Democrat*, later reprinted in pamphlet form, in which he argued that the Soviet government had not taken action against their class enemies until the latter had themselves begun to employ terrorist methods, illustrating his argument with examples of the conduct of various counter-revolutionary forces whom the Allies were actively supporting.

50. Price, M. Philips, *My Three Revolutions*, p. 142.

51. Prince Max von Baden had long been known as a political liberal. When the German High Command realised that Germany could not win the war, the Kaiser appointed Prince Max as Chancellor on 4 October 1918 to preside over the negotiations for an armistice.

52. A decree of 11 June established the formation of elected Committees of Poor Peasants. These were made responsible not only for the extraction of hoarded grain from the better-off peasants, but also for its distribution. Lenin himself described this development as the first time the countryside had begun to experience the November Revolution.

53. The reference is to Colonel Robins, the head of the American Red Cross, whom Price knew well and for whom he sometimes translated when they were attending the same meetings.

54. In May 1918 Lockhart became involved with and began to finance a counter-revolutionary organisation, 'The Centre'. See *Journal of Modern History*, Vol. 3 (1971) pp. 413–19, Richard K. Debo, 'Lockhart Plot or Dzerzhinski Plot?' Lockhart's own account of the 'plot' is given in Chapter 9 of his *Memoirs*. In September 1918 Rene Marchand, Petrograd Correspondent of *Le Figaro*, wrote a letter to President Poincaré giving details of and protesting about an Allied plot to

derail trains and blow up railway bridges leading to Petrograd. A copy of his letter was published in *Izvestia*.

55. The *Kreuz Zeitung* reflected the views of the Prussian Extreme Right and the Director of the Press Bureau himself described Price's reference to it as 'the sting in the tail' of the whole article, suggesting that Price had made an all-too palpable hit.

56. The Spartacists (named after the leader of the Roman slave rebellion) were originally the left wing of the German Independent Social Democrats and the forerunners of the German Communist Party.

57. The evidence for this statement is to be found in the papers of Major General Sir Neill Malcolm, at St Anthony's College, Oxford.

Bibliography

Brogan, Hugh, *The Life of Arthur Ransome* (London, 1984)
Buchanan, Sir George, *My Mission to Russia* (London, 1923)
Carr, E.H., *The Bolshevik Revolution 1917–1923*, Three Volumes (London, 1950, 1952, 1953)
Debo, Richard K., *Revolution and Survival. The Foreign Policy of Soviet Russia 1917–1918* (Liverpool, 1979)
Deutscher, Isaac, *The Prophet Armed. Trotsky: 1979–1921* (Oxford, 1954)
Emons, Terence and Vucinich, Wayne S. (eds), *The Zemstvos in Russia: an Experiment in Local Self-Government* (Cambridge, 1983)
Figes, Orlando, *A People's Tragedy. The Russian Revolution 1891–1924* (London, 1996)
Fischer, Louis, *The Soviets in World Affairs. A History of the Relations Between the Soviet Union and the Rest of the World* (London, 1930)
Fitzpatrick, Sheilah, *The Russian Revolution* (Oxford, 1994)
Getzler, Israel, *Martov: a Political Biography of a Russian Social Democrat* (Cambridge, 1967)
Graubard, Stephen, *British Labour and the Russian Revolution* (Harvard, 1956)
Hosking, Geoffrey, *The Russian Constitutional Experiment: Government and Duma 1907–1914* (Cambridge, 1973)
Ironside, Edmund, *Archangel 1918–1919* (London, 1953)
Jackson, Robert, *At War with the Bolshevkiks. The Allied Intervention in Russia 1917–1920* (London, 1972)
Kenez, Peter, *Civil War in South Russia 1918. The First Year of the Volunteer Army* (Berkeley, 1971)
Kenez, Peter, *Civil War in South Russia 1919–1920. The Defeat of the Whites* (Berkeley, 1977)
Kettle, Michael, *The Allies and the Russian Collapse, March 1917–March 1918* (London, 1981)
Knightly, Philip, *The First Casualty* (London, 1975)
Lerner, Warren, *Karl Radek: The Last Internationalist* (Stanford, 1970)
Lloyd George, David, *War Memoirs* (London, 1933)
Lockhart, R.H. Bruce, *Memoirs of a British Agent* (London, 1923)
Lockhart, R.H. Bruce, *The Two Revolutions. An Eye-witness Account of Russia 1917* (London, 1967
Luckett, Richard, *The White Generals: An Account of the White Movement and the Russian Civil War* (New York, 1971)
Mawdsley, Evan, *The Russian Revolution and the Baltic Fleet: War and Politics, February 1917–April 1918* (London, 1978)
Mawdsley, Evan, *The Russian Civil War* (London, 1987)
Pares, Sir Bernard, *A History of Russia*, undated

Pares, Sir Bernard, *The Fall of the Russian Monarchy* (London, 1939)

Perrie, Maureen, *The Agrarian Policy of the Russian Socialist Revolutionary Party: From Its Origins Throughout the Revolution of 1905–1907* (Cambridge, 1977)

Price, M. Philips, *Siberia* (London, 1912)

Price, M. Philips, *Diplomatic History of the War* (London, 1914)

Price, M. Philips, *War and Revolution in Asiatic Russia* (London, 1918)

Price, M. Philips, *My Reminiscences of the Russian Revolution* (London, 1921)

Price, M. Philips, *My Three Revolutions* (London, 1969)

Rabinowitch, Alexander, *Prelude to the Revolution: the Petrograd Bolsheviks and the July 1917 Uprising* (Indiana, 1968)

Reed, John, *Ten Days that Shook the World* (New York, 1919)

Riha, Thomas, *Paul Miliukov in Russian Politics* (Notre Dame, 1969)

Roobol, W.H., *Tsereteli: A Democrat in the Russian Revolution. A Political Biography.* (Translated by Philip Hyams and Lynne Richards) (The Hague, 1976)

Rose, Tania, *Aspects of Political Censorship, 1914–1918* (Hull, 1995)

Rosenburg, William G., *Liberals in the Russian Revolution* (Princeton, 1974)

Rothstein, Andrew, *When Britain Invaded Soviet Russia: The Consul who Rebelled* (London, 1979)

Ryder, A.J., *The German Revolution of 1918* (Cambridge, 1967)

Sukhanov, N.N., *The Russian Revolution* (Translated by Joel Carmichael) (Oxford, 1955)

Swarz, Marvin, *The Union of Democratic Control in British Politics During the First World War* (Oxford, 1971)

Ullman, Richard H., *Anglo-Soviet Relations 1917–1921.* Volume I, *Intervention and War* (Princeton 1961); Volume II, *Britain and the Russian Civil War* (Princeton, 1968)

Wheeler Bennet, Sir John, *Brest-Litovsk: The Forgotten Peace, March 1918* (London, 1939)

White, Stephen, *Britain and the Bolshevik Revolution* (London, 1979)

Williams, Albert Rhys, *Through the Russian Revolution* (New York, 1921)

Williams, Albert Rhys, *Journey into Revolution. Petrograd 1917–1918*, ed. Lucita Williams, (Chicago, 1969)

Index

Index by Tania Rose